The Marne Campaign of 1914

By

Hermann von Kuhl

Legacy Books Press
Military Classics

Published by Legacy Books Press
RPO Princess, Box 21031
445 Princess Street
Kingston, Ontario, K7L 5P5
Canada

www.legacybookspress.com

This edition first published in 2021 by Legacy Books Press
1

ISBN: 978-1-927537-49-7

First published in English as *The Marne Campaign 1914* in 1936 by The Command and General Staff School Press, Fort Leavenworth, Kansas.

Printed and bound in the United States of America and Canada.

This book is typeset in a Times New Roman 11-point font.

Table of Contents

Publisher's Note

The original English language publication on which this new edition is based had a number of issues within its text. There were multiple misspelling of words, and several place names had inconsistent use of accents. Although great effort has been made to find and correct these issues, some may remain.

In addition, the original publication used in-line citations throughout the text, creating readability issues. For the sake of making the book easier to read, these have been converted to footnotes throughout.

Within footnotes, all references to the editor are referring to the editor of the original 1936 edition.

Foreword

The considerations by which I was induced to attempt a history of the Marne campaign, from the mobilization of the army to the retreat after the Battle of the Marne, are set forth in the Introduction.

The task at the present time is difficult. Omissions and mistakes are unavoidable in the description of a battle waged by millions of troops along a line extending from the upper Moselle through Verdun to Paris.

Many of those who took part in the war have kindly assisted me by contributions, especially Generals von Gronau, von dem Borne, von Kluge, Telle, Groner, von der Marwitz, Sixt von Armin, von Bergmann, von Stocken, Baron von Hammerstein-Gesmold, Sydow, Grautoff, Colonels Auer von Herrenkirchen, Lindenborn and von Caprivi, Lt. Col. Wetzell, Majors von Schutz, Biihrmann, Koppen, Thilo, von Platen and von Voss, as also Captain Konig.

I would be grateful to any readers who send in additional material or suggest corrections.

Berlin. Steglitz,
November, 1920.
VON KUHL.

Introduction

As a result of numerous publications, the Marne campaign of 1914 has acquired a prominent position. The plan of the campaign goes back, on the German side, to the former Chief of the General Staff, Count von Schlieffen. There is a lively controversy in progress as to whether his plan was correct and whether the quick decision which he aimed at was possible. It is said that by our losing the battle of the Marne we lost the whole war. This view has been adopted by a large number of army leaders. The narratives of Field Marshal von Billow and of Generals von Kluck and von Hausen relate mainly to the events occurring in connection with their own armies. From the point of view of the High Command, contributions have been made by General Tappen. An account of the Battle of the Marne has been published by General von Francois.

A uniform description of the whole campaign, based on war records and covering also the operations of the enemy, thus coordinating all the published material, does not exist. An official history, compiled by the General Staff, is not to be expected so soon. We no longer have an historical section nor a General Staff, and it remains to be seen how far their place can be taken by other organizations.

The task is of such difficulty and magnitude that a single individual is scarcely able to master it. It is only by means of a carefully planned collaboration of a number of persons that the enormous amount of material can be sifted, evaluated and worked into shape. This was impossible during the war. There was also a lack of the necessary documents as a basis for setting forth the operations of our enemies. A very great many matters, often of great importance, which were transacted by personal interviews or by telephone could be confirmed only by the statements of those concerned. This explains sufficiently the omission (complained of by General von Hausen in his publication) of an official description of the Marne campaign during the war and before the dissolution of the General Staff. There can be no thought of anything intentional in the matter, for the purpose, say, of concealing damaging evidence against the High Command, of shielding certain personages and of avoiding responsibility. There is no need for "opening up the way to the truth" such as we see announced on the sensational jackets of more recent books. No one is blocking the road to truth. At any rate, it will be a rather long while before an official, exhaustive history of the Marne campaign appears. In the meanwhile, legends form and become established. In the search for a culprit, sharp criticism is employed without sufficient foundation. Many things are belittled, and others are magnified beyond measure. The greatness of our accomplishment pales in the memory of the unfortunate outcome of the War.

Much of importance to the historian is being lost because it rests only on personal recollection. And apart from this, the memory of those who participated in the Marne campaign has been much faded by the events of the succeeding four years of the War. It becomes our duty to fix important events as soon as possible. The historians of the World War are obliged to write under far greater, difficulties than those of previous campaigns. Sources such as those furnished by the correspondence of Moltke in 1866 and 1870-71 we of the later conflict do not have at our disposal. As much as was written during the War, to the dismay of the troops, one will often search the records in vain for documents to explain and give the reasons for the great and most important decisions. They often came about as a result of personal conferences. The voluminous writings of the chiefs of the general staffs which we find in the records of earlier wars, are lacking. Most matters were handled by telephone, or dispatched by officers sent off in motor cars. Of course, this applies more to the time of position warfare when we were equipped with an excellent network of telephones and all the other means of communication, than to the war of movement in August and September, 1914, when the role of the-telephone in communication of the armies between each other and with the High Command was necessarily taken over by radio. But even in this latter period much was done by personal contact.

For these reasons it is hoped that an attempt at a comprehensive narrative of the Marne campaign may find its justification. The sources used have been the publications already mentioned, the war records, and personal recollections of the participants.

The war records have been employed sparingly. As already emphasized, it would scarcely be possible for a single individual, already along in years, to go through them all. I have therefore confined myself to bringing out the connection of the operations, the origin of the determining decisions, and the conduct of the warin its main outlines. Tactical details have been dealt with only where they are of special significance. Emphasis on the deeds of single corps or bodies of troops therefore lies outside the scope of the book.

As a source, the warjournals which contain aconnected report of the events relating to any particular detachment or body of troops are to be used with caution. They are of very unequal value. It all depends on the person to whom the preparation of the report was entrusted. Very often the writer lacked perspective, and often also time. Occasionally the reports were written up subsequently. They contain remarkable errors. Thus, for example, in the war journal of the II Cavalry Corps of September 8, 1914, we read: "At this point Lt. Hentsch of the High Command appears at headquarters and speaks of the operations." As a matter of fact, Lt. Hentsch, in the trip which he was making at that time and to which it was desired to attach such great significance, never appeared at all before the headquarters of the cavalry corps.

The foreign works on the campaign are hard to procure. The French work by Hanotaux is confused. Important and unessential, false and true, are all mixed together. The judgments are often on the level of the layman. But it contains a great mass of material scattered about, and many orders are reproduced textually. Clearer, as well as more valuable from a military point of view, but still not satisfactory, is the French account by Palat. Of English works, the publications of French, Maurice, Arthur, and others have been put to use.

An exhaustive history of the Marne campaign can therefore not be expected in this work, which does, however, aim to recount its main outlines. The fact that the First Army frequently comes into the foreground in this connection is due both to the great significance of its operations to the whole course of developments and to the circumstance that my personal recollections are bound up with it. As to many questions to which no answer can be furnished by the war records, my notes have been the principal source of information.

Chapter I – The Military Situation of Germany Before the Beginning of the War[1]

On July 23, 1914, Austria presented the Serbian government with an ultimatum which was to be complied with within forty-eight hours, and on the 28th she declared war on Serbia. It was plain that Serbia desired to act rapidly and to confront the world with an accomplished fact before the other side could intervene. The struggle with Serbia, which had to come sooner or later, was to be carried swiftly through to a decision. However, it was not to be expected that Serbia's protector, Russia, would merely look on. In a few days the World War was released.

For years this war had been impending; it was merely a matter of the external occasion. The real grounds for the war are clearly visible. They were: in France, the chauvinism which had reached

---

[1] Where the name of a place on the map differs from the name used in the text or from the usual English word, or where it was considered desirable to assist the reader, the helpful word or explanation is enclosed in brackets[].

In the translation the designations "High Command" and "General Headquarters" appear to be used interchangably and are equivalent to the term "GHQ." – Editor's Note.

an extreme point of tension, and the drive for revenge; in Russia, Panslavism, the striving for predominance in the Balkans and for possession of Constantinople; in England, the concern about the German fleet, the jealousy of the competitor in world trade and in industry.[2] The hatred for us united them in spite of all the antagonisms which existed between them. King Edward had started to form a ring about Germany.

What was the *military situation of Germany* with respect to her enemies in August 1914? For many years the enemy military establishments were observed by the Great General Staff and compared with our own forces. The comparison turned out to be unfavorable to us. The intensification of the defensive power of Germany failed to take sufficient account of the difficulty of her situation and of the measure of the preparations in the countries hostile to us. Thousands of men subject to military duty were excused each year, and the defense act of 1913 did not yet embrace all the fit. The "Ersatz" Reserve received no training. And preparedness on the part of Austria was far behind our own.

It is a well known fact that the imperious demands of the general staff in the last few years before the war were not all complied with. Even the additional strength which the army received in 1913 was by no means satisfactory. In particular, the three additional army corps which the general staff regarded as absolutely necessary were not raised. General Tappen reports that in the conferences held at that time some one made the remark: "If the General Staff insists on such demands, we are headed for state bankruptcy or revolution."[3]

On the other hand, France and Russia, in constant understanding and not without mutual pressure, had, since their military convention of 1892-94, increased their war preparations to an extent which may fairly be described as enormous.

In France, every single qualified man was called to the colors. After a hard battle with the representatives of the people, the

---

[2] The author clearly avoids stating the grounds as far as Germany was concerned. – Editor's Note.

[3] "Bis zur Marne 1914"

French government had, in 1913, again introduced the three-year active service. This put a financial and personal burden upon the people which could not be borne permanently. It was calculated upon a war with Germany which was planned for a not very distant date in alliance with England and Russia. *"Within two years they will be obliged either to renounce the three-year service period or else wage war,"* the Belgian ambassador to Paris reported to his government in 1914. Large "special armament credits" were voted for supplementing the war equipment.

Thus the peace strength of the French army, which hitherto had amounted to some 545,000 men (yearly average), had been increased in 1914 to at least 690,000 men in the armed service and 45,000 in the auxiliary service. It could have been increased in the following years, according to our assumption, to 730,000 men in the armed service and 46,000 men in the auxiliary service. Presumably, it could have been maintained for a time at this level, in spite of the fact that the birth rate in France had been regularly decreasing for a long while. In addition there were the Arab troops of Algeria and Tunis, the Senegalese and the Moroccans. According to the official French figures now available, the total peace strength of the French army, including officers, amounted at the beginning of the war to 883,500 men. The corresponding peace strength of the German army (including officers), as of the summer of 1914, did not exceed approximately 761,000 men. The French peace strength (including Navy), which hitherto had amounted to 1.5 per cent of the population, now climbed to 2.10 per cent, whereas in Germany, even after the increase effected by the defense act of 1913, the percentage attained was only 1.20.

The ratio of the French to the German war strength was of the same order. There arose the astonishing fact that France, with a population of 25 million less, by the utmost intensification of her power of defense put more men into the field than Germany. The available French strength (including officers) at the outbreak of the War is officially reported in France as 4,900,000 men. To this number there still had to be added the *armée noire* which could be drawn from Africa. Africa and Indo-China furnished in the course of the war a total of approximately 545,000 men.

Still more astonishing were the preparations of Russia. In the last few years before the war the peace strength had been increased to such an extent that the total could be calculated, as of the summer of 1914, at 1,581,000 men in summer and 2,193,000 in winter. Accordingly, after the complete execution of the increase decided upon, Russian strength would attain the extraordinary figure of 1,803,000 men in summer and 2,193,000 in winter. Even a figure of 2,320,000 was given in the Russian press. The mobilization was accelerated to the extreme limit, and the network of railways was extended for rapid assembly.

Our plan of operations was based upon the passage through Belgium. On this road we had to count on meeting the *English and Belgian armies*. It was known to us, and has later been confirmed, that before the war the English engaged in detailed conferences with the chief of the Belgian general staff and that exact preparatory measures were agreed upon with the French general staff.

We could not rely on *Italy*. To be sure, we had received a promise of five Italian corps and two cavalry divisions, to be sent by rail around Switzerland through Austria to the upper Rhine, but the promise was retracted for a time, In the fall of 1913 the promise was renewed, but the contribution cut down to three army corps and two cavalry divisions. As regards their transportation, a binding agreement was reached in March1914. Count Schlieffen regarded this aid from Italy as an “illusion.” It was his view that even on the Alpine frontier an Italian attack on France could not be taken for granted. Each of the two opponents would there await an attack which the other had not the slightest intention of undertaking. On account of her unprotected coast, Italy feared England. Her relations to France were becoming more and more friendly, to Austria more strained. However, there was room for hope that she might remain neutral.

So then, at the start, we stood alone with Austria-Hungary, faced with a greatly superior force. The following table reveals the crushing superiority of our opponents with approximately 6,200,000 men as against German and Austria-Hungary with approximately 3,500,000:

COMPARISON OF THE ACTUAL PEACE AND WAR STRENGTHS IN THE SUMMER OF 1914 (MAN POWER, INCLUSIVE OF OFFICERS). (1)

	Peace strength	*War Strength (2)*		*Man Power*
		Infantry Divisions	*Cavalry Divisions*	
German	760,908	85 (3)	11	2,019,470
Austria-Hungary	477,859	47	11	1,470,000
Total	1,238,767	142	22	3,489,470
Russia	1,581,000	118½ (4)	40 (5)	3,461,750
France	883,566	75 (6)	10	2,032,820
England	248,000 (7)	6	1 and 2 sep. brig.	132,000 (8)
Serbia	54,600	10	1	285,000
Belgium	61,282	6	1	280,000
Total	2,825,448	215½	54	6,191,570

NOTES

(1) In a comparison with other figures, it must be borne in mind that here, first, all officers are counted; second, that the formations indicated under (2) are subtracted; also that the data relate to the summer of 1914.

(2) Without replacement (Ersatz) formations, *Landwehr* or *Landsturm* in Germany; without territorials in France; without militia in Russia.

(3) Including six mobile replacement divisions.

(4) The Caucasian, Siberian and Turkestan corps are included. (5) Including five Cossack divisions.

(6) 48 active, 27 reserve divisions, two of which were not raised until October 1914.

(7) Regular army in England and the Colonies.

(8) Expeditionary force only.

Only the Expeditionary Corps of England is included, a small opponent, to be sure, but a worthy one. In a struggle in which the world position of England and Germany was at stake, it was to be assumed as a matter of course that England would bring together her full force with the greatest speed and that extensive cooperation would be required of her independent colonies, Canada, Australia, New Zeland and the South African Union.

We were proceeding toward a heavy fight, with insufficient equipment. Only a *quick decision*, first against one, then against the other opponent, could help us; *no wearing-down strategy* would suffice.

Chapter II – The German Concentration and Plan of Campaign[1]

The Concentration

Up to the beginning of the War, I was *Oberquartiermeister* in the great general staff at Berlin, but by the order of mobilization I was named chief of the general staff of the First Army. First Army Headquarters was established at Stettin. On the evening . of August 7 it was transported by rail through Lubeck, Hamburg, Munster to the first headquarters, Grevenbroich, which we entered on the evening of August 9. The enthusiasm which we were privileged to observe among the population throughout the long journey was very affecting. And yet a certain nervousness had already appeared among the people in Stettin, a nervousness which expressed itself in the fear of spies. Even a number of officers of our staff were prosecuted as spies in Stettin. Motor cars were frequently stopped and their occupants menaced with arrest.

The concentration of the First Army (II, III and IV Corps and III and IV Reserve Corps) was effected in the period from August

[1] See General Map No. 1.

7 to 15 in the region of Jülich – Bergheim – Neuss – Krefeld – Erkelenz. To the formations enumerated were added the 10th, 11th and 27th Landwehr Brigades. The First Army occupied the right wing and was faced with a difficult task. It was under the orders of General von Kluck.

The Second Army (General von Bülow; VII, X and Guard Corps, VII, X and Guard Reserve Corps, and to which was assigned temporarily the IX Corps) was as 1sembled in the area: Aix-la-Chapelle – Eupen – Malmedy – Blankenheim – Schleiden – Euskirchen – Düren. Headquarters at Montjoie.

The purport of the concentration instructions issued to the staff of the First Army at mobilization was as follows: "The German concentration against France is based on the following design: the main force of the German army shall proceed through Belgium and Luxemburg to France. Its advance, inso far as the reports at hand concerning the French concentration are proved correct, is thought of as a wheeling movement around the fixed pivot Metz – Thionville. The advance of the movement is to be governed by the right wing. The movements of the interior armies will be so regulated that the cohesion of all the German forces and the contact with Thionville – Metz are not lost. The beginning of the general advance of the main force of the German army will be arranged by the High Command as soon as the right wing (First and Second Armies) is abreast of Liege."

The preliminary condition for the advance was the capture of Liege in a rapid offensive. For this, the command of the Second Army received special instructions. The capture was to be effected by General von Emmich, under whose command were placed, in addition to other brigades hastily pushed forward, two brigades of the First Army. Initially, the Second Army had control of all roads south of the Dutch border. The IX Corps in the neighborhood of Aix-la-Chapelle was later to join the First Army. The First Army could not advance on Aix-la-Chapelle until this corps was moved forward. As soon as Liege was taken, the Second Army was to clear the roads designed for the march of the First Army – roads which led through Aix-la-Chapelle, and then between the Dutch border and Liege over the Meuse. The First and Second Armies were then to be prepared to advance on a line extending through

Liege.

The Second Army was then to advance on Wavre with its right wing and to pass Namur to the north with its left, and the First Army was to march on Brussels and cover the right flank."The advance of the First Army together with that of the Second Army, will determine the turn of the whole force." To the Second Army was also attached, at first, the II Cavalry Corps, whose staff was detrained at Aix-la-Chapelle with the 2d, 4th and 9th Cavalry Divisions. At the beginning of the advance this Cavalry Corps was to come directly under the orders of the High Command and was to proceed to the north of Namur toward the line: Antwerp – Brussels – Charleroi, in advance of the front of the First and Second Armies, with a view to determining the position of the Belgian Army, the landing of English forces and the possible presence of French troops in northern Belgium. The commander was instructed to transmit his reports to First Army Headquarters also.

As we entered Grevenbroich, the situation at Liege was not very clear. Fire was to have been opened on August 5 and the attack begun during the night of August 5-6. But evidently the attack had not proceeded so smoothly as had been expected originally. It had to be resumed with stronger forces. The most contradictory rumors reached us, and even the High Command could furnish no reliable information. The unloading of the active corps, including parks and convoys, was completed on the 4th, that of the reserve corps on the 15th. Already on the 13th, the First Army, on orders from the High Command, started the advance through Aix-la-Chapelle. In due course the situation around Liege was clarified, and the Second Army cleared the roads between Aix-la-Chapelle and the Meuse, north of Liege, for the First Army. The II, III and IV Corps marched in front, followed by the III and IV Reserve Corps. The IX Corps joined the First Army on August 15th.

The advance to and across the Meuse was difficult. On each of three highways, very close together, marched two corps, one behind the other. The whole army had to march thickly pressed through the streets of Aix-la-Chapelle, cross the Meuse in the narrow space between Liege and the Dutch border, and on the other side of the Meuse to spread out quickly to the right. The provisioning of the troops required elaborate measures. The Meuse was reached on the 14th and crossed on the 15th.

The headquarters of the Third Army (General von Hausen) went to Prüm. This army, with the XI, XII, and XIX Corps and the XII Reserve Corps, proceeded through St. Vith – Maxweiler – Neuerburg – Wittlich – Prüm. Once its concentration had been completed, it was required to advance, on orders of the High Command, against the Meuse between Namur and Givet.

The I Cavalry Corps, with headquarters first at Bittburg, was thereupon to assemble in the locality of Laroche – Bastogne, in order to advance south of Namur towards the Meuse, with the main body on Dinant, and to reconnoiter in front of the Third Army and the right wing of the Fourth Army toward Namur and Mézières. At the beginning of the general advance, it came under the orders of the High Command.

The Fourth Army, under Duke Albrecht von Württemberg, was drawn up along the line: Diekirch – Luxemburg – Nennig – Wadern – Treves. Headquarters was at Treves. It was composed of the VIII, XVIII and VI Corps and of the VIII and XVIII Reserve Corps. Once the order of mobilization was issued, the VIII Corps was to proceed into the grand duchy of Luxemburg to assure control of the railroads there. The IV Cavalry Corps, with headquarters initially at Diedenhofen, had orders to proceed to Carignan and Damvillers and reconnoiter towards the course of the Meuse on the front: Mézières – Mouon – Stenay – Verdun – St. Mihiel.

The Fourth Army, echeloned toward the left, with the right flank on Fumay and the left over Attert (north of Anon), had orders to advance on Neufchateau. In the course of the advance, it was obliged to be ready at any time to wheel south toward the Semois and come to the aid of the Fifth Army, which was the first to be exposed to an enemy attack.

According to its concentration instructions, the Fifth Army was to be assembled in the zone: Thionville [Diedenhofen] – Metz – Saarbrücken – Lebach – Wallerfangen, with headquarters at Saarbrücken. It was composed of the V, XVIII and XVI Corps and of the V and VI Reserve Corps, and was under orders of Crown

Prince Wilhelm. The task assigned to this army for the advance was to hold the pivot (Metz – Thionville) in conjunction with the Fourth Army. To this end, it was first to be assembled, while retaining the deeply staggered formation, with its heads of columns approximately along the line: Bettenburg – Thionville. Then, with the troops echeloned far to the left, the advance was to be made on Florenville (south of Chiny), with the right wing from Bettenburg through Mamer – Arlon, while the left wing maintained contact with Thionville. To ward off a counterattack in force from the direction of Verdun, it might become necessary at any time for the army to wheel into a position facing southwestor south.

For the protection of the left flank of the German main forces, in case the troops stationed south of Metz (Sixth and Seventh Armies, and III Cavalry Corps) had to fall back, a fortified position was prepared by civilian workers on the Nied, between Metz and the Saar, and occupied by seven Landwehr brigades and eight batteries of 10-cm guns. This "Nied position" (*Niedstellitng*) was under command of the government of the fortress of Metz, which, together with the government of the fortress of Thionville, was in turn subordinate to the Fifth Army.

Of special importance were the composition and tasks of the Sixth and Seventh Armies. The Sixth Army (I, II and III Bavarian Corps, the XXI Corps and I Bavarian Reserve Corps) was drawn up in the locality: Kurzel – Falkenburg – Saarsburg (Lorraine) – Saargemund, with headquarters at St. Avold.

The Seventh Army (XIV, XV Corps, XIV Reserve Corps), with the exception of the XV Corps, was detrained in Mulheim and Freiburg and was concentrated at Strasburg and on the upper Rhine, with headquarters at Strasburg.

The protection of the left flank of the German forces devolved upon these two armies and the III Cavalry Corps, together with the fortresses, Thionville and Metz. For this purpose, the two armies as well as the III Cavalry Corps, were to be under the command of the commander of the Sixth Army, Crown Prince Rupprecht of Bavaria. The task of this common commander was "to advance toward the Moselle below Frouard and toward the Meurthe, by taking the fortress of Manonviller, in order to hold the French forces concentrated there and to prevent their being transferred to the French left wing. This task could have been rendered impracticable if the French, on their part, had advanced to the attack with superior forces between Metz and the Vosges. In case the troops in Alsace and Lorraine were thus forced to withdraw, the maneuvre was to be effected in such a way as to prevent the menacing of the left flank of the German main forces – which the French could have done by surrounding the Nied position. In case of need, the Sixth Army was to furnish troops for strengthening this position."

In case the Sixth and Seventh Armies did not meet with superior French forces, parts of the Sixth Army and of the III Cavalry Corps might be sent through Metz or to the south into action on the left bank of the Moselle. The question asto how far this possibility could be considered in the arrangement to be adopted for the advance against the Meurthe and the Moselle, was left to the common commander.

In case a French offensive should extend into upper Alsace, this would not be regarded as unfavorable to the operations as a whole, so long as the enemy did not cross the line: Fortress Kaiser Wilhelm II – Breuschstellung – Strassburg. To hold this line and prevent its being encircled to the west of the Fortress Kaiser Wilhelm II was primarily a task for the government of Strassburg.

The protection of upper Alsace and south Baden during the concentration movement devolved upon the commander of the Seventh Army. The nature of this task was purely temporary. The common commander of the troops in Alsace-Lorraine was obliged to be ready at any time to "bring the strongest possible force of the Seventh Army into direct collaboration with the Sixth Army." The covering of upper Alsace was not to result in sacrificing the Seventh Army to a superior French force. An early French advance from Belfort in conjunction with an offensive between Metz and the Vosges was regarded as a possibility. A weak offensive was to be repulsed, "so that the land may not be left defenseless against any action that the enemy may undertake." In case of superior forces proceeding into upper Alsace, the Seventh Army was to fall back on Strassburg and on the right bank of the Rhine. "Then, at the latest, the Seventh Army was to be released in as large numbers as possible for direct cooperation with the Sixth Army. In what direction this was to take place, and whether on foot or by rail, would be determined by the situation of the Sixth Army."

The basic idea involved in these manifold tasks was that a strong French attack was to be expected between Metz and the Vosges, in conjunction with a weaker offensive from Belfort in the direction of upper Alsace. The assumption was that in this case the German troops employed in Alsace-Lorraine would pay for themselves by preventing the movement of the French forces engaged thereto the enemy's left flank. The retirement before a superior French force in Lorraine was conceived somewhat as follows: the Sixth Army would fall back to the Saar, so that the pursuing enemy would be attacked from the north from Metzand the Nied position and, from the south, by the Seventh Army from the Northern Vosges. Naturally it was doubtful whether the enemy would undertake the role thus conceived for him.

The "temporary" task of the Seventh Army was by no means easy. It was not always possible to recognize at once whether the enemy was coming from Belfort with strong or weak forces. An advance of the Seventh Army upon Mülhausen might come to nothing and put in jeopardy the main task of a concerted action with the Sixth Army.

The cooperation of the fortresses Metz and Thionville, the Nied position, and of both armies for the protection of the left flank of the German army, was made more difficult by the various independent headquarters. Today, after the experience acquired in the war, we would embrace them all in an army group under one command.

The strength of the Sixth and Seventh Armies and the task assigned to Crown Prince Ruppercht did not prove favorable to the operations. The center of gravity of the whole operation lay on the right with which the greats weeping movement through Belgium was to be carried out. This flank could not be too strong. The weakening of this flank in favor of a minor task in Alsace-Lorraine constituted adisadvantage. General von Moltke had in mind holding the enemy by an advance with rather strong forces in Lorraine, or, if possible, to defeat him in case be advanced between Metz and the Vosges. The possibility of a later displacement of forces from the left wing to the right was no doubt considered. It was believed, however, that a success might first be attained and the displacement made later. It would be difficult to move the troops on time to the right wing if the Sixth and Seventh Armies advanced toward the Meurthe and Moselle. They could hold the enemy only by an attack, or at least, by feigning one.

The Moltke plan might possibly have led to some success in Alsace-Lorraine. But the basic idea of the sweeping movement through Belgium with a right wing as strong as possible had to be resolutely adhered to, and everything which could be dispensed with moved from the left wing to the right at the proper time. The idea could not be tolerated that stronger German forces should be held in Lorraine by inferior French forces. Everything hinged on the execution of the plan. It was a difficult thing to carry out. Napoleon once said: "Only one thing can be done at a time." In this case we attempted two.

From the beginning it would have been well to concentrate the forces more upon the decisive right wing and to weaken the Sixth and Seventh Armies while at the same time limiting their task; the more so as our forces were considerably inferior on the whole to the combined forces of our adversaries in the west.

To be sure, there was a difficulty to be overcome in this connection. The deployment of our right wing, which had to be extended northward as far as Krefeld, involved utilizing the full capacity of our railways. In order to reach Belgium, the First Army, on the right wing, had to be concentrated on Aix-la-Chapelle, march through this city and cross the Meuse between Liege and the Dutch border. The neutrality of the Netherlands was to be respected under all circumstances. The preliminary condition for the whole movement was that we should have possession of Liege. As already stated, the city was to be seized by a surprise attack before the beginning of the operations. It was a bold idea, and, as we know, it succeeded. The difficulties were overcome by the First and Second Armies. In General Tappen's opinion however, more than the twelve corps of the First and Second Armies could not have been employed north of the Meuse. Certainly not in the first line: that must be admitted. But it was all the more necessary to place in readiness a strong echelon in the second line. Into the third line should have been drawn the Landwehr, the Landstrum, and the replacement divisions (*Ersatzdivisionen*), to take over the observation and besieging of the fortresses, protecting the communications and the services of the rear (*Etappendienst*). To make sure of supplies, our motor transportation should have been assembled on the right flank and specially organized for this purpose. The question of supplies had been thoroughly studied in time of peace.

Origin and Development of the Plan of Operation

The concentration of the army in 1914 did not conform in all respects to the plan of operations established by Count Schlieffen when he was chief of the general staff of the army. The origin and gradual development of our plan of campaign into a two-front war against France and Russia can only be touched on briefly here.

Field Marshal von Moltke still held to the view that we must take the offensive against Russia and stand On the defensive against France. After the French army had been reorganized and the northeast frontier of France had been fortified, reliance could no longer be placed on a quick decision of the struggle in the west. It was therefore preferable to utilize toward the west the great advantages offered to the defensive by the Rhine and our then powerful fortresses and to employ for the offensive in the east all our fighting forces not absolutely required against France. The broad, open, eastern frontier was unfavorable for defense and could be protected only by means of attack. From all appearances, the Russians were contemplating a great offensive against Germany or against Austria-Hungary. We had ground for hope that the Russian attack could be anticipated by a concentrated operation of the German and Austro-Hungarian troops on the right bank of the Vistula.

Count Waldersee also, who succeeded Moltke in 1888, retained essentially the same view.

It was Count Schlieffen who, shortly after assuming the duties of chief of the general staff of the army, first came to the conclusion that the French were the stronger and more dangerous enemy who must be attacked in all force. The defensive power of

France was so high and its offensive spirit had grown to such a pitch that it was necessary to reckon with an early attack from that direction. They had to act in order to win back the lost provinces. Here a quick decision was possible. On the other hand a defensive attitude would have required such forces that it seemed questionable whether we would have been strong enough then for a great offensive in the east. Furthermore, an attack in the east had been rendered much more difficult by the Russian fortifications, and the Russians could prevent a decision by retiring into the broad interior of the country.

Thus Count Schlieffen decided to seek the decision in the west and to confine the eastern operations to the defensive with as small a force as possible. The decision against France had to be obtained in all haste. Therefore the strong French front of fortifications could not be attacked, but had to be detoured by way of Belgium. It was an order prescribed by necessity, there was no other way. With the left flank resting on Metz, almost all of the total forces were to carry out the great detour and sweeping movement. This movement, like a powerful roller, was to proceed through Belgium and northern France and sweep each and every important position of the French in a manner to drive them in an easterly direction against their Moselle positions, the Jura, and Switzerland. To this end, the right flank of our army had to be made as strong as possible from the very beginning and be reenforced continually. Therefore, Count Schlieffen demanded the utilization of the Landstrum, to be called out at once, and of the Landwehr remaining in the interior fortresses, for the occupation of the supply front and for assuring control of the railways. He also demanded that immediately following the order of mobilization, eight army corps be raised from replacement troops. These corps would be brought up behind the right wing as soon as the railway facilities permitted.

Accordingly, the strength of the left wing was to be considerably reduced and the importance of its task diminished. In Lorraine, Count Schlieffen proposed to leave only three and one-half corps, one reserve corps, and three cavalry divisions for the protection of the left flank to the right of the Moselle, and two of these active corps were to be transported by rail as soon as possible to the right flank. In addition to the war garrison, there remained in Metz one reserve division. On the upper Rhinethere were three and one-half Landwehr brigades, and in lower Alsace one Landwehr brigade. The task of the Lorraine forces was to hold as many French troops as possible with the fewest possible Germans. The French might possibly make a counter-attack. It was quite desirable that they should. The great flanking movement through Belgium was to continue just the same; Count Schlieffen assumed that the French would turn back in Lorraine.

Under General von Moltke, the successor of Count Schlieffen, a change was gradually made in the relation of forces between the right and left wings. General von Moltke had been loath to leave Alsace unprotected in the face of a probably successful French attack. The country was not to be vacated at once in case of a war and abandoned to every enemy operation. Initially, the XIV Corps was assigned to the protection of upper Alsace, and later a total of eight corps, in addition to the war garrisons of Metz and Strassburg and a large number of Landwehr brigades, were stationed in Alsace-Lorraine. The tasks of the Sixth and Seventh Armies were accordingly much extended.

The Schlieffen plan was preferable. It was a very simple one. The main thought was brought out with the greatest clarity, and all other considerations were subordinated to it. The course of events in August and September, 1914, has demonstrated the correctness of Count Schlieffen's view.

Critique of the Schlieffen Plan

After our plan of operations had failed in 1914 and the quick decision aimed at in the west became impossible, there arose among us, during and after the War, a sharp criticism of the so-called Schlieffen plan, though it was clear that most of the critics did not know the difference between the concentration contemplated by Count Schlieffen and the one actually carried out in 1914.

It was asserted that the Schlieffen plan was no longer adapted to the conditions of modern warfare, that it was no longer practicable. Others went further, maintaining it was quite out of the question for us to obtain a favorable military decision of the war, that our conduct of the war rested upon a false basis. In view of the fundamental importance of this question, we shall subject it to a closer test. In particular, we must enquire into the question of whether the methods proposed by the other side as more effective might have led to the goal.

In an article entitled "Falkenhayn and Ludendorff" in the *Preussische Jahrbucher*, Professor Hans Delbruck expresses grave doubts as to whether it was possible for us to win the war by the overthrow of our opponents.[2] For a long time, of course, he has developed the doctrine that there are two fundamental forms of warfare, namely, a strategy of annihilation and a strategy of exhaustion or wearing down. Not all wars, to be sure, can be made to fit into this scheme; rather, these basic forms could assume a varying character and merge into each other. But the two main types still remain. Of the great captains of military history Professor Delbruck assigns a portion to the one and another portion to the other school.

As regards the World War, Professor Delbruck sees the same distinction represented by Falkenhayn and Ludendorff. They came from the same military school, of course, and their views were very similar in the fact that they regarded the offensive as preferable to the defensive. But as regards strategy, he says, the two leaders part company. Falkenhayn's ideas on the waging of war are none other than those of the wearing-down strategy of Frederick the Great. Falkenhayn declared that the goal of so crushing the enemy that he is obliged to sue for peace was unattainable in view of the enemy's superiority in means. It was his view that our only permissible aim was to demonstrate to our western opponents that they could not win by wearing us down before they themselves had suffered irreparable damage. When Falkenhayn speaks of the "decision" having to be won in the west, the idea is to be taken only in this restricted sense. The great operation on the eastern front in 1915 was merely designed to break the attack ing force of the Russians

---

[2] May 1920.

for a long while and to protect our rear for the struggle in the west. He rejected the notion that a "thorough job" should and could be done in Russia. He believed that further penetration into Russia would have been an unending affair. He did not approve Ludendorff's plan of advancing through Kovno and Vilna against the line of retirement of the Russians. The attack on Verdun or, rather, "on the Meuse," in 1916 was designed merely to "bleed" the enemy, not to inflict such a defeat upon the French that a decision would be obtained. It is precisely in this undertaking that Professor Delbruck sees a "sort of exhaustion or wearing-down strategy."

Ludendorff, on the other hand, knows nothing but victory or defeat; he wants to "win the war" and rejects the idea of a peace based on understanding. A thorough job was first to be done on the eastern front in order to strive for the decision in the west in 1918 by an attack in France. This was to be accomplished with the aid of submarine warfare in case the land operations had not yet brought about the desired result.

The side on which Professor Delbruck stands is clear from his proposals as to the manner in which we should have conducted the war. "The main thing was that we should stand firm, that we should bring to the consciousness of the enemy, by single blows as strong and heavy as possible, our force and the magnitude of his own undertaking, and at the same time make known our willingness to accept a peace based on understanding." He believes that, in addition to the offensive in France, there was another possibility of attack which, as the prospects in France became darker, should have been given the more consideration. "That was the attack on the English home front." There was in England, he says, in addition to the prevailing war party, a very considerable party which stood for a peace based on understanding, and an attempt should have been made to give this party the upper hand.

Professor Delbruck thinks that if the general staff had had a clearer understanding of the essential nature of Frederick the Great's exhaustion strategy, perhaps our preparation for the world war would have been different. The possibility of a war of long duration would have been weighed, and the political thought of moderate war aims been given more attention. Even if we had been victorious over the French and English in 1914, there would still have been no peace, because the conditions set by us would have been excessive. The attempt to overwhelm France before the Russians pulled us back was not much different, in his view, from that tempting of fate and that over-straining of forces which brought about the failure of Frederick the Great in 1757.

My own opinion is that a *decision was quite possible*. The march through Belgium was by no means a "counsel of despair." The despair was rather on the part of the adversary. General Joffre did not, as is often assumed, try to avoid a decisive battle in August 1914. He has expressly stated, on the contrary, that he aimed at a decision through a great offensive along the whole front. The offensive failed and the general retreat was by no means voluntary. On the contrary, the French as well as the English, were beaten all along the front. Just read in the French and English reports the effect of the defeat and retreat upon the army and upon the statesmen of our opponents. The fact that we were later obliged to fall back upon the Marne has its special reasons. The mistakes in leadership which robbed us of the success of the Marne campaign lay precisely in the fact that the original idea of annihilating the enemy was carried out in a very emasculated form. Otherwise success on the Marne in September would have been assured us. I hope that this will be clear from the narration of the events.

I hold also, as quite within the realm of possibilities, that we could have brought about a decision against Russia and, by means of a skillful policy and by moderating our war aims, attained a definitive peace with the Czarist government in 1915 or 1916. The envelopment of the Russian north wing aimed at by Field Marshal von Hindenburg and General Ludendorff in 1915 was certainly quite possible of accomplishment.

The design of pressing forward here and there with limited objectives, of inflicting occasional blows on the enemy, could never bring us to the goal. To close in on the French at Verdun in 1916, while at the same time the Austrians took the offensive against the Italians, constituted a splitting of forces. Whatever the objective of each of these two undertakings, it would have been much better to concentrate on one or the other, as Professor Delbruck also remarks. The struggle at Verdun, in which the

French were to be "bled," also led to our being bled and did not at all prevent the French from taking a very effective part in the Somme battle. The very design of this bleeding process is characterized by Dr. Delbruck as carrying the exhaustion idea to an extreme.

Our great offensive in the spring of 1918 might very well have been a success. I was then thoroughly in favor of an offensive and can not refrain even today from agreeing with General Ludendorff in the matter, even though I did not agree with him as to the choice of the point of attack. The break-through was certainly difficult. But our preparations which the High Command, particularly General Ludendorff, had worked out with astonishing energy, were brilliant. No one could know the outcome in advance, but the offensive had to be attempted. The Allies were extremely hard pressed, and it was only the Americans who finally saved them. This is becoming more and more evident, now that we are coming to know the situation from the other side through the publications of our enemies.

The sharp weapon of submarine warfare was blunted byourselves. If this submarine campaign had been opened as late as possible and with the maximum surprise effect, after the preparations had been made in all secrecy and a sufficient number of the boats manufactured, and if it had then been carried out with all force and without turning back, it might have had a decisive effect in connection with the spring offensive of 1918.

Of course, after the first great attacks, in which we employed our best attacking forces and equipment, had failed to attain the goal in the spring of 1918, the decision could no longer be reached by continuing the attacks at various separate points. Nor could such attacks break the morale of the enemy. Moreover, his strength was increasing too rapidly from day to day by the arrival of the Americans, while our own reserves were becoming exhausted and the strength of the various formations was vanishing. The time had now come when we had to be satisfied with a temporarizing strategy. But even this strategy I would not call a wasting one. It was not to be expected that the adversary would be worn out or exhausted sooner than we.

The counter-proposals made by Dr. Delbruck have been

mentioned: holding our own or standing firm, isolated blows, announcement of willingness to accept a peace based on understanding, attack on the English home front. Least of all could I have expected anything to come of the latter. That would really be to underestimate too much the tenacity of the English will to victory. One needs only to look into the monograph on Kitchener by Sir George Arthur to see with what elan, breadth of view, and extreme energy the war was taken up in England from the very start. In Kitchener England found a military organizer of the first rank, and in Lloyd George a statesman of the highest power of will. In my opinion, the attack on the mother country would have failed. Nor would it in itself have solved the question of the French war aim, which consisted in winning Alsace-Lorraine.

Our peace resolutions could be regarded by the enemy only as a sign of weakness. With isolated blows, which could not be turned to account, nothing could be gained against the determined will to win on the part of our adversaries. In view of the immeasurable sources of aid which the Allies had at their disposal and in view of our own isolation, a wearing-clown strategy could only lead to a prolonged war and to our own exhaustion. Time was against us, and the hunger blockade was breaking the German people's force of resistance.

On certain points I agree with Dr. Delbruck: Our general situation was such that we should, as a matter of course, have avoided an overstretching of our war aims and have seized any favorable opportunity to come to-an acceptable peace. In the matter of peace terms, some unanimity should have been reached in high quarters, without the necessity of announcing continually to the whole world our readiness for peace. Only as to the restoration of Belgium would it have been possible to make an open declaration, if occasion arose.

It must be confessed that we were mistaken as regards the possible duration of the war. Wes hared this error with the French general staff and Marshal Foch before the war. England too, as will be seen later, was not in the least prepared for such a war on land. We were, furthermore, mistaken regarding the full meaning of a war with armies of millions of men, an economic war, a complete blockade. That a more careful study of Frederick the Great's exhaustion strategy might have furnished us with a hint of the long duration of the late war is not exactly conclusive. All the bases and relations of warfare at the time of Frederick were such as to exclude comparison with the World War. If we had suspected the full significance of a blockade, this would have led us to a quite different economic preparation for the war, and must at the same time have strengthened our determination to bring about a decision as quickly as possible.

It is an old dispute, concerning the exhaustion strategy and the annihilation strategy. We soldiers simply hold with Moltke and continue to see in strategy merely a system of expedients. Moltke's system consisted, according to Count Schlieffen, in the fact that he had no system. Strategy can only aim at the highest goal which the Means at hand make possible of attainment, said Moltke. It can not be expressed more simply and clearly. The individual commanders have not been *a priori* representatives either of the exhaustion or of the annihilation strategy. They belonged neither to the one nor to the other "school," but they acted, if they were real commanders, according to circumstances. They strove, as a matter of course, to annihilate the enemy when their forces sufficed. If this was not the case, they had to limit their ambitions. They changed their procedure in the course of the war, according to the situation. "The most applicable solution must be sought for each case."[3]

At the same time we should not lose sight of the fact that the whole constitution of one commander inclines him more to the ruthless offensive; that of another to a more cautious procedure. This was clearly revealed in their conduct of war. Fabius Cunctator, Daun, Gyulai, Schwarzenberg, Kuropatkin did not wage war in the same manner as Suvarof or Napoleon. It must always be borne in mind, however, that a dallying policy in warfare is likely to lead to success only when there is some hope of a change in the circumstances, of the elimination of one of the adversaries, of reenforcements, of a turn in the situation, or when it is to be expected that the adversary may take the view that the continuation of the war is not worth the sacrifices demanded or, at least, that his

---

[3] Count Schlieffen.

own forces will be exhausted in equal measure.

At the beginning of the second Silesian war, Frederick the Great had set as his goal the overthrow of Austria. By a ruthless offensive into the enemy's territory he wished to bring about the decision and advance upon Vienna in order to "set his foot on the enemy's neck." The plan failed, and the king drew from it and from later events his own lesson. It was impossible for him to break the bonds which impeded his war strategy, and he had to confine himself later to the strategic defensive. He could not say, as did Napoleon in 1812 to the envoys of Emperor Alexander:

"You can not prevent me from offering some resistance. I am spending 30,000 men every month."

The question for us in 1914 was, whether it was possible to strive for a decision or whether the war was to be conducted in a dallying and defensive manner. In the latter case it was presumably lost to us.

It has been asserted that the Schliffen plan was no longer suitable in 1914. The employment of barbed wire and shovels, the modern technique of arms and explosives, are supposed to have resulted in a complete change in the conduct of war. A quick decision had become improbable. The long extended columns required for a flanking movement were promptly discovered by flyers. When the struggle had taken the form of trench warfare in the east as well as in the west, the Schlieffen plan was done for. I hope to furnish the proof that a quick decision was still possible. The significance of barbed wire and the shovel was, to be sure, unknown to us in 1914, but it was equally unknown to our opponents. To become convinced of this, one has only to read the French and English accounts of the war. The strength and extent of our numerous columns proceeding north of the Meuse in August 1914, marching by day, was by no means promptly recognized by the enemy. It has been proved that the adversary was surprised by our sweeping movement and that his whole plan had to be revised.

Count Schlieffen had shown us the only correct way: only in movement was the victory for us to be won, only by victory was a decision of the war to be attained. An exhaustion strategy necessarily led to a war of position. As soon as we had thus lost freedom of movement, technique took the place of the art of leadership, the materiel battle the place of Cannae. In technique and materiel we were doomed to be just as inferior to our enemies as in food supplies after the establishment of the blockade. Germany became a besieged fortress, our battles were reduced to sallies on the part of the garrison to hold back the advance of the siege, until in 1918 we attempted once more to burst the ring by force. When this failed, the war was lost.

Chapter III – The German Operations up to the Failure of the French Offensive on August 23

August 16 – Disposition of the Armies. Information of the Enemy

On August 15, the First Army stood on the far side of the Meuse on the general line: Bilson – Tongres and southward. The first task, and a difficult one, had been accomplished without friction. The two reserve corps arrived in the second line as far as the Belgian border. The IX Corps was transferred on that day to the First Army. Army headquarters was located since the 13th in Aix-la-Chapelle and remained there until the 16th. General von Kluck decided to let the army remain on the 16th on the line which it had reached. The exit from the narrow gap of Liege was attained in quick marches; the army had received word to be disposed for the further march forward and the trains and columns had been grouped accordingly. The reserve corps had been obliged to make long marches immediately after detraining, and heavy losses occurred among the reservists not accustomed to marching. On the 14th the III Reserve Corps had 1100 men affected with foot ailments, but generally these were not of a serious nature. Moreover, the conduct and the marching order of the troops and columns, wherever we caught sight of them, were magnificent. They inspired us with complete confidence in victory.

The II Cavalry Corps proceeded with the 4th and 9th Divisions in the direction of Jodoigne, while, on the 16th, the 2nd Division reached the locality to the south of Hasslet.

On the 16th the last forts of Liege as well as Fort Huy were reduced.

On the 16th also, the right wing of the Second Army, marching by way of Liege, reached the locality of Lantin, northwest of Liege. The army assembled for the advance on the roads leading to the Meuse through Liege as well as from the Ourthe to Hermalle and Huy, but still wished to remain in place on the 17th. Headquarters moved to Spa on the 16th. The two corps of the second line drew toward the Ourthe.

The Third Army remained on the 16th in the line: Malempre (northwest of Houffalize) – Houffalize – Neville (south of Houffalize). The I Cavalry Corps, which was advancing on Dinant, announced that the line: Namur – Dinant was strongly occupied by the enemy.

Up to and including the 16th, numerous reports concerning the enemy had come into the staff of the first army. On the 11th it looked as if the Belgian Army was being concentrated on the line: Antwerp – Louvain – Namur. In the course of the next few days, it was recognized that some three or four divisions were present in the region of Louvain – Wavre with advance guards at Diest – Tirlemont, and one division each in Antwerpand Namur. On the 16th came reports that the Belgians were digging in behind the Gette, on the line: Diest – Tirlemont – Jodoigne, and reserves appeared to be present at Louvain. To the south of Tirlemont it was noted that troops were falling back on Wavre which movements stopped on the line: Tirlemont – Melin – Wavre. Without doubt, the Belgians stood prepared behind the Gette; perhaps, the right wing drawn back to prevent a flanking movement, We assumed that they wished to await the arrivalof the French and English in this position.

We had received numerous reports on the entrance of French troops into Belgium. As early as the 9th, they were reported to have reached Brussels. On the 13th, the French were again detected marching on Brussels, and also on Givet – Namur. Here the French I and II Corps were mentioned on the 16th. A number of French cavalry divisions, advancing from the French Meuse, were observed as early as the 13th in front of the left flank of the Third Army. It was said that the French were drawing up reenforcements from a southwesterly direction toward their left flank, manifestly with a view to opposing the menacing encircling movement through Belgium.

The reports concerning the English were contradictory. At one time they were thought to be landing at Zeebrugge, again at Ostend, Dunkirk, and Calais. It was reported that they were trying to march on Brussels to join the Belgians. Marshal French was reported to have been in Brussels as early as the 12th. We were on a false trail so far as the English were concerned.

On the 11th we learned that the French had undertaken to push forward from the direction of Belfort into upper Alsace, but had been beaten back.

The command of the First Army conceived its task to consist in routing the Belgians as soon as possible, and before their union with the French and English reenforcements could be effected. Whether the Belgians would resist the attack or fall back on Antwerp could not be known in advance. If the French and English failed to come forward in time to aid them, it was to be assumed that the Belgians would retire upon Antwerp. An attempt had to be made to engage them in battle as quickly as possible and to prevent them from retreating, because in Antwerp they could bean embarrassing factor on our flank. On the basis of these considerations, a decision was reached to advance on the 17th into the line: Kermpt (west of Hasselt) – St. Trond, while the two reserve corps would approach the Meuse. Though the Second Army still wished to remain at rest on the 17th, this would not endanger the First Army. Because of this circumstance we were ready more quickly to hold the Belgians by an attack. We had to consider the fact that, in view of the proximity of the Dutch frontier, the strength of the German flank advancing by way of Aix-la-Chapelle and Liege could not have escaped the enemy. By an oversight, during the march through Aix-la-Chapelle, the different streets assigned to the various corps, including the numbers of the corps, were made public.

The question of what sort of operation was to be expected of the French was vigorously discussed in the headquarters staff. Where were they concentrated and how would they meet our great enveloping movement through Belgium?

In the last few years before the war it could be clearly recognized that the designs of the French were becoming more offensive. We had to reckon with the probability that after their concentration was completed they would advance to the attack along the whole line. To this end they seemed to have the design of concentrating one army each at Spinal, Toul and Vouziers – Rethel, supported by a strong army approximately in and west of the line: Neufchateau – St. Menehould. It was supposed that on each of the two wings was a group of reserve divisions. We assumed that troops (one to two army corps and perhaps a few reserve divisions) were being prepared somewhere around Maubeuge to advance on the line: Givet – Namur. On about the 13th day of the mobilization, according to our assumption, the regular and reserve troops could be ready for operations.

The point toward which the main attack would be directed, whether toward Lorraine, or toward Luxemburg and south Belgium, or in both directions, was uncertain. Before the war I considered it more probable that the main attack would come from the general direction of Verdun toward south Belgium and Luxemburg. The High Command inclined rather to the view that a strong attack would occur in Lorraine.

On the French right flank, the invasion of upper Alsace from Belfort (which in the meanwhile had already taken place) was confidently expected by us. It was designed to draw German forces away from the main operation in Lorraine or Belgium. We had conceived the following picture of the probable first movements on the enemy north flank: an advance of the French left flank against the Meuse line: Namur – Givet would be made in conjunction with a concentration of the Belgians to the north of Namur – Liege and an advance of the English toward the Meuse, in order to stop the German right flank which wasexpected to advance south of the Meuse. That agreements had been entered into with regard to the joint employment of the Belgians, English and French on the north flank has already been mentioned.[1]

The English expeditionary corps, with a strength of six infantry divisions and one cavalry division, or a total of approximately 132,000 men, could be disembarked, according to our assumption, at Dunkirk, Calais, or Boulogne around the 15th day of mobilization.

If this picture, which we had formed in peacetime from the presumable operations of our opponents, turned out to be roughly correct, then the First Army had to reckon with the possibility of colliding, on the 16th of August, not only with the Belgians but also with English troops, though scarcely with French. The reports received up to this latter date seemed in the main to confirm our peacetime assumptions.

August 17 – Orders of the High Command. Attachment of the First Army to the Second. Liaison between the High Command and the Armies

While the First Army, on August 17, executed the march up to the line: Kerampt – St. Trond, and approached the enemy's position on the Gette, army headquarters moved from Aix-la-Chapelle to Glons – a small village northwest of Leige. Our way led through Liege, which presented us with the animated picture of a city just taken over. In the hotel where I stopped, I meta large number of officers, including the well known foot-artilleryman, General Steinmetz, who was later to fall in battle. All were in high spirits over the successful occupation of the city and the surprising effect of our heaviest guns. Here, also, the news reached us that a basic order of the High Command had come in for army headquarters.

The order of the High Command to the First and Second Armies read as follows:

> His Majesty commands: The First and Second Armies and the II Cavalry Corps are hereby placed under the orders of the commander

[1] See page 14.

> of the Second Army for the advance north of the Meuse. The march will be begun on the 18th.
>
> The objective of the movement is to drive the enemy troops, reported to be in the position between: Diest – Tirlemont – Wavre, back from Antwerp, while covering on our left flank toward Namur. We have in view employing the two armies later from the line: Brussels – Namur, covering toward Antwerp.
>
> Further orders will be issued for the taking of Namur by the left flank of the Second Army and the right flank of the Third Army. The artillery assigned to the Second Army is to be brought forward for this attack.
>
> The Third Army, with its right flank joining the left flank of the Second Army, will proceed through Durbuy toward the southeast front of Namur.

I betook myself at once to army headquarters in Liege. On the 17th the second Army closed up west of Liege, while the Third still remained in place. The chief of the general staff of the Second Army, General von Lauenstein, was in favor of putting the armies in place for the attack according to a common plan at the outset, as the army was still somewhat behind. In the meanwhile, however, the envelopment of the enemy by way of Beeringen – Paelwas to be got under way. I objected that the enemy would not wait for the execution of this plan, but would evade the enveloping movement in plenty of time, so that the thing to do was to attack at once with the First Army, which was standing in readiness for the task. The command of the Second consented, but insisted on a simultaneous encircling movement in the direction indicated. This movement led into very difficult terrain, could be stopped very easily, and laid great strain upon the II Corps marching on the right flank. The command of the First Army would have preferred to engage the enemy quickly and straight from the shoulder.

This measure of the High Command, subordinating one army to the other, was not a happy one. Such subordinations proved undesirable throughout the war add often led to friction. Such was the case on the Somme in 1916, when the First Army was subordinated to the Second. The views of the different commands often fail to conform, as is quite natural. It is difficult for one army, itself engaged in battle, to put itself completely in the place of the other, fighting along side of it, and to take account of the whole situation in a uniform manner. We were not yet familiar with the organization of *groups of armies*. Just as an army group would have been required on the left wing in Alsace-Lorraine, such an organ of command would have been needed also by the right wing. Relying too much on modern means of communication, we had probably given too little attention in peace time to liaison between the armies and the High Command; perhaps we were also misled by the familiarity of the general staff journeys and the great strategical exercises. In these, each evening the supreme commander could, without trouble, issue his orders and directions to the most distant armies in all desired minuteness of detail. Although the General Staff had carefully prepared itself for the war, we had not attained a satisfactory organization in the technique of leading an army of millions of men. The movement of such masses from a position cannot be accomplished on such short notice as was possible to the elder Moltke in 1866 and 1870-71.

In August and September 1914, we suffered continually from the *defective liaison between General Headquarters and the commands of the different armies*. The telephone sections were much too weak and were not sufficiently equipped with new apparatus. It was only exceptionally that the First Army succeeded in getting a telephone connection with the High Command over the wire of the service of supplies. Because of the rapid advance it was not always possible to connect the army in time with the farthest forward station of the supply front. Of course, one could then attempt to reach this station by motor car. But then again the line inside the supply front itself was out of order or would break just when needed, or conversation was impossible because of faulty construction due to too much haste.

The communications of the First Army during the battle of the Marne were therefore nearly all by radio. The staff of the First Army had at its disposal two stations of different systems, one of which afforded connection direct with the High Command, the other only by way of the second Army. In the latter case considerable delays arose. But even in the case of the direct connection, a wait of several hours was often necessary before the radio message could be sent, as the High Command was equipped with only one receiving set, on which the messages of all the armies flocked together. Storms, which arose rather frequently on hot days, would break the communication, as also would interference by the Eiffel Tower. Frequently a message had to be repeated three or four times before it went through satisfactorily. To this had to be added the time required for decoding. This explains the fact that at decisive moments 24 hours were required for important messages. An exchange of views was out of the question.

A further difficulty arose from the fact that the High Command was much too far from the front even on the decisive days. On August 30, General Headquarters betook itself to Luxemburg on the outermost flank of the army. Long, mimeographed instructions which now and then were conveyed to us by motor car from Koblenz or Luxemburg were frequently out of date before they arrived. The occasional despatch of officers to the armies, from General Headquarters, could offer no substitute for the direct understanding which was lacking.

Neither the chief of the general staff of the field army nor the chief of the operations section of the High Command nor the general quartermaster aver visited the headquarters of the First Army prior to the end of the battle of the Marne. No discussion ever took place. Compare with this, as the narrative proceeds, the restless personal activity of General Joffre. In the French and English reports one finds him mentioned at every moment. Wherever an important decision is to be made, wherever accord between armies must be established, he is on the spot, here urging on, there holding back, everywhere clarifying matters. He has an astonishing mobility, without loss of constancy in the leadership. This presupposes, to be sure, a chief of staff working with a sure hand under the orders of the generalissimo and more attached than he to the main headquarters; a chief of staff who quietly and steadily directs the machine of the staff and keeps it in motion. It requires also perfect railway and telephone connections, which were always at the disposal of the French commander-in-chief.

Our own supreme commander was His Majesty the Kaiser. General von Moltke was chief of the general staff of the field army, and the chief of the operations section was Lieutenant-

Colonel Tappen. The supreme commander was moderate in the exercise of the commanding power, and is-sued only the most important orders. The chief of the general staff of the field army was authorized to issue operative orders in the name of the Kaiser and thus, with certain restrictions, actually occupied the position of a commander-in-chief. In order to have the necessary freedom of movement, such as was peculiar to the French generalissimo, he should have had under him a general vested with the required authority, fulfilling the real tasks of a chief of the general staff and not burdened with any other tasks. The general quartermaster, even though he might be thought of as taking the place of the chief of the general staff of the field army, still had other important duties to perform. It is far from my thought to wish to pronounce a judgment on personages who worked in the staff of the High command. We are here concerned merely with a question of organization.

In contrast with the French commander-in-chief, the chief of the German general staff was obliged from the very start to wage war on two fronts, and later even on several others. *The location of the Great Headquarters* in Coblenz, Luxemburg, Mézières, Pless, and Spa was influenced by this fact. It is a moot question whether the High Command should not have remained at-Berlin in 1914 and appointed a supreme commander for the west, as there was later a supreme commander in the east. But this would have involved a renunciation. The decision was expected to come in the west. It is easily understood that the chief of the general staff should wish to take over the leadership here in person. He also preferred, after the decision had provisionally come in the battle of the Marne, to retain for the time being the leadership of the operations in both the east and west.

During the time the High Command remained in Koblenz and Luxemburg during the months of August and September, 1914, it should, at least, have despatched liaison officers regularly to the different armies. It ought also to have shoved forward an intermediate office as a station for the collection of messages and for the conveyance of orders,, and kept in close touch with it. From that point the connection with the armies could have been maintained by motor cars. From Luxemburg it was impossible, in the manner attempted, to keep the leadership of the armies firmly in hand.

Such a firm hold on the reins was, however, demanded. We shall meet with the need for it at every step in the course of the further operations. It had constantly been emphasized by Count Schlieffen, who had said that the plan of the supreme commander should be adopted as their own by the army leaders, and that a single thought must penetrate all the armies. On the visits of inspection by the general staff, he criticized, in fact, the lack of the drill quality in the movements, stating that they should be made as in the battalion drill. Particularly in connection with the great enveloping movement through Belgium and northern France, he often expressed the opinion that the armies should march aligned like battalions. We had not realized that this could not be attained without the intervening link of army-group commands. We shall see that we got far off the track in 1914. It was very decidedly not a battalion drill.

Nor was the French general staff acquainted with army groups in 1914. As the narrative will show, the lack of them made itself felt as disadvantageously in their case as in ours.

Late in the evening of August 17, I arrived at Glons from Liege. Here the newspaper reports spoke of an advance of the French through Charleroi in the direction of Gembloux. It was quite late before the army order for the staffs of the various army corps could be issued. In spite of all the good intentions, such was rather frequently the case from this time onward. This was a great disadvantage to the troops and was much regretted by the army command. We had been trained at the staff in time of peace to communicate to the subordinate commands the most essential part of their task as soon as the decision for the next day was determined, so that they might regulate the falling in of the troops. When a comprehensive army order, which moreover was found to be quite necessary, had been prepared, it was to be transmitted by messenger or/and dictated by telephone. The assembly of liaison officers at Headquarters was regarded as an anachronism, and their long wait for the issue of an order as a defect.

We took the greatest pains to act accordingly. But due to the enormously rapid advance of the army and the continually changing situation (often several times in a day), it succeeded only occasionally. As early as August 17, the chief of the general staff of the II Corps, on order of his commanding general, wrote me a letter which I here reproduce:

> The tactical orders have hitherto reached us during the night hours. The customary brief orientation regarding the designs for the following day, and which was exceedingly welcome, has not come in during the last few days. Since the situation did not indicate clearly whether we were to march or not, the simple expedient of preparing the troops for the advance in the early morning at a determinate hour, was not applicable. The wire connection between the corps and the army is not working. We lack gasoline for our motor vehicles, and the army has taken no steps to supply the need. This auxiliary means of liaison can accordingly not be utilized. It is therefore impracticable for the corps to go for the orders of the army in due time. His Excellency the general in command of the corps requests, in these circumstances, a general instruction which shall be valid for the next time interval of the impending battle against the Belgian army, and within the framework of which he will be enabled to act in consonance with the designs of the army command. Otherwise it is impossible to assure the execution of the orders of the army, either as to time or space.

That the fulfillment of these desires was unfortunately not always possible is already clear from the narrative of the occurrences in the course of August 17. The army was suddenly subordinated to another command, whose orders it was obliged to get. As regards the impending operations against the Belgians there were differences of opinion which had first to be cleared up. On my arrival in Glons I had to obtain the decision of the Supreme Commander before the army order could be issued. The disadvantages of a tardy issue of orders had to be taken into the bargain. It will frequently be seen hereafter, from the records of the various corps, that they could not conform to the prescribed timesfor setting out.

On August 20 we called the attention of the subordinate commands to the fact that in view of the rapid advance of the army the'materials required for operating the means of communication could often not be brought forward to the staffs in time; that the connection by means of telephones and motor vehicles had accordingly often failed in the last few days, and especially that the inhabitants continually destroyed the connections provided. We were therefore obliged to have recourse to the former expedient; that is, at a certain hour each day a liaison officer, who had to be correctly informed regarding the situation of the corps in question and who brought the latest news of the enemy, would be appointed by each army command to come for the orders. A brief preliminary order was also to be given when a wire was available.

August 18 – Beginning of the General Advance. Advance against the Belgians

On the 18th began, in accordance with orders of the High Command, the *general advance* of the main body of the German forces.

The First Army proceeded on this day to the attack against the enemy reported to be on the line: Diest--Tirlemont---Jodoigne. The corps were formed in two columns. The II Corps sought to invest the enemy by way of Beeringen. The march was a very long and strenuous one. The enemy evaded the attack in time; it was only at Diest and Tirlemont that he offered stubborn resistance. He retreated by way of Rillaer (east of Aerschot) and Winghe St. George, as also to the west of Tirlemont. The first Army followed in the general direction of Louvain up to the line: Hersselt--Tirlemont. The II Cavalry Division, attached to the First Army, was to proceed through Veerle against the roads along which the enemy was retreating. Army headquarters was transferred to Stevoort (west of Hasselt).

By a forced march, the Second Army reached the locality east of Jodoigne up to the line: Opheylissen – Wansin – Wasseiges, with headquarters at Marlinne (southeast of St. Trond). The left wing (guard and guard reserve corps) covered toward Namur.

The Third Army reached the upper Ourthe along the line: Barvaux – Laroche--Erneuville, with headquarters at Vielsalm.

The corps on the right wing of the Fourth Army got as far as Wiltz.

The fifth Army marched with the right flank on Arlon, while the left maintained contact with the pivot (Thionvine).

August 19 and 20 – The Belgians Fall Back before the First Army toward Antwerp. Preparations for the Attack of the Second, and Third Armies against the French at Namur

The First Army continued its advance on the 19th to the west of Louvain; on the 20th, to the line west of Brussels to Waterloo. The right wing (II Corps) could not keep up, after the strenuous exertions of the flanking attempt in difficult terrain, and got no farther than Vilvorde (northeast of Brussels).

Army headquarters was moved on the 10th to Louvain, where it remained until the 21st, inclusive. Early in the morning of the 19th the army headquarters broke camp before the troops had advanced far enough to make sure of the road on which we were to travel. This is a thing to be avoided, as we learned to our sorrow. From Stevoort we wanted to drive to Louvain via Diest, but on the road between Diest and Winge St. Georges we ran into a barricade which was manifestly occupied. The staff deployed for a fight on foot, and under this protection the long column of automobiles was withdrawn. We had to make a long detour via St. Trond – Tirlemont. When we stopped for a short time along the way and were preparing to work in the open, shots fell close by: the inhabitants were firing on our hussars. At that time it was impossible to drive or walk without a carbine or revolver in hand; no one was safe anywhere from the insidious onsets of the inhabitants, in which even the women participated. From any bush, from any house a shot might suddenly break. Naturally, the troops had to protect themselves against this state of affairs and adopt strict preventive measures. The fact is so notorious that one has to be astonished at the nerve of our enemies, who simply deny it. General Mangin, for example, in his article "Comment finit la guerre" simply denies that there was an organized armed resistance on the part of the Belgian inhabitants.[2] We alone were responsible, in his view, for all the cruelties which occurred in connection with the counter measures.

In Louvain I had occasion to witness a sight which I still remember with pride and joy. It was the passage of the IV Corps through the city. On a street corner stood the generally respected commanding general Sixt von Armin, and before him the troops marched in magnificent array, after a hard day's march. One could not help admiring the troops; with them, victory was inevitable. Such was the thought of all of us.

The enemy had fallen back farther and had even evacuated the Dyle after light fighting. On the evening of the 20th, it was clear that the Belgians had retired on Antwerp. We had not succeeded in cutting them off. An excellent airplane report on the forenoon of August 20th was to the effect that all roads in the area: Louvain – Brussels – Alost – Termonde – Antwerp were free of enemy troops; only one column was still located marching northward from Wolverthem. It appeared that one division was at Termonde. According to another airplane report, of the 20th, all roads were completely unoccupied in the area: Brussels – Alost – Ghent – Ostende. On the railway between Vilvorde and Malines (Brussels – Antwerp line) there was heavy northbound traffic.

Now, however, came in the first news of the impending approach of the English. It appeared from the newspapers that the landing of the English Expeditionary Corps in French ports was completed on the 18th. Nothing was known of the direction of its approach, but it was apparently still at some distance. A striking circumstance was that according to letters seized from the field mail of a Belgian division the English were expected to enter into action on the left wing of the Belgian Army.

On the 20th, the head of the government of Aix-la-Chapelle communicated by telephone that he had just learned "from an apparently reliable source" that the English had landed in France two days before, to march into Belgium, and that the king and queen of Belgium were in Antwerp where apparently large

---

[2] *Revue des Deux Mondes*, beginning in April number 1920.

numbers of troops were concentrated. As regards the French, it was added that a French army was stationed between Namur and Dinant. The report was strikingly accurate.

The II Cavalry Division, assigned to the First Army, was, on the 19th, still behind the right flank and, already suffering from a shortage of oats, reached Aershot on the same day. It was not until the 20th that they arrived at Wolverthem on the right flank. It will be clear, from the further course of the narrative, that a change in the command to which the army cavalry is assigned, usually leads to different employment and to its being shoved about from place to place, which is detrimental to its efficiency. To this II Cavalry Division was assigned the task of proceeding between Antwerp and Brussels to observe the approach of the English.

On the 19th the Second Army reached the line: Sart Risbart – Perwez – Mehaigne, between Wavre and Namur. The attack on Namur was entrusted to Generalvon Gallwitz, to whom accordingly was assigned a remarkably strong force – the guard reserve corps of the Second Army and the XI Corps of the Third Army. In the locality north of Charleroi, parts of the French 1st, 3d, and 5th Cavalry Divisions (C.C. Sordet) were observed.

On the 20th the Second Army continued the timing movement on the left around Namur. The II Cavalry Corps reached the vicinity of Marbais (southeast of Nivelles). On the evening of August 20, the following order of the High Command came into army headquarters at Jodoigne:

> His Majesty orders:
>
> The First and Second Armies, covering towards Antwerp, will close up on the line reached August 20. Attack on Namur will be started as soon as possible. The impending attack on the enemy west of Namur, to be coordinated with the attack of the Third Army against the Meuse line: Namur – Givet, must be left to the commands of the two armies. In the further operations of the right wing, employment of strong cavalry west of the Meuse is required. The I Cavalry Corps is therefore assigned the task, after notifying the Third and Fourth Armies, of clearing in front of these armies and to initiate the movement around the north of Namur. On reaching the north bank of the Meuse, the I Cavalry Corps will be subordinated to the command of the Second Army. The present order will be transmitted to the I

Cavalry Corps by the Third Army.

VON MOLTKE.

The Second Army then notified the II Cavalry Corps to unite again under its orders all three divisions (including the 2nd Cavalry Division assigned to the First Army) and to transfer itself via Ath to the front of the right wing of the First Army in order to reconnoiter toward Thourout – Lille – Condé. It reached the vicinity of Ath on the 22nd. In order to reach the locality of Nivelles and reconnoiter in the direction of Condé (sur l'Escaut) – Maubeuge – Philippeville, the I Cavalry Corps was obliged to march around Namur to the east and north.

Thus, almost from the very beginning of the movements, heavy demands were placed on the army cavalry.

The Third Army had come up on the 18th in the general direction of Dinant, and on the 20th, with advance guards on the line: Spontin – Ciergnon, had approached the Meuse. In the Third Army also, it had become the general view that west of the Meuseline: Namur – Givet, and south of the Sambre around Charleroi not only the French I and II Corps but also a whole army was stationed. Thus the Third Army, in its further progress, came up against a Meuse sector which was very strong in itself and was occupied by considerable forces. After detaching the XI Corps, it had in the front line only two corps (XII and XIX), followed in the second line by the XII Reserve Corps with the corps headquarters which reached Erezée on the 20th. Army headquarters was at Marche.

On the 19th the Fourth Army reached Bastogne – Fauvillers – Arlon; on the 20th, Amberloup – Leglize – Ste. Marie.

The Fifth Army continued its advance in the direction of Longwy.

The estimate of the situation by the First Army on the Evening of the 20th

According to the instructions issued by General von Bülow up to this time, the First and Second Armies were to have wheeled into the line: Ninove – Gembloux. According to my notes the staff of the First Army appraised the situation on the 20th in the following manner:

The Belgians, French, and English were evidently acting in accordance with a prearranged plan. The Belgians had waited for French and English support and had retired before our attack behind the Gette and Dyle, first in a westerly direction approximately on Brussels. They had expected the approach of the French on their right flank from the direction of Charleroi – Gembloux, the entrance of the English on the left flank, perhaps from Alost. After crossing the Dyle, to continue the retreat in a westerly direction would have meant the loss of connection with Antwerp. By reason of our rapid advance, our adversaries had been prevented from joining forces.

Apparently the English had completed their landing as early as the 18th and were now being brought up by rail. But in what direction? We assumed the landing and the advance of the English to be farther to the north than was actually the case. If our right flank advanced to Ninove, it would be too far forward and exposed to a flanking attack by the English.

Therefore, the First Army considered it better to-advance only a small distance on the 21st and to assume a strongly echeloned formation right and left so as to be prepared for all emergencies. It was not yet desirable to form the army facing in a definite direction. It was especially desired not to wheel left too early. We had to remain in a position which would enable us to execute a sufficiently broad sweeping movement. The prescribed turn could not be resumed until we were sure that the English approach did not threaten our flank. The English were to be attacked by surrounding their left flank, throwing them against the French, and cutting them off from the ports. This was already regarded as a necessary condition for the further operations. If the design succeeded, it would, at the same time, initiate the surrounding of the French left wing in the most effective manner.

According to the instructions of General von Bülow, both our reserve corps were to be held in readiness for use against Antwerp. There was danger already of a considerable splitting up of the forces for accessory tasks, for which troops of the second line, following behind, should have been available. We began to doubt whether we had enough troops on the right flank for the broad sweeping movement such as had been planned by Count Schlieffen, while the left flank of the German forces, the Fifth Army, was obliged to maintain contact with Thionville. We assumed, however, that another echelon would soon follow behind our right flank.

On August 20 we brought to the attention of Captain Brinckmann, who had been sent to us from the command of the Second Army, our doubts concerning the advisability of moving our right wing forward to Ninove. In the afternoon the chief quartermaster of the Second Army, General Ludendorff, also appeared in Louvain, and he shared the view of the First Army.

That is the sense of the order issued by General von Kluck for the 21st:

> To be prepared for its further tasks, the First Army will make only a short march forward on the 21st, covering toward Antwerp.

This order was in harmony with the instructions of the High Command which reached the Second Army on the evening of the 20th.

August 21 – Information of the Enemy. General von Bülow's Plans for the Attack on the Enemy at Namur. Coordination between the Second and Third Armies

On August 21, the First Army advanced to the line: Castre – Hal – Braine le Chateau, while the right wing (II Corps) brought up at Ganshoren (a very short distance northwest of Brussels) and, therefore, was in strongly refused echelon. Our design of having this corps in echelon coincided with the desire of its commander, who had issued instructions not to cover more than 15 kilometers because of the strenuous marching of the last few days. The III Reserve Corps in the region south of Aershot – Werchter (northeast of Brussels) covered toward Antwerp; the IV Reserve Corps reached Louvain. The 2nd Cavalry Division had been detailed to look for the English in the direction of Alost, but, as already stated, was no longer under our command.

On the evening of the 21st we received by phone via Liege from the High Command a resume of the information available in Coblenz on the 20th with regard to our opponents. It was to the effect: On the Meuse, between Namur and Givet, were the French I and II Corps, perhaps also the X. South of the Sambre, between Namur and Maubeuge, enemy forces were on the way, including at the time (i.e. the 20th) one, or at most two, corps in the vicinity of the Sambre. West of the line: Charleroi – Fumay, some three corps, probably including reserve divisions, were advancing toward the north. They had presumably not yet reached the line: Philipeville – Avesnes. There appeared to be no troops in front of our center between Fumay and Charleville, or,, at most, only very small detachments. Between. Charleville and Verdun there were some four corps, behind which perhaps four reserve divisions had been called up.

As to *the English*, we were to bear in mind that they had probably landed at Boulogne and would be employed from the direction of Lille.

> There is a tendency here, however, to believe that landings on a large scale have not yet taken place.

The data with reference to the French were in accord with our assumption of *a strong French army advancing between the Meuse and the Sambre*. This was also very near the truth, while, as we shall see later, between the locality north of Verdun and Charleroi two French armies were making ready to advance on the 21st from the line: Longwy – Mézières to the attack on Arlon, Neufchateau, and west.[3]

On the other hand, with regard to the English, we were of a quite different opinion. According to an article of the war reporter Repington in the "Times" of August 20, which came to our knowledge, the English army had already landed on French soil,

---

[3] See Sketches 1 and 2.

but had first to concentrate and arrange its trains before the advance could be begun. From this, together with the other reports at hand, we counted on the appearance of the English in the next few days.

On the 21st, aviators reported the country clear of enemy troops up to the line: Ghent – Audenarde – Tournai. The II Cavalry corps reported on the evening of the 21st: "Country as far as Grammont – Ath – St. Ghislain clear so far. Tomorrow, a joining of forces between Ath and Renaix."

In the evening another radiogram reached us: "Great victory in Lorraine by the Sixth Army. Thousands of prisoners."

According to my notes of the 21st, the situation was appraised as follows by the staff of the First Army:

> With its left wing the Second Army begins the attack on Namur and prepares to wheel southward in order to open a passage for the Third Army over the Meuse. The English have certainly landed but are not to be expected from the direction: Ghent – Courtrai – Audenarde. There is no longer any danger to our right flank. After the retreat of the Belgians on Antwerp, it is not to be assumed that the English will advance in a direction so far from the French left wing. They will have to be expected farther to the south, more in liaison with the French. We can now proceed in the prescribed direction with the right wing via Ninove, and tomorrow approximately on Ath, so as to maintain liaison with the Second Army; ready to wheel southward in case of need, hence in echelon formation to the left.

On August 21, the Second Army closed up and prepared to wheel southward by bringing its left flank to face in that direction. On the same day the VII Corps reach Nivelles, followed by the VII Reserve Corps. The X Corps reached the Sambre at Pont de Loup and Tamines, the guard corps at Auvelais and Jemeppe. The enemy had fallen back across the Sambre, and the previously named crossings were occupied by the X Corps and the guard corps.

General von Bülow desired, at the outset, to continue to wheel southward with the First and Second Armies, and only then, with the greatest possible combination of forces (including the Third Army), "to carry out the attack against the enemy forces reported south of the Sambre and west of the Meuse."

The staff of the First Army began to have doubts regarding the advisability of sending the First Army directly to the south. Such a swing of the German right flank might jeopardize the great encircling plan. In the view of Count Schlieffen, the movement through Belgium and northern France should have been so broad as to envelop not only the French troops of the first order of battle but also any later position, whether behind the Aisne and Somme or behind the Oise or Seine.

The plan for carrying out the attack against the French, who occupied the angle between the Sambre and the Meuse (it was the French Fifth Army of General Lanrezac), was left by the High Command to be agreed on between the second and Third Armies. Experience has shown that such understandings are usually arrived at only in incomplete form and with loss of time. Each particular army has its own interests and its own conception of the situation. They can be completely harmonized only by higher authority.

This was shown here also. After the above order had come in from the High Command on the 20th, General von Hausen sent a general-staff officer to the Second Army. After releasing the XI Corps for the attack at Namur, he had at his disposal only two corps in the front line and was therefore obliged to move the XII Reserve Corps out of the second line into the first before proceeding to the attack against the strong Meuse sector occupied by the enemy. Therefore, in his view, it would be the 21st at the earliest, when fire could be opened in accordance with plans. It was not until the 21st that an agreement was reached to the effect that early on the 23rd the Second Army was to open the attack, with the left flank resting on Mettet via Jemeppe.

On the 21st the Third Army reached the line: Spontin – Furfooz – Ciergnon, the XII Reserve Corps being still behind the right wing.

We shall see later that the understanding between the second and Third Armies could not be adhered to. There can be no doubt that on the 21sta strong hand was required on the right German flank. The reins of the High Command were already slackening. From Coblenz it was quite out of the question to regulate in detail the tactical cooperation of the Second and Third Armies in the attack beyond the Sambre and Meuse and the participation of the

First Army in this task. This could be effected only by the headquarters staff of an army group. The role of the High Command would then have consisted merely in prescribing the governing principles for the progress of the great operation and in maintaining liaison with the movements of the whole German force.

If the Second Army struck southward over the Sambre west of Namur in the vicinity of Charleroi, while the Third Army passed the Meuse at Dinant in a westerly direction, the two armies might easily become crowded together in the angle between the two rivers. That the First Army should keep too close to the Second and wheel too much to the south was also to be avoided. We were not concerned merely with a "unified blow" against the French Fifth Army but also with hemming this army in and surrounding the oncoming English. The undesirability, for the further progress of the operations, of bringing the armies too close together had already been experienced by Prince Friedrich Karl at Münchengratz. in 1866. The measures adopted by the Third Army appeared somewhat complicated but, nevertheless, were probably justified if we consider the difficulty of crossing the Meuse at Dinant. Therefore at the very beginning, this army should have been recommended to take the direction leading to Givet instead of Dinant, so as to strike the enemy in the flank and rear, while the Second Army wheeled toward the Sambre to deliver a frontal attack. In any case, the First armyitself should have executed a sufficiently broad sweeping movement to envelope the extreme left wing of the enemy.

The High Command, to be sure, was of the opinion that for the moment the English need not be reckoned with. The veil was soon to be raised.

On August 21st the Fourth Army got as far as Resteigne – Libin Bas – Ste. Marie.

The Fifth Army reached the line: Etalle – Chatillon – Arsviller.

The Operations of the Belgians up to the Retreat on Antwerp

The proceedings on the side of the Belgians during the foregoing

German operations are revealed to us by the official Belgian report.[4]

Of the six Belgian divisions, four, according to, this report, were shoved forward at the beginning of Augustin the directions toward which danger was presumed to exist: one to Flanders against England, one to Liege against Germany, two against a French attack on Namur from the direction of Maubeuge – Lille. To each of these divisions was assigned the task of offering the first resistance until the other divisions had time to come up. Whether this deployment facing all fronts really came to pass, and whether it was intended seriously, must be doubted. Probably only the appearance was to be preserved. The many negotiations which took place between France, England, and Belgian before the war were all exclusively with a view to common action against the Germans.

After it became certain, on the night of August 3-4, that the Germans were invading Belgium, the 3rd Division at Liege was instructed to act in accordance with the general plan, while in the course of August 4-5 the 1st was called to Tirlemont, the 5th from Mons to Perwez, the 6th from Brussels to Wavre, the 2nd from Antwerp to Louvain. The 4th Division remained at Namur. The cavalry division, assembled around Gambloux, proceeded toward Waremme.

On August 6 the army was ready with four divisions on and behind the Gette and with one division each at Liege and Namur, in all about 117,000 men. The plan of operations prescribed that the army should stop the enemy in advantageous positions. The army was to be regarded as the vanguard of the French and English armies. The junction with these latter was therefore to be awaited. But if this junction was not possible before the arrival of the hostile forces in mass, the army was not to expose itself to a defeat but was to fall back. At the same time, however, it was not to lose sight of the possibility of joining forces later with the French and English for a concerted action.

After the attack on Liege had begun, the 3rd division was

---

[4] *L'Action de l'Armée Beige.* Rapport du commandement de l'armée.

likewise withdrawn from there behind the Gette River, so that five divisions were concentrated in the locality: Tirlemont – Louvain – Wavre [Wawre] – Perwez, while one division was left in Namur. The Gette is described as the natural line of defense; it rested to the left on the Demer River and to the right projected along the Meuse line: Namur – Givet. Here the Belgian army was to wait "until the military forces of the guaranteeing powers occupied the intermediate space between the Gette and Namur, as also the Meuse [Maas] River above Namur, in case they came in time." At the same time liaison could be maintained with the base of operations, Antwerp, from which in no circumstances should the army let itself be cut off.

The army formed in the line: Jodoigne – Tirlemont, with three divisions in the first line and two behind near and south of Louvain. The cavalry division fell back from Waremme upon St. Trond, then upon the left flank into the line: Tirlemont – Diest. A mixed brigade protected Huy.

On August 18 an attack was delivered all along the front: the cavalry division on the left flank had to fall back from Diest upon Winghe St. Georges; Tirlemont and vicinity were evacuated with heavy losses. The situation became critical. The German enveloping movement through Diest on Aerschot threatened to cut the Belgians off from Antwerp. At Huy and below, new German masses advanced steadily. The French were still far off; one of their corps had occupied the crossings of the Meuse from Namur to Hastiere, another the Sambre in the middle point between Namur and Charleroi, while three others were not to reach the locality of Philippeville until the 19th. But it was well known, on the other hand, that a German army was advancing upon Dinant on the 17th.

Under these circumstances it was no longer possible to remain in the chosen position in order to carry out a joint operation with the Allies. On the 19th the Belgians would have been attacked on the flank and in front by superior forces. So on the afternoon of the 18th it was decided to retreat in a northwesterly direction. On the 19th the army stood behind the Dyle [river] on both sides of Louvain, but because of the menace of the German envelopment by way of Aerschot the retreat on Antwerp was continued, Antwerp was reached on the 20th. Henceforth they conceived their task to consist in supporting the Allies by holding back strong German forces. The 4th Division was left at first in Namur, to which place also the Huy brigade was called up. After the attack on Namur was started on the 21st, this division was withdrawn on the 23rd and reached Antwerp in twelve days after a long detour via Mariembourg (southwest of Givet).

August 22 – Appearance of the English in Front of the First Army[5]

On the basis of the above conception of the situation, the commander of the First Army had decided to continue the march on the 22nd in a southwesterly direction, with the left wing passing slightly to the west of Maubeuge, when on the 21st the following order of General von Bülow arrived.

Vieux Sart, Aug. 21, 1914.

> On Aug. 22 the Second Army will proceed to the line: Binche – Jemeppe, for the purpose of advancing over the Sambre on the 23rd and opening a passage for the Third army over the Meuse.
>
> The First Army, by covering toward Antwerp and leaving a garrison in Brussels, will participate in this movement so far as to be able in a given case, by investing the north and northwest fronts of Maubeuge, to come into action west of this fortress for the purpose of supporting the Second Army.

Captain von Brauchitsch was sent to Vieux Sart by the command of the First Army with written instructions for presenting its different conception of the situation. It was emphasized that the direction of approach of the English army had not yet been determined; that the First Army had selected its marching objectives in such a way as to be able to face south, west and northwest; that it wished to maintain the cohesion of the front, but, initially, to keep sufficient maneuvering space to prevent the First,

---

[5] See Sketch 1.

Second, and Third Armies from being crowded together in the course of their further forward movement; and finally, that the prescribed turn required an extremely strenuous effort on the part of the left wing of the First Army, upon which great demands had been placed already.

The chief of staff of the Second Army, General von Lauenstein, however, held to the idea that the First Army should face more to the south in order to invest Maubeuge and to be in a position to support the Second Army. The result of the negotiations was finally summed up as follows: "*Support the attack of the Second Army by investing Maubeuge*; hence, approach the Second Army more closely."

Therefore General von Kluck was obliged to issue the following order for the 22nd: "The First Army will wheel to the left to the support of the Second Army." On the 22nd the army moved up to the line: Silly – Soignies – Mignault, with the IV, III, and IX Corps. The II Corps on the right wing remained far in the rear and came only as far as Ninove. The III Reserve Corps took up a position on both sides of the Dyle Canalon the line: Louvain – Maliens, to assure covering toward Antwerp. Corps headquarters was to be located at Thildonck (north of Louvain). The IV Reserve Corps reached Brussels, where only two battalions were left as a garrison. That was a bold measure, but we wished to keep the forces of the army asconcentrated as possible after a corps had already been left facing Antwerp. The marches effected by the troops were already considerable, but there could be no thought of giving them a day's rest. The II Cavalry Corps united its divisions in the region of Ath.

On the 22nd, the staff of the First Army journeyed to Hal by way of Brussels. It was a memorable moment for us as we stood on the lovely square of the Hotel de Ville in Brussels, associated with so many historical occurrences, to discuss with General von Jarotsky, appointed provisional governor of the city, the task assigned to him.

At 11 o'clock in the forenoon the cavalry corps transmitted by radio the following report: "Patrol taken under fire on the canal6kilometers east of Mons. Roeulx (northeast of Mons) clear. Country clear as far as Escaut." Another radio message received at

11:50 a.m. was of great importance: "Patrol of the 4th Cavalry has positively identified an English squadron at Casteau, northeast of Mons." The 4th Cavalry Division transmitted the following report by radio at 4:40 p.m.: "English at Maubeuge."The IX Corps sent the following report at 3p.m.: "According to declarations of inhabitants, Mons is occupied by English troops." At 9:50 p.m. this corps supplemented its report as follows: "18th Division reports that the passages of the Canal du Centre between Nimy and Ville-sur-Haine are occupied by the English."

Thus the English were suddenly opposite us. All doubt disappeared when the 5th Division, brought down at Enghien, an English aviator of the 5th Squadron, who had come from Maubeuge and had been assigned the task of reconnoitering in the direction of Ninove. But just where were the English located? An air report which reached us at Hal at 9:45 p.m. read: "No sort of military activity in the sector: St. Ghislain – Mons." As regardsthe other sectors of the front, it was learned in the course of the daythat audenarde – Renaix – Grammont, as well as the country toward Ath – Tornaiwere free of enemy troops and that the railway lines around Lille showed no particular activity.

The manner in which the command of the First Army viewed the situation is revealed by my personal notes, of the following tenor: Our assumption that the English had disembarked long ago and were advancing toward us had been confirmed. They were presumed to be in the region between Valenciennes and Maubeuge and perhaps still farther back. They were coming, then, to take up a position beside the French. The direction: Lille – Tournai, was free of enemy troops. However, the situation was not quite clear. It was impossible to bring the First Army close up behind the Second. It was necessary that we should advance by the side of the second Army, the First army itself in echelon to the right and left, ready to face in any direction from which the enemy should appear. General von Bülow's order of the 21st, according to which the First Army was to invest Maubeuge on its north and northwest fronts, did not appear to conform to the new situation.

Doubts arose as to whether the First Army was still subordinate to the command of the Second Army in any manner. His Majesty's order had prescribed this subordination only for the operations to the north of the Meuse. A general-staff officer in Liege succeeded in getting us a telephone connection with Lieutenant Colonel Tappen of the High Command at Coblenz. Lieutenant Colonel Tappen declared that the First Army remained under the orders of the Second Army and that General von Moltke approved the instructions of the Second Army according to which our left wing was to invest Maubeuge. He added that we were to remain in strict liaison with the Second Army for the attack on the line of the Sambre and that we could not continue the sweeping movement until the enemy had been beaten.

The command of the First Army considered that it would be too late to make the sweeping movement if we waited until the enemy was beaten on the Sambre. Captain von Schutz was sent to the Second Army to set forth our objections: "If the Third Army moves in a westerly direction between Namur and Givet, the Second in a southerly direction between Binche and Namur, while the First also is brought up to the east, there will result in the course of the movements, and from the very first days such a heaping up of masses of troops that the unimpeded continuation of the operations will be rendered extremely difficult and in any case will be certainly retarded. We run the risk of seeing the left wing of the First Army (IX Corps) landlocked in front of Maubeuge and failing to take part in the decisive combats. But the determining objection is that the First Army will be turned aside from its great task, the envelopment of the enemy north wing, including the English. This is all the more to be taken into consideration as the English have just made their appearance, on the 22nd, for the first time."

General von Lauenstein did not approve our proposition which aimed to have the left wing of the First Army pass through Mons, but at least he renounced the idea of investing the northeast front of Maubeuge and contented himself with requiring that a division should be placed at Givry (north of Maubeuge) to support the left wing of the Second Army. He justified this measure by alluding to the heavy fighting which the Second Army was going into on the Sambre and the Third Army on the Meuse. He hoped that marching routes situated farther west could be assigned to the First Army as early as the 23rd. He added that the great task of the First army had not been lost sight of.

A radio message from the Second Army sent at 7:55p.m. stated: "On the 23rd the First Army will reach Givry, northeast of Maubeuge, with its left-wing corps."

While the army order was being prepared at Hal for the day of the 23rd, a telephone conversation with the chief of staff of the II Corps brought to our knowledge at 8p.m. that aviators of that corps had observed large bivouacs between Lede and Grootenberge (northwest and southwest of Alost). Those might have been Belgians menacing our communications in the vicinity of Brussels. This city was very feebly occupied. It was decided, nevertheless, not to adopt any special measures. On the 23rd at 7:35 a.m. we received from Hal the following telephone message: "Camp fires at Grootenberge phony – no troops."

The army order for the day of the 23rd was finally completed at Hal about 9:30 p.m. The foregoing events contribute further to show that it was not always possible to take into account the justified complaints of the corps in the matter of the late arrival of orders. Neither was it possible, in circumstances such as those of the 23rd, to issue brief preparatory orders.

General von Kluck ordered that on the 23rd the army would continue its advance into the region northwest of Maubegue, covering toward this fortress. The IV Corps was to reach the region northeast of Condé [on the Escaut] (Basécles and Stambruges not shown on map), the III Corps was to reach St. Ghislain and Jemeppe [near Tamines west of Namur]. The heights to the south of the canal were to be carried. On the right wing the II Corps, starting from Ninove, was to follow the turning movement only as far as La Hamaide (west of Lessines not shown on map)by way of Grammont. On the left wing the IX Corps, was to assure covering toward Maubeuge; to this end, it moved beyond the line: Mons – Thuin toward the north and northwest fronts of Maubeuge, the bulk of the forces on the right wing. The IV Reserve Corps followed via Hal as far as Bierghes (southwest of Hal). The task of the III Reserve Corps was, as before, to cover the right flank and the communications of the army in the direction of Antwerp.

The II Cavalry Corps was not at our disposal. In reply to its communication stating that its intention was to move on Courtrai, we could only say that we could not see the point of such a move, that the First Army was moving with its right wing on Condé against the English who were presumed to be to the northwest of Maubeuge and that the cavalry corps was needed for action in the direction of Valenciennes. We could not see the possibility of any advantage from an advance in the direction of Courtrai. According to all the information received from flyers, there was no important enemy force whatever in this direction. The English were identified before our front. Although the task of the cavalry corps consisted in assuring strategic reconnaissance and the covering of the flanks, it should nevertheless have avoided getting so far away that its cooperation would be impossible at the time of great decisions aiming at envelopment and pursuit.

So, on August 23, the First Army moved against the English, without knowing exactly where they were located. They were supposed to be farther south. Accordingly, it had been impossible to issue an order of attack on the 22nd. But, as a matter of fact, the English were close to Mons. The battle was engaged in this region on the 23rd, and the English were hurled back. Unfortunately, due to the fact that we had received the order to move our left wing on Maubeuge, we struck the English position frontally.

The Second, Third, Fourth, and Fifth Armies on August 22. Beginning of the French Offensive

Meanwhile, the attack on the Sambre, which by agreement with the Third Army, was set for the 23rd, was released by the Second Army on the 22nd. Whereas until that time, on the basis of information furnished by the High Command, it was believed that important French forces were already stationed to the south of the Sambre.[6] Toward noon of the 22nd, General von Bülow received the impression that, apart from the three divisions of cavalry already identified, there were only small detachments of infantry to the south of the river. He consequently decided to take

---

[6] See page 53.

advantage of this opportunity and to cross, that very day, the extremely difficult sector of the Sambre with his left wing before the arrival of new enemy forces. The army was expected to reach the line: Binche – Mettet before the close of the day. This decision was in conformity with the tactical situation. The Third Army also was urged by radio to move forward as rapidly as possible.

The Second Army actually succeeded on the 22nd in getting a foothold on the right bank of the Sambre. The attack was continued on the 23rd beyond Fontaine Valment – Mettet, the right wing covering toward Maubeuge.

The Third Army had not been able to comply with the request of the Second inviting it to join in the movement on the 22nd. This request, by radio, stating that a rapid advance of the right wing of the Third Army on Mettet "was urgently desirable," was not received at army headquarters until 11 p.m. The orders for attacking at 5a.m. of the 23rd had been issued long before that time, and it was no longer possible to change them. Only XIX Corps was advised that it had been assigned the task of: taking possession (still on the night of August 22-23) by means of the 40th Division of the crossing at Hastière – Lavaux, in order to be prepared to take up the pursuit in case the enemy was forced to retreat as a result of the advance of the Second Army. The nearness of the Third Army to Mettet was unfavorable to the operation.

The Fourth Army had meanwhile been obliged, on the 22nd, to wheel its columns southward with the left wing passing through Bouillon to meet strong enemy forces advancing from the south.

Important enemy forces having been observed coming from the direction of Montmedy – Etain, the Fifth Army decided to attack them.

So then, here also, the French were coming to the attack. *We were plainly confronted with a great French-English offensive.*

On the 22nd the commanders of the Second and Third Armies were not, according to their reports, precisely pleased with each other. General von Bülow awaited in vain the cooperation requested of the Third Army General von Hausen did not understand why the agreement effected with regard to the date of the attack was suddenly modified. Both facts are explained by a knowledge of the general situation.

August 23 and 24 – The Battles of Namur, Neufchateau, and Longwy[7]

August 23 was the principal day of the battle of Namur, or, as the French call it, the battle of Charleroi. The assumption made by the Second Army on the 22nd, that it was faced by a very small enemy force, had not been confirmed; it had really come up against a strong force and had arrived on the evening of the 23rd, after heavy fighting, as far as Merbes le Chateau – Thuin – St. Gérard. *It was obliged to call upon the two neighboring armies for direct support*. The first army was ordered tosendthe IX Corps around to the west of Maubeuge on the 24th for an attack against the left flank of the French 5th Army and to have another corps follow in echelon. But the First Army had become engaged on the 23rd with the English expeditionary force and was not in a position to execute the order.

Faced with the great difficulties presented by the crossing of the Meuse at Dinant, the Third Army adopted the decision, quite logical from the strategical point of view, of taking a more marked southwesterly direction. A radiogram received from the High Command on August 23 suggested that the Third Army have its available units cross the Meuse to the south of Givet in order to cut off the retreat of the enemy forces facing it. This direction should have been taken not only by the available units of the Third Army but also by its whole mass. Now it was too late. However, on the same day, the 23rd, the command of the Third Army set the available elements of the XIX Corps, which were on its left flank, in motion toward Fumay. Its plan for the 24th was, after forcing the passage of the Meuse on both sides of Dinant with the main body of its forces, to take the direction of Philippeville – Mariembourg. As early as the afternoon of the 23rd, however, the Third Army received the following appeal from the Second Army: "Advance of Third Army over Meuse today still urgently desired." At 4o'clock in the morning of the 24th, a staff officer of the Second Army appeared before General von Hausen and declared that it was

[7] Sketch 1.

"highly imperative" to support the attack of the Second Army by an advance in a southwesterly direction. The Second Army estimated that the enemy forces which faced it consisted of five corps. The commander in chief of the Third Army thought himself obliged to conclude from this urgent request, twice repeated, that the Second Army was in a critical situation. He reflected that if he took the southwesterly direction while the Second Army possibly suffered a defeat, the result might be a wide breach between the two armies. He decided to comply with the request of the Second Army. Accordingly, on the 24th, after crossing the Meuse in the vicinity of Dinant, the Third Army took the westerly direction. There was still time to turn it in the direction of Philippeville when, in the early hours of the morning, aviators had announced that the enemy was in retreat on a broad front beyond the line: Beaumont – Philippeville – Givet. In the evening the army reached Florennes – Romerdenne. The left wing of the Second Army also advanced to Florennes, its right wing as far as Beaumont. Thus the interpenetration of the two armies was still prevented. As for the undertaking in the direction of Fumay, it had not succeeded.

According to the report of Field Marshal von Bülow, the Second Army had inflicted a decisive defeat on the enemy on August 24th, with nothing but its own forces (that is, without the support of the neighboring armies) and after heavy fighting. But according to French statements, General Lanrezac evaded the encircling movement by a retreat decided upon as early as the evening of the 23rd and begun on the morning of the 24th.

The thing that was lacking in our operations on the Sambre, the Meuse, and in the region of Mons was a supreme command. The understandable efforts of the Second Army to draw to itself the First and Second Armies so as to be supported directly by them in the impending battle did not have a favorable effect on the operations. If from the very beginning the Third Army had been summoned to take the direction: Givet – Fumay with the main body of its forces while the First Army swept more widely westward to surround the English left wing, a great decision could have been obtained. The, disconnected French attacks had put Lanrezac in an extremely delicate situation. There was already a possibility of annihilating the enemy left wing and of hurling the French army to the southeast against the fortresses of the Moselle, as had been desired by Count Schlieffen.

The anonymous author of "*Kritik des Weltkrieges*" thinks that the Second Army made a mistake in attacking the enemy forces of the Sambre as early as August 22.[8] He says that "it should have waited until the First Army had advanced sufficiently and the Third Army had opened up for itself the passages of the Meuse. Attacked too early in the front, the enemy recognized the danger of having its two wings surrounded and got itself out of the difficulty by beating a retreat." I believe, on the contrary, that the defeat of the English on the 23rd at Mons and an advance of the Third Army in the direction of Givet--Fumay might very probably have led General Lanrezac not to wait any longer for Bülow's attack. He was always very much concerned about his flanks. By attacking him on the 22nd, the Second Army at least succeeded in beating, if not in annihilating him. The encirclement can rarely be accomplished by holding back the center until the two wings have formed the circle. Count Schlieffen used to say in connection with such attempts, that the enemy is not in the habit of playing the role which it is desired to assign him. The disadvantage of the operation lay in its arrangement, in having brought the First, and especially the Third Army too close to the Second.

Meanwhile, heavy fighting had also occurred in connection with the Fourth and Fifth Armies.

The Fourth Army had been obliged to wheel in order to face the French Fourth Army which was moving up beyond the Semois in the direction of Neufchateau and to the west, and which had been defeated at Neufchateau on August 22-23. The enemy was pursued in the direction of the Meuse toward the line: Sedan – Mouzon – Pouilly, where violent fighting was resumed.

The Fifth Army collided with the French Third Army coming from the region north of Verdun and marching on Longwy – Arlon and hurled it back in the battle of Longwy on August 22-23. The fighting lasted in the region of Longuyon and on the Othain (river) up to the 27th.

---

[8] Verlag Köhler, 1920, page 88.

Chapter IV – The French Operations up to August 23

The French Concentration and plan of Operations

The French concentration included 44 divisions of infantry, 1 Moroccan division, 3 divisions of the colonial corps, 25 reserve divisions (including the general reserves of the forts), 13 territorial divisions and 10 divisions of cavalry. The army of the Alps was immediately brought up, as we had assumed it would be.

New and detailed information has been published recently on the French concentration. The report of the French commission charged with investigating the causes of the loss – so serious for French industry – of the basin of Briey has been published in the Journal Official. It contains detailed data on the designs and orders of the French High Command in August 1914. Furthermore, Marshal Joffre has written a brochure ("*La Preparation de la Guerre et la Conduite des Operations Jusqu'd la Bataille de la, Marne*") for the information of the commission and published by the *Archives de la Grande Guerre* in November 1919. A work by Thomasson, "*Le Revers de 1914*," deals likewisc with the French concentration and the operations of August 1914. Though numerous incidents are not yet clarified and, in spite of certain contradictions between the works in question, it is possible even at the present time to obtain a sufficiently accurate general view of this question.

The French concentration and first operations were based on "Plan 17" dating from the spring of 1913. Whereas prior to "Plan 16" the French left wing extended only to Verdun, the concentration had been extended farther northward in "Plan 16" and still more in "Plan 17." General Berthelot formally declared, before the investigating commission referred to, that even in "Plan 17" the left wing did not go beyond Mézières and that this measure had been adopted with a view to avoiding the very appearance of a design to enter Belgium.

Four armies comprising eighteen active corps and eight reserve divisions, distributed among the armies, were concentrated in the first line between Belfort and Mézières as follows:

The First Army in the region Belfort – Epinal, the Second Army in the region Toul – Nancy, the Third Army in. the region of Verdun, and the Fifth Army to the northwest of Verdun up to Mézières.[1]

Seven cavalry divisions were distributed between the armies, three others were brought together in the cavalry corps of Sordet which concentrate1 to the north of Sedan. In the second line, the Fourth Army, three corps strong, was to be drawn up in the area: Saint Menehould – Bar-le-Duc – Vitry-le-Francois – Suippes.

A group of reserve divisions was assembled on each of the wings: the First Group at Vesoul, the Fourth Group to the east of Laon, between Vervins and the Aisne River. This concentration was in general accord with the picture which we had formed, except that the forces were distributed less in depth and, from the very beginning, deployed more upon a single line. The reserve army was more concentrated toward the north and considerably weaker than we had supposed. The arrangement was therefore not so much one of counter-offensive in deep echelon as an arrangement designed for direct strategic offensive, as we had likewise assumed before the war. In fact, this arrangement

---

[1] See Sketch 2.

answered to the designs of the French command: *As soon as all the forces were assembled, the offensive was to be taken at once.*

The First and Second Armies were to advance with their main forces between the Vosges Mountain[2] and the Moselle River, First Army in the direction of Saarburg, Second Army in the direction of Morhange, while the VII Corps, and the 8th Cavalry Division were to debouch from Belfort and the Vosges upon Colmar in such manner that the extreme right could rest on the Rhine.

The Fifth Army and the cavalry corps were to advance north of the line: Verdun – Metz. To this end, the army was obliged to close up toward the right and to move up on Thionville [Diedenhofen] between Verdun and the Belgian frontier.

In the center, the Third Army was designed to assure liaison between the two directions of attack, to hurl back any enemy forces advancing from Metz and possibly to invest this fortress.

The Fourth Army was to follow.

The First Group of reserve divisions was either to cover against a violation of Swiss neutrality or else to protect the right flank of the First Army and contribute to the investment of Strassbourg [Strasburg] and Neubreisach.

The employment of the Fourth Group of reserve divisions was reserved with a view to supporting one of the armies of the center or of the left wing.

The general objective of the operation was, by investing Metz, to proceed toward the Rhine.

But this particular concentration and the succeeding operations was destined to be discarded. A variant of the concentration had been provided in advance, allegedly to provide for the possibility that the Germans would violate the neutrality of Belgium. The plan in this case provided that the Fifth Army close up sufficiently to the left upon Mézières so that it could enter Belgium to the east of the Meuse. The Fourth Army was to be shoved into the vacant space thus formed between the Third and Fifth Armies so as to be able to move approximately in the direction of Arlon. The cavalry

---

[2] Not on map. This range extends north along the French border from Belfort through Saarburg – Editor's Note.

corps of Sordet was designed to be assembled to the east of Mézières, to march in the direction of Naufchateau, to reconnoiter in front of the German columns advancing through southern Belgium and to stop them. A regiment of infantry was to come under its orders, march rapidly upon Dinant and occupy the bridges of the Meuse between Namur and Givet.

This variant went into effect as early as August 2 when on that day the German ultimatum announcing the march of the German armies through Belgium had been sent to Brussels. Consequently, the detraining of the Fourth Army was shifted : to the north, so that this army could take a position to the north of Verdun between the Third and Fifth Armies. On August 5 Dinant was occupied as had been planned. As the transportation was not to set out, according to the plan, until August 5, the theory that, on the basis of the variant, a rerouting of the transportation and a shifting of the concentration already begun was made as a result of the news of the entrance of the German troops into Belgium, is absurd. It seems probable that the concentration indicated in "Plan 17" existed only on paper and that it served particular political ends. It was desired to lay the blame on us for violating Belgian neutrality, and to this end it was possible to maintain that "Plan 17" respected this neutrality and was based on a frontal advance of the French on both sides of Metz in the direction of the Franco-German frontier. The previously cited declaration of General Berthelot likewise alludes to this point. Now an attack of the sort supposed to have been projected according to "Plan 17" had very slight chances of success, and the fact was no doubt realized by the French staff itself. This offensive was broken up into two frontal attacks completely separated one from the other by the fortified system Metz – Thionville; that of the north lacked space for deploying, that of the south came up against great difficulties between Metz and the Vosges.

The genuine concentration was therefore certainly a priori the one provided for in the variant. Its left wing extended so far to the north and was so located with reference to the Belgian frontier, that the employment of the left wing was inconceivable except on the condition of penetrating into Belgium and Luxembourg. It was formally stated, moreover, that in the case of the variant also, the design was to take the offensive as soon as the concentration had been completed.

As regards the French publications with reference to the concentration and the first strategic designs, do they contain all that might be said on the matter or have many things been passed over in silence? That still remains an open question.

It is evident that in the measures projected, it was assumed that the advance of the German right wing would proceed exclusively along the right bank of the Meuse and not farther to the north. However, in case it should become necessary to prolong the French left wing, the enemy had at his disposal not only the English and Belgian Armies but also other forces drawn from the frontier of the Alps, from Algeria, and from Morocco.

As regards the measures to be adopted by the Belgians in case of violation of their neutrality by the Germans, the French maintain that they were in doubt on this point. Marshal French has confirmed this in his memoirs. He declares it was assumed that the Belgians would oppose a German invasion, but that nothing in the matter of cooperation had been settled. Such a statement is hard to reconcile with the detailed discussions which took place in time of peace between the English, Belgians, and French with reference to joint use of their fighting forces.[3]

To say that as soon as the concentration was completed the offensive would betaken all along the line was, in words, a very simple, clear and precise matter; but, in fact, it was not at all simple so long as the designs of the enemy were unknown. There was much doubt as to how far the German right flank extended northward and also regarding its strength. It is interesting, therefore, to follow the changes introduced into the designs and orders of the French generalissimo in conformity with the gradual arrival of information regarding the Germans.

---

[3] See pages 13-14.

The French Offensive

On August 8, General Joffre still assumed that the main body of the German forces were assembling in the region: Metz – Thionville – Luxemburg, while an army of five corps was preparing to enter Belgium. Hence he seriously underestimated the German enveloping wing. His designs in the matter of the attack of the First and Second Armies, of the VII Corps and of the 8th Cavalry Division, as well as to the employment of the First Group of reserve divisions remained the same as in "Plan 17." At the center and on the left wing the Fourth Army was to concentrate to the west of Verdun (on both sides of Clermont-en-Argonne [Clermont]), the Fifth Army between Vouziers and Aubenton (east of Vervins),[4] the Fourth Group of reserve divisions at Vervins. General Joffre assumed that the English would suffice for operations against any small German forces which might advance to the north of the Meuse. As for the Third Army, the order remained as before, namely, to take a position facing Metz, but also to hold itself ready to wheel northward while covering toward Metz and throwing its left wing through Damvillers.

On August 13, information on hand indicated that German troops were advancing north of the Meuse. General Joffre considered, however, that there was no great danger of being surrounded in that region and that it could be averted by the Fourth Group of reserve divisions pushed forward on Hirson in addition to the English and Belgians. His plan was to pierce the German center while the extreme German right was executing its broad sweeping movement.

This main attack was to be executed by the left wing, which was reenforced to this end: the Third Army by reserve divisions; the Fifth Army by two African divisions, the Fourth Group of reserve divisions, and a corps (XVIII) which had come from the Second Army; the Fourth Army by two divisions (one division of the IX Corps of the second Army and a Moroccan division). The Fourth and Fifth Armies were to arrange themselves, with a view

---

[4] Not on map – Editor.

to this attack, behind the line of the Meuse between Dun [Sur-Meuse] and Mézières. The attack was conceived in the form of a counter-offensive. The dependence on the movements of the adversary was already visible; there was no longer any thought of the offensive which was to follow immediately upon the concentration. It was only in case the adversary was still far off that the two armies were to enter Belgium. The task of the Third Army remained unchanged.

Before the release of the main attack, the thrust into Alsace from Belfort and the secondary attack of the First and Second Armies in Lorraine were to retain as large a German force as possible and keep them removed from the decisive theater of combat. The First and Second Armies consequently received the order for the attack, which was to begin on August 14th. The thrust of the VII Corps in Sundgau [region south of Mulhausen] had already started on the 7th.

But the commander of the Fifth Army on the left wing, General Lanrezac, held, in opposition to the opinion of the generalissimo, that the danger of envelopment which menaced this wing was much greater, and addressed him a letter to that effect. General Joffre was gradually constrained to shift his forces more and more toward the left as the strength of the German right wing advancing to the north of the Meuse became known. General Lanrezac was first authorized to push the I Corps to the left upon Dinant in order to guard the Meuse, and later to wheel left with his army so as to advance west of the Meuse against the Sambre.

On August 15 and 18, new orders, answering to the new situation, were issued. According to these, the main attack, from which the High Command expected the decision, was to be released on the 21st, once the concentration was completed.

The Fifth Army was to advance to the west of the Meuse upon Philippeville and, in conjunction with the English and Belgians, go to meet the enemy forces advancing between Givet and Brussels. The cavalry corps of Sordet and the Fourth Group of reserve divisions were placed under its orders.

The Fourth Army was to hold itself in readiness to attack to the right of the Meuse in the direction of Neufchateau and to the west, starting from the line: Mésières – Sedan.

The task of the Third Army then became more aggressive; its principal role was to participate in the attack. . On the 17th an army detachment of Durand was drawn from it and on the 18th an army of Lorraine, under the command of General Maunoury, was formed to take its place; to this latter was assigned the task of covering toward Metz and of investing it later. The Third Army could thus make ready in the region of Jametz – Etain (northeast of Verdun) to attack in the direction of Longwy – Arlon.

The English were invited to march upon Soignies, to the north of the Sambre.

The French commander in chief held, then, to his original design of breaking through the German center with the Third and Fourth Armies, while farther north the Fifth Army, in conjunction with the English, would hold the enemy, and the Belgians with the corps of cavalry would thrust against the flank of the German right wing. General Joffre assumed that that wing would pass to the south of Brussels. But the English concentration was not completed until August 23, and on the 18th the Belgians decided to fall back on Antwerp. In this way the plan was already frustrated, due to the rapid advance of the German First Army.

The offensive of the French First and Second Armies, begun on August 14, had failed by the 29th. General Joffre continued nonetheless to hold to his project. On the 20th, he issued his final orders as to the dispositions to be taken for the decisive attack which was to start on the 21st from the line: Longwy – Mézières. Even then he had not yet realized the actual strength and the extent of the German right wing north of the Meuse, and still believed that it could be met by the English and Belgians. According to the report of the investigating commission previously referred to, it was supposed that only those German troops pursuing the Belgians in retreat were north of the Meuse, so that south of the Sambre and Meuse the enemy could be gripped between the Fourth and Fifth Armies. It was a costly illusion.

The darkness was suddenly lighted. On the 21st, information of a non-contradictory nature was received: powerful enemy forces were marching westward north of the Sambre; they were bearing on Charleroi, Nivelles, Waterloo, as well as from Brussels on Ninove and Hal. The Belgians announced that they would debouch at the proper time from Antwerp, to which they had fallen back. General Joffre did not permit himself to be disconcerted. He still believed, as he had reported to Paris on the 23rd, that he held the numerical superiority. He declared that the strategical maneuver was ended, that the mass of the enemy was going to be struck at its most sensitive point, and that nothing remained but to let the subordinate commanders do their work. The fourth Army was to continue its movement toward the north and attack any enemy force with which it came in contact. Its aim was to hurl back against the Meuse all the enemy forces which it encountered in this region between Dinant, Namur, and the Ourthe [river]. The Third Army was to follow in echelon and cover the flank of the Fourth Army against any enemy forces present in Luxemburg. Such were Joffre's orders on the 21st. He evidently believed that, with his attack in the generally north direction, he could strike in the flank, by surprise and with superiority of numbers, any enemy forces entering Belgium in the westerly direction.

It was soon to be realized that this was completely erroneous.

On August 22, the French Third and Fourth Armies came up against an enemy force which was moving toward them and which was muchstrongerthan had been supposed. The French armies were beaten back.

General Joffre still hoped that the Fifth Army would win a success. On the 23rd, this army's offensive likewise failed completely against the Germany Second Army in the battle of Charleroi. The English were repulsed at Mons by the German First Army and fell back on Maubeuge – Valenciennes.

The Battle of Namur

The course of the Battle of Namur on the French side reveals the difficult situation into which General Lanrezac (Fifth Army) had fallen.[5]

On August 21, at the time when he was to start his offensive,

---

[5] See Sketch 1.

General Lanrezac had at his disposal, in the first line, to the south of the Sambre, only two corps: the III to the south of Chatelet – Charleroi, and the X at Fosse. The I Corps assured the protection of the right flank on the line of the Meuse between Givet and Namur. It was to be relieved by a reserve division of the Valabregue group, which did not arrive until the evening of the 22nd. Hence, this corps failed to take part in the fighting of the 22nd. On the left wing of the army, the XVIII Corps, sent from the region of Toul by the Second Army and detrained on the 18th to 20th, assembled on the 21st in the region south of Thuin. Still farther left, the two other reserve divisions of the Valabregue group were called up from Vervins to defend the Sambre at the Belgian frontier, to the west of Thuin, and to assure liaison with the English.

Of the two allies with which Lanrezac was to cooperate, the Belgians had fallen back on the 19th upon Antwerp and the English were not yet ready on the 23rd. The Fourth Army was advancing along a route which was separated from him by a broad interval, so that his right flank was seriously menaced by the approach of the German Third Army. He decided nevertheless to make ready to attack on the 23rd. But he was anticipated by the German attack on the 22nd and hurled back on the 23rd. The defeat of the III Corps was particularly serious. According to the French data,[6] its masses swarmed back on the evening of the 23rd in indescribable disorder, their cohesion broken. The XVIII Corps also had suffered heavily. Lanrezac himself confesses that certain units displayed a "shameful weakness."

On the evening of the 23rd, Lanrezac independently formed the decision to retreat behind the line: Philippeville – Beaumont – Maubeuge, "in order to avoid another Sedan." The orders were issued between 11 o'clock and midnight. The army was to have begun its retreat behind the line indicated before daybreak of the 24th. General Lanrezac is given credit by the French for having saved his army from complete encirclement by a timely retreat. It appears that at first General Joffre was not at all in agreement with

---

[6] Palat: *La Grande Guerre sur le Front Occidental*, Vol. III, page 304.

his subordinate, but on the 24th approved his decision. From our point of view, this rapid retreat is to be regretted. The fourth Army had been beaten on the 22nd and was falling back toward the Meuse; Lanrezac was accordingly in an isolated and far advanced position, exposed to the concentric attacks of the Second and Third Armies. August 25, the last forts of Namur were carried. The English had been in full retreat since the 24th.

It is unfortunate that the German Third Army was induced to march directly on Dinant and to cross the Meuse precisely at the point where the crossing was most difficult and the river most strongly defended, instead of keeping on in a southwesterly direction. To be sure, Lanrezac was obliged on the 23rd to have parts of the relieved I Corps face again toward the Meuse in order to defend itself against the attack of the Third Army at Dinant, but the aim he was Pursuing was nevertheless attained: he was saved from "a mortal danger."[7]

Palat remarks, however, that although the defeat was not decisive, it was a defeat nonetheless.[8]

The employment of the cavalry corps of Sordet (1st, 3rd and 5th Cavalry Divisions) is very instructive. Setting out from the Meuse, it had crossed the Belgian frontier as early as August 6, had penetrated deeply into Belgium, but after a very exhausting ride it had made a half-turn without having been of very great use. Before the battle, it was stationed first in front of the right wing of the Fifth Army, but on the 23rd it, received the: order to move as quickly as possible to the English left wing which appeared to be menaced by the advance of the German First Army. Although the horses were still exhausted from their Belgian excursion, the corps was expected to reach Maubeuge that same afternoon. In the course of the march, the governor of Maubeuge informed the corps that it could not have quarters inside the fortress "because its proper place was in the open country." In the middle of the night it arrived at Beaufort (south of Maubeuge) where it bivouacked. In

---

[7] De Thomasson, loc. cit. , page 215.

[8] Loc. cit., page 213.

spite of extreme exhaustion, it proceeded on the 24th in the direction of Avesnes to reach the English left wing; but its horses were so fatigued that advance was no longer possible. It was not until the 25th that the corps had reached the vicinity of Walincourt (southeast of Cambrai) after an exhausting march, associated with numerous reverses, and after having passed through the midst of the English army in retreat.

Thus was revealed once more the difficulty of getting the army cavalry to the proper spot when it has already been employed in another direction. The instructions designed for it require to be studied with great care. Shifting this cavalry from place to place takes much more time than one is inclined to assume, and easily leads, to premature use. We shall find this view confirmed in connection with the employment of our own army cavalry.

No other recourse remained to the French generalissimo than to indicate to each of his armies their direction of retreat. General Maunoury was ordered to hold the line Verdun – Toul; the Third Army was to fall back on Montmedy – Damvillers – Azannes; the Fourth Army on Givet--Beaumont – Maubeuge, while the English would detain the enemy between Valenciennes and Maubeuge and in case of necessity fall back on Cambiai.

The Events in Alsace-Lorraine

On August 7 began the advance of the VII Corps and the 8th Cavalry Division on Mülhausen. On the 8th, the French succeeded in entering the city; an initial success seemed assured and restored enthusiasm. A counter-offensive on the 9th threw them back, and during the night of the 9th and 10th they began to retreat on Belfort.

It was decided that the offensive would be resumed with larger forces, in order, in conjunction with the operations of the other armies, to detain as large a German force as possible and to cover the right flank of the First Army. General Pau, already in retreat, was given command of the army of Alsace, composed of the VII Corps, the 44th Division (from Africa), the First Group of reserve divisions (58th, 63rd and 66th), the general reserve of Belfort (57th

Reserve Division), the 8th Cavalry Division and five battalions of chasseurs employed in the Vosges. The movements began on the 15th; Mülhausen was occupied again on the 19th. The German Seventh Army having meanwhile been called up to join the Sixth Army, there still remained in upper Alsace only landwehr and replacement (*ersatz*) troops, which endeavored in vain to repulse the French. In the meantime there took place on the fronts of the other French armies the events which culminated in their retreat. These events and the critical situation of the French left wing where the decision seemed to lie, led the French High Command on the 26th to abandon again in large part the ground occupied in upper Alsace and on the 28th to order the army of Alsace disbanded. The VII Corps (14th Division and 63rd Reserve Division) was called to the new Sixth Army which was to be formed to the north of Paris; the 44th Division passed to the First Army. In place of the army of Alsace, the Vosges group (subordinate to the First Army)and the group of Belfort, were constituted.

The offensive in upper Alsace had been fruitless; the decision lay elsewhere. Even by the French, this operation is judged severely.

The attack of the Second Army and of the left wing of the First Army began on the 14th in the general direction of Saarburg and Saarbrücken. In the course of the great *Battle of Lorraine* (August 20-22) the French were beaten by the crown prince of Bavaria and fell back in disorder behind the Meurthe, as Palat confesses. But, as we shall see later, the French had attained their aim: that of detaining large German forces.

Retrospect – The Situation After the Failure of the Offensive

As with us, so also among the French, numerous points of friction had arisen in the movements of the armies during the period of the operations just described. After the Army of Lorraine had been formed on August 19, General de Castelnau, commander of the second Army, knew nothing of its existence, while, on the other hand, the commander of the Third Army, General Ruffey, believed that General Maunoury was under his orders. The latter, in his turn, was not sufficiently informed regarding the tasks of the Second and Third Armies. The result was that his army remained inactive during the battle waged by the Third Army on August 22-25.

The liaison between the Third, Fourth, and Fifth Armies had, furthermore, been entirely insufficient. Between the Fourth and Fifth Armies there had been no contact; the Fifth Army had pushed forward quite alone, seriously menaced on right and left. As with use, on the French side arose complaints that the High Command remained too far from the front. It had installed itself at Vitry-le-Francois.

The French leadership had not been at all brilliant. General Joffre was obliged to report to the Ministry that the offensive had failed: "*In spite of the numerical superiority which we possessed, our corps have not displayed in the open field the offensive qualities which we had expected following the initial successes. We are consequently forced to the defensive*, resting upon our fortresses and on strong points of the terrain." The report of the investigating commission, mentioned above, contains the following remark: "The Germans had concentrated all their offensive forces on their right wing and it was there that their best corps were employed. Faced with that right wing, composed of the elite of the German Army, the French right wing had been brought together from various directions, it was of unequal value, without a joint command and in an untenable position. Thus occurred the inevitable."

The legend according to which Joffre methodically avoided a decisive battle during the last ten days of August, in order to draw us on after him until we were surrounded, is destroyed. From Mülhausen to Mons, we had wrested a great victory in the decisive struggles sought by both sides. The French admit a "heavy defeat," as a result of which "the retreat along the whole front became necessary."[9]

It had happened as Count Schlieffen had foreseen. He was expecting a counter-offensive. We could not fail to benefit by it, he

---

[9] General Mangin: loc. cit.

thought. Our various corps would march in concentrated order. Their left wing would be as well supported as possible, their right wing would be strong. It was not likely that the French, who would first be obliged to concentrate their corps, would have the whole of their army as closely grouped as ours.

It now remained to be seen whether he would still prove to be right in what followed.

The French, he had predicted, will fall back into a new position, behind the Somme or the Oise, perhaps even behind the Marne and the Seine. We must attempt at all cost to drive them back in a westerly direction against their fortresses of the Moselle [Mosel], the Jura [the mountainous region bordering Switzerland near Lake Geneva], and Switzerland by attacking them in the left flank. The essential thing for the development of the whole operation is to constitute a powerful right wing for winning the battles and forcing the enemy to yield again and again by pursuing him ceaselessly with that powerful wing.

The situation at the end of August was entirely favorable to us. The report of the French investigating commission ends by saying that after the general retreat of the French the road to Paris was open to the Germans. On the night of August 24-25 the Minister of War ordered General Joffre to send to Paris an army of at least three active corps to protect the capital.

But we had not yet obtained the decision of the campaign, the annihilation of the enemy. He had avoided being encircled. The second part of the Schlieffen plan still remained to be executed.

Were we strong enough on the right wing for our new task? Were we on the proper path and was our movement sufficiently sweeping? Count Schlieffen, himself, wished to throw his right wing on Amiens, if necessary on Abbeville, in case the enemy again took up a position behind the Somme. If he fell back behind the Oise, the Marne or the Seine, then this position was to be encircled to the west around Paris. He considered that seven corps would be required for this operation.

After the battles of August, one was already justified in entertaining doubts. The right wing of the German Army was too weak from the beginning. There would still have been time, however, to strengthen it.

Chapter V – The Operations of the First Army Against the English at Mons and Le Cateau

Kitchener and French – Transport and Concentration of the English Expeditionary Force

When the English government had decided to enter the war against Germany, the command of the English Expeditionary Force was confided to Marshal French, while Lord Kitchener was appointed secretary of state for war.

It happened that Kitchener had come back to England from Egypt in July 1914. England was destined to find in him a man who would organize the war with an astonishingperspicacity and anunequaledforceofwill. As forus, we were going to find in him our most dangerous adversary. As Sir George Arthur (loc. cit.) has said of him, he had prepared India for the war, won over the opinion of South Africa to England; Australia and New Zealand owed to him their military organization, and Egypt was protected. He realized at once that his great task was "to make Great Britain a military power of the first rank." The fleet and the expeditionary force were ready; the promise made to France to send to the continent six divisions and one or two others later could be fulfilled. But no thought had been given to such a complete transforming of the military organization as would have been necessary for a war of such long duration and extending to the most remote theaters of the British empire. Sir George Arthur assures us that the English had entered the war rather light heartedly and without an idea of its duration. Kitchener's first remark on taking over the war office was: "But we have no army." The small expeditionary force was entirely insufficient for the gigantic task it was called upon to fulfill. First of all it was necessary to create an army. Kitchener formulated his plan at once; to raise 70 divisions which would attain their maximum power during the third year of the war, at a time when the enemy forces would be diminishing. "Kitchener was thinking in millions of men where the others were thinking in thousands." He was the only statesman, says Sir George Arthur, who had the courage to declare that England must make ready to "fight to the death."

It was decided, first of all, to keep at home two divisions as a safety measure until the territorial army was sufficiently trained and to send to France four divisions of infantry and one division of cavalry, or in round numbers 100,000 men. On August 10 a deputation of French officers went to London to reach an understanding in the matterof their employment. It was Joffre's desire that they should be assembled on the left wingbetween Maubeuge and Le Gateau. General Douglas Haig wished to retard their landing until after the war had started and it had become possible to judge regarding the point where the English cooperation. would be most beneficial. Kitchener held that the concentration in the region of Maubeuge would be too far forward. He feared a failure in case the Germans, as was to be expected, attempted to surround the left wing of the Allies. He considered that the effect produced on the troops would be unfavorable if, on the first occasion in fifty years when they were to come in contact with a European adversary, they were obliged to fall back. He consequently pronounced himself in favor of a concentration around Amiens. He finally submitted, however, to the urgent proposal of the French, which was concurred in also by Marshal French.

Before his departure, Marshal French received from the government written instructions in which he was urgently enjoined, in view of the small strength of his army, to avoid useless losses and not to expose his army more than was necessary. If tasks of excessive magnitude were assigned to him, he was to consult the government in due time. He was independent, and in no circumstances was he to be placed underanother command.

As regards the transportation of the English Army into the Belgian theater of operations, we are more exactly informed – thanks to the publication of the first part of the official English history of the war on the sea. The two divisions left at home for the protection of the country were the 4th and 6th, which had been stationed in Ireland and which were now transported to England. All measures with reference to the transportation of the troops and their disembarking in France had been prepared in detail in time of peace. The principal port of embarkation for the troops leaving England was Southhampton. From there the mass of thetransports proceeded to Le Havre, someto Rouen and asmall number to Boulogne. The troops were then routed by rail in the direction of Le Cateau. A new proceeding wasemployed in ocean transport. Although the transports had to be got under way before the Allies had obtained decisive superiority in the territorial waters, recourse was nevertheless not had to a convoy (a fleet of transports under the protection of the battle fleet). The transports traveled singly or two together. Safety rested upon the measures adopted to cover the transportation generally. The transportation zone in its entirety was protected against attack by closing the two mouths of the Channel – to the east by torpedo boats and submarines, to the west by the Franco-English squadron of cruisers. The fleet remained on the sea throughout the duration of the transportation and was arranged in such order as to enable it to attack at once the forces of the German high-seas fleet in case they moved forward.

The transportation began on August 9. The advance parties were moved on the first three days, and then, from the 12th to the 19th, the mass of the troops. All transportations were to be completed by the 20th. Meanwhile it had been decided to transport another division, the 4th. Its movement immediately followed that of the other divisions and was completed on the 23rd. The 6th Division was not transported until September.

French arrived at his headquarters, Le Cateau, on August 17.

His army was made up of the following units: I Corps (1st and 2nd Divisions), General Douglas Haig; II Corps (3rd and 5th Divisions), General Grierson, who died, however, before the beginning of the operations and was replaced by General Smith-Dorrien; cavalry division, General Allenby.

To these units were added the 19th Brigade, then the 4th Division which was detrained on August 25 at Le Cateau and which then, together with the 19th Brigade, formed the III Corps. The 6th Division did notarrive until after the troops werestationed on the Aisne.

The concentration of the English army to the south of Maubeuge was completed on August 20. General Maurice estimates its strength at 70,000 men, in round numbers,[1] a figure which is too low. The number 100,000 is no doubt nearer correct.[2] The task which this army was called upon to accomplish in liaison with the French operations has already been mentioned.[3] The Belgians having meanwhile fallen back upon Antwerp, their cooperation to the north of the English was now out of the question. Kitchener anxiously asked himself whether the concentration of the English army was sufficiently covered, and questioned Marshal French on the matter a number of times. He pointed outin this connection the menace created by the German enveloping movement and gave it as his opinion that the French should be reinforced on their left wing to avoid a thrust between Maubeuge and Lillie. Marshal French's reply was directed to reassuring him: the French cavalry to the north of the Meuse [Maas] was to be transferred to the left wing; the French general staff was calm and full of confidence. On the 22nd, he reported that his concentration was completed and that on his right the French Fifth Army was ready to attack; adding that it was hoped to be superior to the Germans.

But as a matter of fact, on the English left wing were only a

---

[1] *Forty Days in 1914*, London, 1919.

[2] See page 85.

[3] See page 75.

few French territorial divisions dispersed over the vast space stretching from Valenciennes to Dunkerque [Dunkirchen] via Lille.

On August 21 the English army moved into the region of Maubeuge, and on the 22nd to Mons.

The Battle of Mons (August 23)

On August 22, French, according to his own narrative "*1914*," adopted the view that three German corps were marching against him and that the most westerly of these corps had reached Ath. The situation of General Lanrezac appeared unfavorable: he wanted French to move against the flank of the German forces which were attacking him. French refused, and declared that it was his design to hold his position another 24 hours, but that then he would have to consider retreating upon Maubeuge because of the envelopment by which he was menaced. He added that the arrangement of his troops was pushed as far forward as possible and that he would not be ready to attack before the 23rd. At the same time he asked, as we have already said, that the cavalry corps of Sordet be moved to his left wing.

On the morning of the Battle of Monsthe II Corps was stationed behind the Canal du Centre, from Condé [on the Escaut] through Mons to Obourg, the right wing drawn back toward Saint Chislain. The I Corps was arranged in echelon behind the right wing. The 19th Brigade was still coming up from Valenciennes. The mass of the English cavalry was stationed on the left wing one brigade in the region of Binche to assure liaison with the French.

It was on a day of fog and rain that the German First Army marched, on August 23, to its first combat with the English army. We were in a state of considerable uncertainty. Our aviators had been ordered to reconnoitre Avesnes, Le Cateau, and Cambrai – localities in which we supposed the English were disembarking. But they were unable to take the air. As for the II Cavalry Corps, it proceeded, on orders of the Second Army, from Ath upon Courtrai, to the great regret of the First Army.

The headquarters staff of the First Army was still at Hal when, at 9:20 a.m., a message (sent from Ath at 6:30 a.m. by the II

Cavalry Corps) was received, and which announced that important detrainings of troops had taken place at Tournai since the 22nd and that patrols had there been fired on. What could that mean? What was to happen now? According to my personal notes, the command of the First Army wondered whether any English had really been detrained at Tournai. They could certainly not detrain at that point exclusively. Was Tournai now the center or the right or left wing of the detrainings? Now, according to all appearances, there were some English troops near Maubeuge. Could they turn up at Tournai as well? That did not seem likely. To detrain so far forward, under the nose of our cavalry corps, seemed to us too audacious. Perhaps it was the garrison of Lille. It is impossible to modify immediately the movement of an army on the receipt of each bit of information. Granting that our echelon formation in rear and to the right put us in a position to ward off any danger menacing our right flank, the continuation of our advance might deprive us of the possibility of surrounding the English. That is why the command of the First Army ordered, at 9:30 a.m., that the advance be suspended temporarily and that the road: Leuze – Mons – Binche should not be passed: At 10 a.m. it instructed the II Cavalry Corps by radiogram to determine the north wing of the enemy detrainments, and asked: "Are these detrainments of English troops or of French?"

At 11 a.m., the headquarters staff went to Soignies. There it found information to the effect that, according to the inhabitants, on the previous evening 30,000 men had proceeded from Dour (not on map, 14 km. SW. of Mons) upon Mons. A letter which fell into our hands indicated that another column had passed through Blaregnies (8 km. NE. of Bavais). Along the road through Genly (not on map, 13km. south of Mons) 40,000 men were said to be marching northward. Hence it was possible to count with certainty upon the presence of considerable English forces in the region of Mons. On the other hand a report arrived from the cavalry corps announcing that Tournai was clear of enemy troops and that a French infantry brigade had fallen back upon Lannoy (northeast of Lille). The hypothesis which we had formed, namely, that we here had to do with French troops of the garrison of Lille therefore appeared to be confirmed. The army could now resume its forward march.

The IX Corps was the first to enter into action, toward noon, at Nimy – Obourg, on the bend of the canal.[4] The III Corps was then urged, at 1:15 p.m., to move to the attack by way of Saint Ghislain (not on map 9 km. W. of Mons) – Jemappes (5 km. SW. of Mons), the IV Corps received the order to continue its movement on Thulin (15 km. W. of Mons, not on map) – Hensies (on Condé Canal 19 km. W. of Mons) to support the III Corps. The passages of the canal were to be carried in the course of the same day. In view of the distance at which the IV Reserve Corps was located, it did not appear possible to bring it up in time for the battle; nor did such action seem necessary.

The IV Corps was very late in arriving on the field of battle. By the end of the day, after violent combats waged by the III and IX Corps the army had reached the canal between Condé and Saint Ghislain and had succeeded in crossing it at Jemappes, Mons, and Saint Symphorien. In this covered terrain, cut by numerous ditches and barbed wire entanglements, the attack on the powerful obstacle represented by the canal had been very difficult. The II Corps, still far in the rear, got as far as La Hamaide; the IV Reserve Corps remained in the locality of Bierghes (southwest of Hal).

The situation on the 23rd as it appeared to the command of the First Army was somewhat as follows: By reason of the strong resistance offered by the enemy in the course of the day, it was necessary to continue the attack on the following day, the 24th. It was necessary also, first of all, to force the passage of the canal on the right wing. Furthermore, it was necessary, in the course of the further forward movement, to expressly avoid permitting the army to be jammed up around Maubeuge. A most strenuous effort would be made to prevent the enemy from retreating westward and to throw him back upon Maubeuge.

Hence General von Kluck directed, for the 24th, that the army should resume its attack at 5o'clock in the morning. In the course of the further advance, the left wing of the III Corps was to pass close to the west of Bavai while the IX Corps would throw the

---

[4] See Sketch 3.

enemy back upon Maubeuge and invest the north and northwest fronts of this fortress. The II Corps was pushed forward, in a night march, upon Condé, while the IV Reserve Corps destined to replace it as an echelon on the right wing, was directed toward Ligne.

On the 23rd, at 12:30 p.m., the First Army received a radiogram from the High Command prescribing that it employ the III and IV Reserve Corps as a covering force facing Antwerp until the IX Reserve Corps, which was on the way, had arrived in Belgium. Furthermore, Brussels was to be strongly occupied until further orders. Now the IV Reserve Corps had in fact just left Brussels in order to move upon Bierghes. Therefore, it was necessary for the First army, to its great regret, to bring the garrison of Brussels up to one brigade with the aid of new battalions of the IV Reserve Corps. On September 5, at the beginning of the Battle of the Ourcq, when the IV Reserve Corps was engaged in hard fighting, its Brussels brigade had not yet rejoined it.

On the evening of the 23rd we sent repeated and urgent requests by radio to the II Cavalry Corps to proceed upon Denain in order to cooperate in the action of our right wing and cut off the retreat of the enemy toward the west. We also added the following phrase to the report which we addressed on the evening of the 23rd to the High Command with regard to our further designs: "We ask that the II Cavalry Corps cooperate in direction Denain: it desires, unfortunately, to move upon Courtrai." The II Cavalry Corps was then placed under the orders of the First Army and acceded to its demand.

The order which General von Bülow addressed directly to the IX Corps – an order which has already been mentioned[5] and which was likewise received by the First Army toward midnight – came near to making a serious derangement in the measures we had adopted. This order said: "The Second Army will continue tomorrow (24th) its attack, with right wing starting from Merbes le Chateau. The IX Corps will be despatched at once to the west of

---

[5] See page 66.

Maubeuge in order to execute an enveloping attack against the enemy left flank. The III Corps will follow the IX Corps in echelon. The IX Corps will be alarmed at once upon receipt of the present order and shoved off in the direction indicated, in ease the First Army has not already given orders to this effect." The tactical situation made it impossible to carry out this order. From the strategical point of view, such a movement would have led us in an unfavorable direction. The matter was settled by the IX Corps itself, which replied to the Second Army that it was already in direct contact with the enemy and that consequently it could not execute the prescribed movement.

The German First Army on August 24 and 25

Early in the morning of the 24th, staff officers of the First army were sent to all the corps to exert their influence continuously to prevent the army from being attracted to and held up before Maubeuge and to insure that it would remain in its entirety obliquely to the right.

The II Cavalry Corps had wheeled off by way of Tournai – Orchies upon Marchiennes and wished to attain Denain in the night of the 24th-25th. Along the way it dispersed the French 88th Territorial Division, which according to its report "had been brought up from Paris only the day before," and parts of the 82nd Division. French territorials were thereafter identified at numerous points on our right flank. No particular importance could be attached to them for the moment.

Let one think of the strain imposed upon the II Cavalry Corps when, engaged in action from Ath upon Courtrai, it performed a double march in order to move upon Denain. The performance of the von der Marwitz Cavalry Corps during the months of August and September is astonishing. None of the tasks imposed upon it were beyond its capacity. Its commander had a broad comprehension of the strategical situation. The role of the cavalry corps during those days deserves special detailed study. Not only would it prove that the great bodies of cavalry possess an enormous importance even in modern warfare, but it would also furnish impressive lessons for the organs of command under whose orders they are placed, enabling them to employ such troops judiciously and considerately.

The retreating enemy offered us strong resistance on the 24th by means of his rear guards, so that we advanced but slowly. In the course of the day the army succeeded in forcing the passage of the canal between Jemappes and Condé and in advancing up to the line Maulde – Condé – Onnaing – Givry.[6] The point where the mass of the enemy forces was stationed could not be distinguished clearly.

The situation as it appeared to the command of the First Army on the evening of the 24th is shown by the report which it addressed to the High Command at 9 p.m. from Soignies: "The First Army has thrown back in the direction of Curgies – Bavai two or three English divisions after violent fighting. Principal enemy position thought to be on the line: Bavai – Valenciennes. First Army will attack this line on the 25th by surrounding the enemy left wing." We believed, accordingly, that we would not meet with the resistance of the main body of the English forces until we had advanced farther southward.

Consequently, in accordance with the order issued at8:30p.m., by General von Kluck, the III and IV Corps were to advance on the 25th between Bavai and Valenciennes while the IX Corps would assure cover facing Maubeuge. The II Corps was ordered to cross the forest of Raismes [Wald von Raismes], situated between Condé and Saint Amand, in order to surround the enemy. The IV Reserve Corps was pushed forward upon Condé.

But the picture changed before the morning of the 25th. On the evening of the 24th, when the army order had already been dispatched, the II Corps announced that, according to orders fallen into its hands, we had had in front of us between Condé and Monsfour English divisions and one cavalry division and that a French territorial brigade had been stationed between Condé and Flines.

In the course of the night, important air reports arrived. On the afternoon of the 24th, enemy columns had been sighted marching

[6] See Sketch 3.

from the north and northwest upon Bavai and from Bavai upon Pont-sur-Sambre. According to another aviation report, enemy columns had been seen in retreat on the evening of the 24th not only from the northwest but also from the west (from Bellignies, La Flamengries, Wargnies and Gommegnies), on the roads leading to Bavai. The roads from Le Quesnoy toward the southwest and south as well as all the roads passing through the great forest of Mormal [Wald von Mormal], which extends from. Bavai to Landrecies, were clear of enemy troops. "*Impression as a whole: general retreat upon Maubeuge.*"

It thus appeared that the English were falling back through Bavai upon Maubeuge. A new army order was sent at 8:15 a.m. and rapidly transmitted by automobile to all its corps. The columns of the II, IV and III Corps were wheeled in the southerly direction upon Le Cateau – Landrecies – Aulnoye; the II Cavalry Corps was ordered to advance toward the region northwest of Guise (about 30 km. E. of St. Quentin). In this way we could hope to cut off the enemy and then proceed against the French left wing.

The command of the first Army betook itself at 10 a.m. to the region of Condé where, at noon, it received an aviation report saying that during the morning "long columnsof all arms had been observed marching from Bavai on the highway leading to Le Cateau," rear at 9:30 a.m. at Bavai, advance guard 1 kilometer northeast of Croix (northeast of le Cateau). "Numerous smaller columns, isolated companies, squadrons, batteries, automobiles were crossing the region of the Selle brook, to the south and north of Solesmes, on the roads leading to the southwest." Hence the enemy was marching in a direction almost exactly opposite to that which we had supposed in the morning. It was again necessary to form a new decision in all haste if we were not to let him escape. The question was one of attacking him in the course of his retiring movement and of cutting off his retreat by barring the route. The II Cavalry Corps was ordered to get in front of the enemy column, the IV Corps to advance with its right wing upon Solesmes – Le Cateau, the II Corps, to march to the west of this line the III Corps to transfer the base of its forces to its right wing. The task of the IX Corps remained as before, to cover the movements toward Maubeuge.

In the evening, after a hard march, the army reached the line: Bouchain – Solesmes – Landrecies – Aulnoye. At Solesmes and Landrecies the IV Corps in the evening again came up against strong resistance. At Bouchain the von der Marwitz Cavalry Corps hurled back some French territorial units.

The staff of the First Army wished to move in the afternoon to Solesmes. This point had been selected too far forward. When we approached Solesmes the locality was still the object of fighting. We were obliged to install ourselves in a very haphazard fashion in a little house on the side of the road, to the north of Solesmes. No cornmunications were available, and the liaison agents had difficulty in finding us. It was not until near midnight that the army order for the 26th could be despatched. We reached Solesmes on the morning of the 26th.

The army order prescribed that the pursuit should be continued. Great marching efforts had to be required of the troops once more. The movement was to be continued in the southwesterly direction, beyond the line: Cambrai – Le Cateau. The IV Corps was to come into the front line after a hard march. The IX Corps was to assure cover facing the south and southwest fronts of Maubeuge, and with its remainingforces to follow the III Corps upon Landrecies.

On the 26th the army was set in motion in accordance with orders. At 10 a.m., the following report of the 9th Cavalry Division reached the staff of the First army: "Cavalry corps engaged in heavy fighting at Solesmes and Le Gateau; offensive taken by the enemy at places. Support requested." We had again got contact with the enemy; the Battle of Le Cateau was beginning.

The English on August 23-26

At noon of the 23rd Marshal French had been attacked in the manner previously indicated. In the afternoon his II Corps was obliged to evacuate the salient of the canal near Mons and later the city; his left wing held out on the canal till nightfall and then it also fell back upon a rear position. The Germans had not yet exerted any pressure upon Condé and there was still no danger of being surrounded. In the evening French was informed by Marshal Joffre of a report to the effect that at the least three German corps and two divisions of cavalry were marching against the English army, that it was necessary to look out for an enveloping movement via Tournai and that the Germans had seized the passages of the Sambre in front of the French Fifth Army.

The English generalissimo then decided to retreat into the position Jenlain – Maubeuge, which was reconnoitered beforehand. The I Corps was instructed to cover, from a position near Givry, the retirement of the II Corps which was to begin during the night. General Allenby, at the head of the 19th Brigade, covered the retreat of the left wing. On the 24th the II Corps was hard pressed in its retreat. On the evening of the 24th the army reached the region on either side of Bavai (La Longueville – Bavai – Jenlain).

Marshal French went to Avesnes on the 24th and appeared at the headquarters of the I Cavalry Corps, stationed near Maubeuge, in order to ask General Sordet to take up a position on his left wing. Sordet declared that his horses were completely exhausted and that he could not move for another 24 hours.[7]

The detraining of the English 4th Division was beginning at Le Cateau.

Marshal French was perfectly aware of the fact that the Germans intended to surround his left wing and throw him back upon Maubeuge. He considered for a moment whether he ought to put himself under the protection of the fortress. The recollection of the fate of Bazaine at Metz prevented him from committing that error. He decided to continue his retreat.

The English army got under way before daybreak of the 25th and moved forward on either side of the great Mormal forest, the I Corps on Landrecies, the II Corps on Le Cateau. Fighting occurred once more at Solesmes and Landrecies. The I Corps in particular was violently attacked at dusk at Landrecies by the German IV Corps. The hard-fought struggle lasted into the night. General Maurice particularly recognizes the vigor of this attack. If the Germans had attacked everywhere with equal violence, he says,

---

[7] See page 79.

the English army would have been put in a bad situation.

It is admitted on the English side that the retreat exercised a considerable influence on the English troops. The great strain of the marches, the heat, the lack of sleep, the continued fighting, the ceaseless preparation of positions, fatigued the troops to the highest degree. The danger which constantly menaced them, the depressing realization of the retreat of which they did not understand the necessity, profoundly lowered their morale.

The French Troops on the Left Flank of the English

On the left wing of the English, between Dunkerque (Dunkirchen) and Maubeuge, at the time of the Battle of Mons there were nothing but troops of small combat value: the 81st, 82nd and 84th Territorial Divisions, to which was added, on the 22nd, the 88th Division which had heretofore belonged to the garrison of Paris. Their task could consist only in forming a barricade against cavalry patrols and automobiles for the purpose of protecting the communications. Their forces were not sufficient to become dangerous to the left flank of the First Army. To these troops, placed under the command of General d'Amade, were further added the garrisons of Lille and Maubeuge. Hanotaux evaluates the effectives of the garrisons of Lille and Maubeuge at 40,000 men and the territorial troops of d'Amade at 60,000,[8] which is probably quite high.

Of these troops, on the 23rd, the 84th Division was at Valenciennes, the 82nd in the region of Lille, the 81st farther north to Dunkerque, while the 88th was in process of being detrained to the south of Lille. Advance guards of the territorial divisions had been pushed forward to Condé and Tournai. These were the French troops with which, as has been said, we had come in contact. In particular, parts of the 82nd and 88th Divisions had been dispersed, on the 23rd and 24th, by the German army cavalry at Tournal and Orchies, and the parts of the 84th Division pushed forward on

[8] *Histoire Illustrée de la Guerre de 1914.*

Condé had been hurled back, on the 24th and 25th, in the direction of Cambrai by the German II Corps and by the von der Marwitz Cavalry Corps.

A Retrospect of the English and German Operations from Mons to Le Cateau

The original idea of the First Army, to march with its left wing in the direction of Mons – Bavai, had been correct. Its close juxtaposition to the Second Army and the march of its left wing upon Maubeuge proved unfavorable. It thus collided frontally, on the 23rd, with the strong canal position of the English, while the II Corps, which was advancing in, order to surround the enemy arrived much too late by reason of the preceding operations, and the von der Marwitz Cavalry Corps was not on hand. French was in constant fear of seeing his left wing surrounded.

On August 24, the First Army was on the right track when it ordered the left wing of the III Corps to take the direction west of Bavai and brought up the II Corps by a night march. Unfortunately, we made but little progress that day. We had an opportunity to note the great power conferred by modern arms upon the methodical resistance of the rear guards, particularly in difficult and covered terrain. We had a fairly accurate idea of the direction of the enemy's retreat and of the new position which he intended to take up. If, as we assumed, the whole expeditionary force had arrived in the meanwhile, we could count on new resistance from the enemy.

For the day of the 25th also, the First Army was well stationed. But the wheeling about, on the morning of the 25th, upon Le Cateau – Landrecies – Aulnoye was disadvantageous. The enemy fell back that day upon, Landrecies – Le Cateau. We would accordingly have collided with him frontally again, and our left wing would have beaten upon the void. The air report to the effect that the enemy was falling back upon Maubeuge was false. Furthermore, it was not credible that the enemy would commit such a serious error as to fall back on that fortress. The First Army should have continued its march in the direction prescribed on the previous evening, in spite of the air report. If, contrary to all expectations, the enemy had, after all, fallen back upon Maubeuge, there would still have been, time to wheel in the direction of the fortress and such a turn would have been only the more effective.

The aviators corrected their. error. Their noon report indicating that the enemy was marching from Bavai upon Le Cateau was correct. The First Army was still able to wheel at the desired time toward the southwest.

Three army orders were issued for the movements of the day of the 25th, and the direction of march was changed twice in the course of the day. The marching efforts required were considerable for the III and IV Corps, particularly for the former whose itinerary lay through the difficult forest of Mormal. It greatly impeded the movements of the columns and trains.

The command of the First Army attached but little importance to the fortress of Maubeuge, which was still more antiquated than we had thought. We held that it was not necessary to invest it with heavy forces, and that observation of it sufficed. It was a case of holding the troops together for the operations. In this respect, we were not quite in accord with the command of the Second Army. In fact, the garrison of Maubeuge exercised no direct effect whatever upon the operations of the First Army; the fortress did, however, limit our movements by affording a certain protection to the English right flank. As for its complete investment and besieging, which were necessary by reason of the railway communications, these matters were to be left to rear echelons of our field army.

The great uncertainty in which both sides found themselves with regard to the enemy, in spite of the modern means of obtaining information,, is striking. Cavalry was available in large quantity. But the Sordet Cavalry Corps was exhausted, and the von der Marwitz Corps was employed in another direction. General Maurice, in his book, criticizes the fact that the German cavalry was employed in seeking far to the west the flank of the Allies instead of being held ready to fulfill the task which lay at hand. But it also appears that the cavalry of Allenby did not fulfill its task either, and that it kept close to the canal Condé – Mons rather than going to look for the enemy. It seems to have been from Afire especially that French got his information regarding the enemy.

On various occasions General Maurice criticises the decisions of General von Kluck. He declares that during the Battle of Mons there was no precise plan on the German side; that General von Kluck threw into the battle the troops which were nearest, although half of his corps were still so far away that they could not enter into action before the evening of the 23rd: hence, he attacked before being ready and before having sufficient troops to assure success. He had recourse to an enveloping movement which was to be executed by troops which were still too far away. Instead of that, he should have brought this army up in such manner as to be in a position to attack with his other corps as well. He would still have been able to take the enemy by surprise before 5 o'clock in the evening; later, after French had received from Joffre information revealing the great strength of the German forces marching upon him, he could not do so.

But this latter circumstance is absolutely opposed to the proposition of General Maurice, according to which the First Army should first have been brought up and concentrated. If the German leader had still waited on the 23rd, if he had first concentrated his forces and made ready for a methodical attack, the knowledge of this circumstance, which could not have escaped French, would certainly have led the latter, considering also the information received from Joffre, to beat a precipitate retreat as he was already disposed to do anyhow.

We are acquainted with the view held by the German command with regard to the enemy at the time of the forward movement on the 23rd. General von Kluck acted correctly in attacking the enemy as soon as he was encountered, in order to hold him.

The Battle of Le Cateau (August 26)

On the evening of the 25th the English I Corps arrived at Landrecies; the II Corps at Le Cateau, with the exception of the brigade which had been detained at Solesmes by the, German attack and which did not arrive until during, the night. The army headquarters was transferred to Saint Quentin, very far in the rear. Marshal French was faced with the question: whether to accept combat at Le Gateau or whether to continue his retreat. On his right wing the French were in continuous retreat; his left flank was menaced with being surrounded and was not sufficiently protected by the French territorial troops; liaison with Le Havre might have been lost. For preparing a defensive position, time waslacking. The English generalissimo consequently decided to pursue his retreat upon Saint Quentiti – Noyon so as to arrange his army behind the Oise and the Somme. He hoped that there he might rest his troops and prepare them for the further operations.

In fact, on the 26th, the I Corps continued the retreat from Landrecies upon Guise while the II Corps, reenforced by the 4th Division which had just come up, and supported by the cavalry division of Allenby, rested upon a position in the region: Le Cateau – Caudry. General Smith-Dorrien had in fact become convinced during the night of the 2526th, that his troops which, in part, had arrived but late in the night, after exhausting marches and fighting, could not continue the retreat at dawn. Furthermore, the enemy was in direct proximity to his front. He consequently decided to accept combat on the morning of the 26th. According to information at hand during the night of the 25th-26th, Cambrai was still held by the French (the 84th Territorial Division had fallen back on that city after the battle of Mons). French had gone to Saint Quentin on the 26th to confer with Joffre and Lanrezac; but he had previously, upon receipt of information that the II Corps was becoming engaged in combat, sent an officer to General Smith-Dorrien with the definite order to break off combat and to retreat. According to his account, it was not until evening that he learned of the difficult situation into which the II Corps had fallen.

Thus for the second time General von Kluck was furnished the opportunity to force the English to fight.

First, it was the von der Marwitz Cavalry Corps, coming up in the nick of time, which attacked the English left, wing in order to detain the enemy and which waged combat in that region with complete success until the arrival of the IV Reserve Corps and of the II Corps.

Because of the direction of march which had been prescribed

for it, namely, upon the region: Caudry – Reumont, the IV Corps fell in first with the enemy and attacked him at 9a.m. On the right and left, the IV Reserve Corps and the III Corps were, according to the designs of the army command, to push forward in the direction which had been assigned them until they should attain the enemy flank. The planned envelopment was not, however, to be realized. After executing an extraordinarily long march from Valenciennes, the IV Reserve Corps came upon the enemy at Haucourt and Esnes. Night fell before the greater part of its divisions could become engaged. The enemy retired undercover of darkness. The III Corps got no farther than Honnechy. The II Corps collided with French forces at Cambrai and drove them back. The brunt of the fighting thus fell upon the IV Corps. The commander of the III Corps, General von Lochow, who in the afternoon had arrived upon the fighting ground of the IV Corps, offered his support to General Sixt von Armin. But the latter rightly held that direct support was not required. The best assistance which the III Corps could lend him was to continue its march toward its objective. The III Corps which had been turned about on the 25th in the southeasterly direction upon Aulnoye and on the 26th was to march toward the southwest through Landrecies, had been obliged to arrange its two divisions one behind the other in a single column. Its approach and deployment required so much time that it was late in coming into action on the left wing of the army.

On the English side, the morning of the 26th, the major part of Allenby's cavalry was on the right wing between the Sambre and Le Cateau; the 5th Division was between Le Cateau and Troisvilles, and appeared to have with it the 19th Brigade; the 3rd Division was at Caudry; the 4th Division, which had just arrived, was stationed farther left at Haucourt; and finally, there was a brigade of cavalry on the left wing.

According to the English account, the situation. of General Smith-Dorrien was critical at noon. After the retreat of the I Corps, his right flank was in danger of being surrounded. In the course of the afternoon he was obliged to decide to give the order to retreat in the midst of combat. The English accounts also admit that in these conditions the retreat became precipitate and not at all voluntary. The 5th Division received the order to retreat precisely at the moment when it was being violently attacked. The order failed to reach all the units, and disorder was the result. In other words, Smith-Dorrien suffered a heavy defeat.

The retreat took place by way of Saint Quentin behind the Somme near Ham, where the troops arrived on the morning of the 28th. The cavalry tried to cover it. The troops marched day and night, often without food. Only brief halts were made.

Marshal French remarks that it was only due to the bravery of the troops and to the support furnished by Allenby's cavalry, the Sordet Cavalry Corps and the territorial troops of General d'Arnade, that the II Corps was saved: otherwise, it would have been encircled. French places the losses for his army at 15,000 men, 80 cannons and much materiel. "The condition of the army," says French, "was pitiful. The remote consequences of the losses which we suffered in the battle of Le Cateau were felt up to the battle of the Marne and up to the first operations on the Aisne." He adds that the further retreat had become more difficult and that it was no loner possible to halt behind the Somme and the Oise or even north of the Marne.

The English generalissimo ordered first of all, on the evening of the 26th, a retreat upon La Fère – Noyon. Army headquarters moved to Noyon. On the evening of the 28th the I Corps was south of La Fère between the forest of Saint Gobain (in the area: St. Gobain – Laon) and the Oise, the II Corps at Noyon. On the French side,[9] the 84th Territorial Division, which had fallen back from Valenciennes upon Cambrai, had taken part in the fighting around Cambrai. The Sordet Cavalry Corps had finally succeeded, by crossing the marching routes of the English army, in reaching the left flank of this army in the region of Cambrai and in getting into action there. It fell back later upon Péronne. Two reserve divisions, which had hitherto been a part of the garrison of Paris, the Gist and 62nd Reserve Divisions had rejoined the army of General d'Amade and had been detrained at Arras. One brigade of the 62nd Reserve Division is reported to have been in action on the 26th at Cambrai. After the 26th, these two divisions also fell back, by way of

---

[9] See General Map.

Bapaume, upon Péronne, but on the 27th and 28th they were attacked along the way by the II Corps in the region of Combles and thoroughly beaten. Most of the 61st Reserve Division fled in the direction of Bapaume and Arras, and what remained of it was assemble with difficulty at Saint Pol. The 62nd Reserve Division escaped by way of Amiens and was later drawn back upon Pontoise (northwest of Paris). The 61st and 62nd Reserve Divisions later formed part of the garrison of Paris. The territorial divisions of General d'Amade were drawn back, by way of Abbeville, behind the lower Somme.

Remarks

General Smith-Dorrien's decision to accept battle on August 26 has been judged in very diverse manners in England. French himself approved the general's conduct in his 1914 report, immediately after the events, but censured him in his book which appeared later. According to Hanotaux, General Smith-Dorrien defended himself to a news reporter in 1917 by saying that he could not help fearing that the continuation of the retreat with exhausted men would lead to a collapse, and that the only means of holding back the enemy was by showing him their teeth.[10] General Maurice sides vigorously with General Smith-Dorrien, saying that by his decision he saved the English army from a catastrophe, that it was impossible for him to retreat early in the morning before the beginning of the German attack and that, since he had at his disposal three divisions and one brigade of infantry as well as a division of cavalry in a strong and prepared position, he was justified in expecting to be able to hold out until evening and falling back under cover of darkness.

On the other hand, it may be said that after the departure of the IX Corps General Smith-Dorrien was faced with a very great danger of being surrounded on both sides. If he believed it impossible to set out prior to the enemy attack and then impossible

---

[10] Loc. cit. Vol. VII, page 294.

to fall back once it had begun, he was nevertheless finally forced to break off the battle in broad daylight, in much more difficult conditions, precisely at the moment when the enemy was delivering a violent attack. He was obliged to impose on his troops, after heavy fighting, much greater marching efforts than if he had broken camp before daybreak under the protection of rear guards. The English themselves emphasize the unfortunate effect of the battle of Le Cateau. The combat might easily have taken a course similar to that of Woerth in 1870.

But where was the English High Command on that day? One of his corps falls back; the other remains in place, contrary to orders, and accepts an unequal combat. The commander in chief himself is at Saint Quentin and learns in the evening of the sad situation of his II Corps.

As for the English troops, one has to admit that they bore themselves bravely and that they succeeded in effecting their retreat in the midst of combat, although at the price of heavy losses. It is true that their numerical inferiority was not very great, considering that a large part of the German First Army did not engage in the battle. The decisive circumstance was the danger of being surrounded.

The second battle waged against the English had accordingly ended, like the first, in their serious defeat, but it had not led to the annihilation which we were seeking. It was not until the Marne that we were again to enter into an important action with them.

According to the report which it addressed on the 26th to the High Command, the German First Army was of the opinion that it now had facing it the entire English expeditionary force – six divisions of infantry and one division of cavalry – as well as three French territorial divisions.

On the evening of the 26th the First Army was stationed to the southwest of Cambrai – Le Cateau on the line: Hermies – Crevecoeur – Caudry – Honnechy. Hence there had been no pursuit on the part on the center and left wing; but the right wing, executing a broad sweeping movement and a hard march, had pushed beyond Cambrai.

The fortress of Maubeuge continued to occupy us. It now had to be attacked. One, division each of the VII Corps and VII

Reserve Corps of the Second Army was assigned to this task, and the First Army was also to furnish a division. The question was discussed at Solesmes on the 26th with a liaison officer of the Second Army. The First Army took the position that one to two reserve divisions were enough in front of Maubeuge and also that to divide a corps in halves was not advisable. We were obliged, however, to consent in furnish one division of the IX Corps, though this meant a serious weakening of our army in the midst of a period of operations.

On several occasions recently the conclusion has been drawn, from the course of the World War, that the importance of fortresses had disappeared and that it would not be necessary in the future to construct permanent fortifications. In opposition to that, let one consider the embarrassment and difficulties which had been occasioned us up to that time by the French fortifications and the numbers of troops which they had drawn to themselves and which we lacked for the operations. The taking of Liege had been a necessary condition for the success of the forward movement of our right wing. In front of Antwerp, where the Belgian army was stationed, the First Army had been obliged, shortly after the beginning of the operations, to cover itself with the III Reserve Corps, which was definitely lost to us. A corps from each of the Second and Third Armies – the reserve corps of the Guard and the XI Corps – were engaged in an attack on Namur. The fortress was not carried until the 28th, and the XI Corps could again be put at the disposal of the Third Army, and the reserve corps of the Guard could rejoin the Second Army. Now it was the turn of Maubeuge. We shall see later that the little barrage fortress of Givet again withdrew a division from the Third Army. We shall also have to examine the role to be played by the fortresses of Laon and La Fère, though they were both completely antiquated, without counting the part played by Paris. The influence even of defective fortresses upon the operations is manifest. We were obliged to take possession of a large number of them in order to clear the railway lines. If the second and third line formations which followed our field army were not sufficient in number for fulfilling this task, that was an error in concentration.

Even fortresses which we did not attack exerted a great

influence upon the operations. Was it not the mere existence of the line of fortresses: Verdun – Toul – Epinal – Belfort which led us to make the great detour through Belgium?

Chapter VI – The German Operations up to the Battle of the Marne

The Second and Third Armies on August 25 and 26. Continuation of the Movement toward the Southwest. Despatch of Two Corps to the Eastern Front

The surrender of one division to the Second Army for the attack on Maubeuge led the command of the First Army to put the following question to the High Command: "The Second Army wants to attack Maubeuge with 3 divisions, and asks fora division belonging to the First Army. Is the First Army still subordinate to the Second?" On the morning of the 27th the High Command replied: "*Subordination of First Army to Second is countermanded.* Maubeuge will be invested by the Second Army alone."

As a result of the operations on the Sambre and Meuse the Second and Third Armies were marching toward each other, almost at a right angle. It was now necessary to reform them in a markedly *southwesterly direction* in order to keep them from jamming together and to maintain contact with the first army which was executing a sweeping movement with a view to surrounding the enemy.

The Second Army, which on the evening of the 24th had stood to the east of Maubeuge, on the general line: Beaumont – Florennes, pursued the enemy on the 25th and 26th in the southwesterly direction and on the 26th reached the line: Aulnoye – Boulogne (south of Avesnes) – Ohain. The I Cavalry Corps and the 14th Division which was marching on the right wing (the 13th Division had remained in front of Maubeuge) were both ordered to take the direction through Aulnoye – Le Cateau so as to get into the rear of the English.

The Third Army did not follow exactly the movement of the Second, but marched in a more southerly direction; on the 25th it reached the region of Mariembourg, on the 26th the region of Rocroi (on the line: Regniowez – Rocroi – Les Mezures). There existed the menace of a gap being opened between the Second and Third Armies.

The siege of Maubeuge was confided to General von Zwehl, who for this purpose had under him the VII Reserve Corps and the 13th Division. The latter, however, was soon sent back to the Second Army, leaving in front of Maubeuge only a reenforced brigade.

On the 26th a fateful *order of the High Command* reached the Second and Third Armies: "*With a view to being transported as quickly as possible toward the east, the following units will be got under way on the 26th: available portions of the Guard Reserve Corps* in two columns, divided into divisions, bound for Aix-la-Chapelle [Aachen]: *available portions of the divisions of the XI Corps bound for Malmedy (or Saint-Vith).*"

The strength of the Third Army was thus reduced to two and one-half corps when, beginning August 26, the 24th Reserve Division had been detached to besiege Givet.

August 27-29 – The First Army Starts in the Direction of Péronne. The French Counterattack against the Second Army at Saint Quentin. The Fourth and Fifth Armies Fight for the Crossings of the Meuse

After the battle of Le Cateau, there was no precise idea as to the direction in which the English were retreating. On the morning of the 27th we did have information indicating the march of strong enemy columns from Landrecies in the direction of Guise (the English I Corps did in fact follow that direction on the 26th) and the march of a column upon Saint Quentin by way of Estrées (northwest of Saint Quentin), which is the route followed by the English II Corps on the 26-27th. According to statements of prisoners which were received on the 28th, French had been at Noyon up to the 27th. In that city there were said to have been 4000 to 5000 men and larger forces at Saint Quentin. It was possible, however, from the situation as a whole, that the English would take a more southwesterly direction in order not to let themselves be cut off from the ports. For this reason and in order to continue the enveloping movement of the right wing of the German Army in the southwesterly direction – a movement which was interrupted by the Battle of Namur – on the 27th the First Army struck in the direction of Péronne. The IX Corps, which had been held back in front of Maubeuge, was brought up by forced marches upon the left wing. To the right wing (II Corps and II Cavalry Corps) was assigned the task of proceeding through Combles and preventing the escape of the enemy north of the Somme below Péronne. On the evening of the 27th the army reached the line: Combles – Joncourt (north of St. Quentin) and on the 28th took possession of the Somme sector from Bray to a point north of Nesle. Army headquarters moved to Villers-Faucon.

On the 29th the First Army advanced up to the line: Villers-Bretonneux – Chaulnes – Nesle.[1]

In the course of these days the French forces, which until that time had been numerically rather weak and of small value, were appreciably reenforced *on the right flank.* On the 27th and 28th encounters had taken place in the locality of Combles with the 3rd Cavalry Division, the 61st and 62d Reserve Divisions and a French territorial division, in the course of which the French were beaten. On the 29th the II Corps collided at Proyart with strong elements of the French VII Corps as also with battalions of Alpine reserve chasseurs, which were thoroughly beaten and thrown back beyond

---

[1] See Sketch 4.

Villers-Bretonneux. Other encounters took place southwest of Chaulnes.

We had an impression that the enemy was throwing all remaining available troops in front of the First Army in. order to hold up its advance. Up to that time we had identified in all: the 61st and 62nd Reserve Divisions, which appeared to have fallen back from Arras upon Péronne in order to reach the Somme ahead of us further, as before, the 81st, 82nd, 84t11and 88th Territorial Divisions, Sordet's Cavalry Corps (1st, 2nd and 5th Cavalry Divisions), a number of reserve battalions of Alpine chasseurs, which according to statements of prisoners had been detrained at Amiens the 14th Division of the VII Corps, called up from Mülhausen to Amiens by way of Paris, detrained on the 27th and pushed forward upon Proyart. Detrainments of troops seemed to have taken place on the 29th at Amiens, Moreuil, and farther south. Roye was reported occupied by the enemy. According to orders falling into our hands, the abovementioned troops formed the army detachment of General d'Amade, to whom, thus reenforced, was assigned the task of covering the left flank of the English.

The II Cavalry Corps was accordingly ordered to proceed toward Montdidier and reconnoiter in the direction of Amiens, Paris, and the Oise. For covering the flank and the communications of the army, the 4th Reserve Division was sent toward the locality of Combles. It proceeded to Albert and threw back some small enemy forces. The corps had no aviators at its disposal and at the time only three reserve squadrons, the three others being employed elsewhere. The reconnoitering on the flank could therefore not fail to be insufficient. It would have been well to have left a division of the II Cavalry Corps on the right wing.

The staff of the First Army betook itself on the morning of the 29th to Péronne. Important detachments of the French units mentioned had already been badly beaten. The idea was first to disperse completely "the French group in process of being assembled" before it had received new reenforcements. But following that, the First Army had to reach a decision regarding the further operations. The English appeared to have fallen back through St. Quentin in a south and southwesterly direction. Hence the First Army could not continue in the markedly southwest direction which it had followed up to that time. Such a course might have led to a dispersion of the German forces. It was the general operations against the French that now came into the foreground. It was assumed that they were retreating to a position extending behind the Aisne, then through Reims – Laon – La Fère toward the Somme. This position had to be surrounded.

A staff officer was accordingly sent on the afternoon of the 28th to the Second Army to propose *a change of front toward the Oise*, the right wing of the Second Army marching upon Quierzy and Chauny, First Army upon Compiegne – Noyon, in extended echelon to the right against Paris, the cavalry bearing in part upon Paris and in part upon Soissons. In this manner the English would at the same time be cut off in the most effective manner. The officer informed the Second Army that in the opinion of the command of the First Army the fortifications of Laon, La Fère, and Fourdrain were neglected, of small value, without offensive power, and probably not armed.

Whether the time had come for the First Army to wheel left could be determined only by the High Command. In any case, it could hardly keep on in the direction: Amiens – Roye. It could already be seen that its forces would not be sufficient for such a broad sweeping movement. But such a sharp turn toward the Oise as the First Army was proposing was probably out of the question. If the English were really falling back by way of St. Quentin, say upon Chauny – Noyon, it had to be assumed that the French, by uniting with them, would bend back the left wing of their La Fère – Laon position upon Compiegne by way of Chauny or else that they would continue their retreat. In either case it was not yet clear that we should wheel toward the Oise. If the French troops which had recently turned up on the Somme were dispersed, it would have been preferable for that reason to march first in the general direction of Montdidier – Noyon *via* Roye. Further measures had to be left to the future.

On the evening of the 28th, however, the First Army received explicit instructions of the High Command which gave it a quite different direction. And on the evening of the 29th it received at Péronne the following radiogram from the Second Army: "Second Army engaged on the line: Essigny le Grand – Mont d'Origny –

Voulpaix – Haution (hence, south of St. Quentin up to the region of Vervins) in hard fighting with apparently superior forces. Urgently request early support by portions of first Army in direction of Essigny [Essigny le Grand]." A little later a staff officer of the Second Army appeared and declared that the fighting in which his army was engaged was particularly severe and that the aid of the IX Corps in the direction of Mont d'Origny was urgently needed; adding that the IX Corps was already apprised.

Hence, the battle of Namur had not yet brought about the decision: the enemy was attacking again.

On the 27th, the Second Army had continued its march in the southwesterly direction, its right wing passing through Landrecies, and had attained the region extending from Sain Souplet to south of La Capelle. It wished to remain there on the 28th to await the arrival of the Third Army which threatened to lose connection.

On the 26th the Third Army had got as far as the region of Rocroi, and on the 27th to Girondelle – L'Echelle – Lonny. In the course of the 27th, the Fourth Army, whose right wing was fighting south of Sedan, the left wing at Repay, and was making no progress,, urgently asked for its assistance. Accordingly, General von Hausen wished to proceed that day upon Signy l'Abbaye – Thin le Moutier in order to support the right wing of the Fourth Army by passing close to the west of Mézières; and in his turn he asked to have his rear covered by the Second Army. The latter was obliged to refuse. As the First Army wished to proceed on the 26th. upon Nesle with its right wing, the operation was in danger of falling apart. The Second, Army was, in fact, in a difficult situation. Its conduct was not, in the words of General von Hausen (loc. cit.), "peculiar and no doubt largely determined by particular interests."

General von Bülow consequently decided, for the 28th, to leave his left wing (X Corps and Guard Corps) at Guise and eastward, facing the Oise whose south bank was still occupied by the enemy, but to push his right wing upon Saint Quentin so as at least not to lose connection with the First Army. Such a drawing apart of the Second Army was certainly not desirable. When, therefore, the Third Army announced in the course of the 28th that by order of the High Command it was not facing about in the southeasterly direction but would advance toward the southwest, the left wing of the Second Army (X Corps and Guard Corps) received the order to cross the Oise. . The enemy forces stationed to the south of the river appeared to be very small. In the evening, however, information was received to the effect that fighting was still in progress for the passages of the river. It was thought that these were rear-guard combats. The army, desired accordingly to make ready on the 29th for an attack on La Fère.

But on the 29th it was attacked by a *vigorous counter-thrust of the French in the direction of Saint Quentin.*

As a matter of fact, the Third Army had received from the High Command the order already mentioned directing it "to continue its movement in the general direction of the southwest." General von Hausen had consequently renounced on the 27th his idea of continuing the march in the direction of Signy l'Abbaye and Thin le Moutier; but on the 28th he decided, nevertheless, upon receipt of a new appeal for assistance from the Fourth Army, to face about upon Vendresse – Luvergny, when a new enemy arose in front of him at Moncornet--Rethel. The change of front to the left was deferred until the situation was clarified. This having occurred, the march upon Vendresse was got under way at noon of the 29th; but at 4 o'clock in the afternoon the Third Army also received a communication from the Second Army saying that it was engaged in a violent combat on the line: Guise – Etreaupont and that it requested support of the Third Army in the direction of Vervins. The command of the Third Army was unable to change once more its dispositions, and was holdingto its decision to support the Fourth Army, when the latter announced, on the evening of the 29th, that the enemy facing it had begun to retreat by way of Vendresse – Sauville. The Third Army then advanced, on the 30th, upon Chateau Porcien – Rethel – Attigny to attack the retiring enemy and in the evening found itself engaged on that line.

An *a posteriori* critique will conclude from the foregoing that the Third Army would have supported the Second Army in the battle of St. Quentin – Guise as well as the Fourth Army in its struggles for the crossings of the Meuse if it had not obliqued either to right or left but had continued its march unbroken in the southwesterly direction. That is what Count Schlieffen had taught should be done in such a case. But the Third Army could not embrace the whole of the situation, and it merits no reproach whatever. On this occasion it was the leadership from above that proved defective.

After the victory of Neufchateau (August 22 and 23) the, Fourth Army had struck out in the direction of Sedan – Stenay, but on the Meuse came up against stubborn resistance. The enemy was delivering violent counterattacks. From the 26th to the 29th the Fourth Army engaged in some heavy fighting in order to cross the Meuse, and the attempt finally proved successful between Sedan and Stenay.

In front of the Fifth Army the enemy had fallen back on the Meuse after the battle at Longwy – Longuyon and on the Othain sector (August 22-27). After the needed rest had been granted it, the army set out toward the Meuse in the direction of Dun [Dun sur Meuse]. Its left wing was drawn back upon Consenvoye – Azannes to assure covering toward Verdun. The main reserve of Metz invested theeast front of Verdun. Until the enemy fell back slowly, the Fifth Army, also, had to engage in some hard fighting in the region of Dun in order to cross the Meuse.

Instructions of the High Command on August 27. The Advance on Paris is Continued. The First Army Proceeds toward the Seine River below Paris

The First Army had been aware of the relations just described in connection with the Second, Third and Fourth Armies. It had been kept informed in part by the Second Army and in part by the radio messages on which it had listened in. Reports indicating decisive victories had been followed by urgent calls for support; the situation struck us as being rather confused. We had heard of the despatch of two corps to the east by order of the High Command.

It was in such conditions that the command of the First Army had to examine, in the course of the day of the 29th, the written and very detailed instructions of the High Command issued on the 27th and delivered on the 28th by an officer of the High Command, and to arrive at a decision with regard to the further operations.

The general instructions of August 27 to the First to Seventh Armies, inclusive, for the continuance of the operations,[2] read:

> The enemy, formed in three groups, has attempted to halt the German offensive.
>
> On his north wing, facing our First, Second, and Third Armies, and supported by the English Army and portions of the Belgian Army, he has adopted in the region: Maubeuge – Namur – Dinant an attitude which is primarily defensive. His plan of flanking the German right wing has failed through the sweeping movement of our First Army.
>
> The central enemy group was stationed between. Mézières and Verdun. Its left wing had taken the offensive and had advanced beyond the Semois sector against our Fourth Army. This offensive having proved unsuccessful, it then attempted to drive back the left wing of our 5th Army from Metz by an attack from Verdun. This attempt has also failed.
>
> A third powerful enemy group has attempted to penetrate into Lorraine and into the valley of the upper Rhine, in order to press forward against the Rhine [Rhein] and the lower Main, passing on either side of Strasburg. Our Sixth and Seventh Armies in the course of stiff fighting, have succeeded in victoriously repulsing this attempt.
>
> All the active French corps, including two divisions newly formed (44th and 45th Divisions), have already been engaged and have suffered considerable losses; the majority of the French reserve divisions have also been engaged and are badly shaken. We are as yet unable to determine the present capacity of resistance of the Franco-British army.
>
> The Belgian Army is in process of dissolution; it can no longer consider taking the offensive in the open field. At Antwerp there may be approximately 100,000 Belgian troops, both field and garrison. They are badly shaken and have little capacity for offensive undertakings.
>
> The French, or at least their north and center groups, are in full retreat in the westerly or southwesterly direction, hence on Paris. It is quite possible that in the course of this retreat they will again offer stubborn resistance. All the information coming from France confirms our assumption that the French army is fighting to gain time and that its aim is to hold the largest possible part of the German forces on the French front in order to facilitate a Russian offensive.

---

[2] See Sketch 5.

The Anglo-French groups of the north and center may, after the loss of the Meuse line, offer new resistance behind the Aisne, the extreme left being perhaps pushed as far as Saint Quentin – La Fère – Laon, and the right wing west of the Argonne approximately in the region of Sainte Menehould. The next line of resistance would probably be the Marne, the left wing resting on Paris. It is also possible that forces are being concentrated on the lower Seine.

On the French south wing the situation is not yet clear. It is not impossible that the enemy, in order to relieve his north wing and his center, will resume the offensive in Lorraine. If this south wing should fall back, it will continually attempt, by resting on the fortified triangle: Langres [on the Marne, 60km. N. of Dijon] – Dijon – Besancon, to flank the German armies from the southerly direction or to assemble forces for a new offensive.

We must reckon with the French army being brought back to original strength and receiving new units. Although for the moment it has at its disposal, in addition to the small strength represented by its depots, only the class of 1914, it must yet be assumed that it will have recourse to the next class of recruits and that it will bring up to the front, all the available units in North Africa as well as marines. The French government will probably soon order the formation of bands of franc-tireurs.

England, too, is actively striving to form a new army from volunteers and territorial troops. However, it is hardly conceivable that this army will be in a condition for use within the next four to six months.

Our task accordingly is *by quickly advancing the German army upon Paris, to give the French Army no respite*, to prevent the formation of new units and to deprive the country of the greatest possible means of combat.

Belgium will be organized as a general government under a German administration. It will serve our First, Second and Third Armies as a rear zone for the supply of provisions and will thus considerably shorten the lines of communication of our right wing.

His majesty orders that the German Army advance in the direction of Paris.

The Third Army (Sketch 5), to which the II Cavalry Corps is subordinated, will advance west of the Oise toward the Lower Seine. It must be ready to go to the aid of the Second Army. It is also charged with protecting the flank of the German forces. It will prevent in its zone of action the formation of new enemy units. The detachments left in the rear to invest Antwerp (III and IX Reserve

Corps) will be directly under the High Command. The IV Reserve Corps is again at the disposal of the First Army.

The Second Army, to which the I Cavalry Corps is subordinate, will cross the line: La Fère – Laon and advance upon Paris. It will invest and carry Maubeuge, and later La Fère and Laon, this latter in conjunction with the Third army. The I Cavalry Corps will reconnoiter before the front of the Second and Third Armies. Its reports will be sent to both armies.

The Third Army, crossing the line: Laon – Guignicourt (west of Neufchatel), will advance upon Chateau-Thierry. It will seize Hirson as well as Laon and the fort de Condé (not on map), the two latter in conjunction with the Second Army. The I Cavalry Corps, operating before the front of the Second and Third Armies, will furnish reports also to the Third Army.

The fourth Army will march via Reims upon Epernay. The IV Cavalry Corps, which is under the Fifth Army, will also make reports to the Fourth Army. The siege material required for carrying Reims will be put at the disposition of this army. The VI Corps goes to the Fifth Army.

The Fifth Army, to which the VI Corps is assigned, will proceed toward the line: Chalons sur Marne – Vitry le Francois. It will assure the protection of the left flank of the armies by assuming an echelon formation to rear and left, until the Sixth Army is in a position to take over this task west of the Meuse. The IV Cavalry Corps will remain under the Fifth Army; it will reconnoiter before the front of the Fourth and Fifth Armies and will also keep the Fourth Army supplied with information. Verdun will be invested. In addition to the five landwehr brigades of the Nied position, the 8th and 10th Replacement Divisions will also be assigned to the Fifth Army as soon as they are no longer absolutely needed by the Sixth Army.

The Sixth Army, to which the Seventh Army and the III Cavalry Corps are subordinate, is first, by resting on Metz, to oppose an enemy irruption into Lorraine and upper Alsace. The fortress of Metz will come under the orders of the Sixth Army. If the enemy falls back, the Fifth Army, with the III Cavalry Corps under it, will cross the Moselle (Mosel) between Toul and Epinal and will advance in the general direction of Neufchateau. This army is then charged with the protection of the left flank of the German forces. It will invest Nancy and Toul and will cover sufficiently toward Epinal. In this case the Sixth Army will be reenforced by portions of the Seventh Army (XIV and XV Corps, a replacement division). On the other hand, it will yield the 8th and 10th Replacement Divisions to the Fifth army. The

Seventh Army will then be independent.

The Seventh Army will at first be under the Sixth Army. If the Sixth Army crosses the Moselle, the Seventh Army will become independent. The fortress of Strassburg (Strazburg) and the works of the upper Rhine with their garrisons remain under its orders. The task of the seventh Army will then be to prevent any enemy irruption between Epinal and the Swiss frontier. It will be well for it to construct substantial defensive positions in front of Epinal and from this fortress up to the Vosges as also in the valley of the Rhine, connecting them with Neubreisach, and that it arrange the major part of its forces behind its right wing. The XIV and XV Corps, as well as a replacement division will then be transferred to the Sixth Army.

Limits of the zones of action: . . . . .

All the armies shall act in mutual understanding and support each other in the struggle on the different sectors. If the enemy offers strong resistance on the Aisne and later on the Marne, it may become necessary to have the armies wheel from the southwesterly into the southerly direction.

It is urgently desirable that the armies move forward rapidly so as to leave the French no time in which to reform and organize a new resistance. The armies will accordingly communicate to us when they will be ready to start their advance.

The order concerning the removal of the XI Corps and the Guard Reserve Corps had reached the Second and Third Armies on August 26. On the 28th the armies received the instructions of the 27th. Hence the orders followed very closely upon each other and evidently arose from the same conception of the general situation.

On this point, Lieutenant-General Tappen reports that the entirely favorable news which had arrived each day up to August 25 had led the High Command to believe *that the great decisive battle of the western front had ended in our favor*, and that under the impression of this "decisive victory" the chief of staff of the field army *had decided to send six corps to the eastern front*. Certainly, such a displacementof forces had been held in view for a long while, to be effected as soon as the decision was definitely obtained in the west. Now that we know the course of events, no further discussion is needed to prove the error involved in assuming that such a time had already come. It should have been considered that essentially the enemy was only thrown back frontally. The great decision, the encircling of the French Fifth Army, the hurling back of the whole French force toward the Swiss frontier, were things which were perfectly susceptible of accomplishment as we have proved, but this goal which Count Schlieffen had set for the operations had not been reached. We deceived ourselves on that point, and that led to our losing the Battle of the Marne.

Lieutenant-General Tappen expressly declares that it was not the bad situation in the East which gave rise to General von Moltke's decision. And furthermore, the trans port of six full corps had not been contemplated. Encouraging news had already been received on the 26th, and on the 27th, the first information announcing great successes in the east was at hand. Accordingly, the High Command was in a position to hold back the army corps destined to be sent first, namely, the XI Corps and the Guard Reserve Corps. These corps were marching toward Aix-la-Chapelle (Aachen), Malmedy, and Saint Vith, where they did not arrive until the 30th.

In a memoir composed in 1915 General von Moltke bases the sending of the two corps upon reasons different from those given by General Tappen.[3] He says: "While the First to Fifth Armies were advancing victoriously beyond the Meuse and the Sambre, the situation on the eastern front, where the Russians, contrary to expectations, had rapidly invaded Prussia, obliged us to send reenforcements to that front *before* a final decision could be obtained in the west."

The despatch of the two corps, taken from the right wing itself, has been justified by saying that after the carrying of Namur they were immediately available and that the eastern front had to be rescued quickly. Hence, the bad situation of this front required, after all, quick support. It is a matter of regret that the corps were taken precisely from the right wing, which on the contrary should have been reenforced in every possible way. Nor can it be admitted, in view of the great distance which the corps had to

---

[3] Foerster: "*Graf Schlieffen und der Weltkrieg,*" Part I, page 34. E.S. Mittler & Sohn, Berlin, 1921.

traverse on foot in order to reach their embarcation stations, that they were the first which were ready for transport. Certain corps of the Sixth Army, much better placed for being embarked, could have been taken more quickly. General von Hausen has come out in opposition to the statement of General Tappen to the effect that he had named the XI Corps as available.

It must be granted, however, that the reports of the armies often spoke of "decisive victories" though such an expression did not always conform to the situation. Under the term "decisive victory" one understands something more than a mere frontal hurling back of the enemy or the fact of having victoriously repulsed an attack. After the failure of the French offensive, the chief of staff of one of our armies had announced that "the enemy was shattered all along the front of this army." Such reports may have contributed considerably to giving the High Command the erroneous idea which it had formed of the enemy. It must also be recalled in this connection that the enemy actually sought the decision all along the German front, but that he had suffered a heavy defeat.[4]

The same reasoning which had led to the despatch of two corps to the east was also at the bottom of the long instructions of the High Command issued on the 27th.

There the view taken of the enemy was the same. All the French active corps had already fought and suffered serious defeats, the major part of the reserve divisions was said to be seriously shaken. The Belgian army was in process of dissolution. The French were fighting to gain time they wished to hold the main body of our forces and were awaiting the effects of the Russian offensive. To this end, they were going to offer resistance on favorable sectors. It was assumed that the French were falling, back in the southwesterly and southerly direction upon Paris. In Lorraine, it is true, there was still some expectation of a new French offensive, but it was plainly assumed that the French would also fall back in that region if the Fifth Army advanced west of the Meuse in the southwesterly direction. It was supposed that the

---

[4] See pages 81-82.

Lorraine forces would then fall back upon Langres – Dijon – Besancon, that is, toward the flank.

On the basis of these hypotheses, the task assigned to the German armies was that of preventing the French from recovering after their defeats and of not allowing them time either to reform or to offer serious resistance or to constitute new formations.

Since, as a result of the fighting, certain armies had been led to face in a more southerly, direction, the great sweeping movement of the right wing of the German army toward the southwest was now to be resumed on a more extended front. The First Army was even to advance toward the Seine below Paris. Hence it appeared that the Schlieffen plan was going to be carried out in its scope. But in view of the distribution of forces resulting from the initial concentration, such a broad sweeping movement of the right wing was possible only in case the pivot of Thionville (Diedenhofen) or later that of Verdun was abandoned. And this also was plainly taken into consideration: the Fifth Army was to isolate Verdun and, in echelon to the left, march upon Chalons-sur-Marne – Vitry – le Francois. But such a march was possible only in case the French abandoned all contact with Verdun and the Meuse on the part of their right wing and also fell back in Lorraine under the pressure of the advance of the Sixth Army west of the Meuse and as a consequence of the retreat of the mass of their army upon Paris. The Sixth Army was then to follow the enemy beyond the Moselle in the direction of Neufchateau and take up the task of protecting the left flank.

The advance as conceived in the instructions of the High Command presented only outwardly the picture of the Schlieffen operation. There was no conformity with it whatever as regards the distribution of forces. While the Fifth Army had been reenforced, the right wing remained much too weak. Whereas the Second Army was marching upon Paris, the First Army was advancing toward the lower Seine with only five corps. It could hardly be hoped with these forces to break through the powerful obstacle of the river, in case the enemy actually fell back (as it was assumed he would) with the main part of his forces upon Paris and thus found himself established in a defensive position on the Seine on either side of the capital. To advance against a French position:

Oise – Aisne – Paris, Count Schlieffen had considered it would be necessary to employ twenty-five active corps, two and one-half reserve corps, and six corps newly formed. Of these forces, seven corps were to be employed in encircling Paris on the west and six new corps were to invest the fortress on its western and southern fronts.

On the other hand, the left wing of the German army remained, as before, much too strong. It was to advance upon Chalons-sur-Marne – Vitry-le-Francois – Neufchateau. The Sixth. and Seventh Armies were assigned the secondary task of covering the left flank in the direction of Dijon, of investing Nancy – Toul, and of assuring cover toward Epinal and also between Epinal and Switzerland. Essentially, then, it was a frontal push with a relatively weak right wing and a powerful left wing, against the enemy who was falling back on Paris, supposing the assumption made regarding his direction of retreat was confirmed. The great enveloping movement executed with a crushingly superior right wing, the hurling back of the enemy toward the southwest; was not realized.

The decision of the High Command is nevertheless perfectly natural in view of the circumstances and the assumptions made. A displacement of forces from the left to the right wing no longer seemed practicable, now that the enemy. had begun to retreat all along the front and was also, as it assumed, going to fall back from the Moselle front. In that case the best thing to do was to push straight ahead beyond the Moselle with the Sixth and Seventh Armies.

But the assumptions were erroneous. The enemy did not fall back to the west and southwest upon Paris but in the southwesterly and southerly direction. He did not give up the contact with Verdun and he ordered his First and Second Armies to hold out on the Moselle. The enemy was anticipating the designs of Count Schlieffen. What brilliant prospects our maneuvers would have had if it had been planned and executed in this sense from the very beginning. To attain our great goal, the shoving back of the enemy toward the southeast, all that would have been needed was to continue wheeling while holding on to Verdun as a pivot, and at the same time adopting a defensive attitude in Lorraine. The preliminary condition for that was that the right wing should be as strong as possible from the very beginning and constantly reenforced, while the weak left wing in Lorraine would remain on the defensive.

But these preliminary conditions were not realized. It would still have been possible in a certain measure to get out of the difficulty if, immediately after the battle of Lorraine, that is, around August 23, we had been content to remain on the defensive in that region and if a certain number of corps had been transported by rail in the direction of Aix-la-Chapelle to follow the right wing as a powerful echelon of the second line. Empty rolling stock was held in readiness by the chief of the field railway service fora displacement of five to six corps.

However, if the wheeling movement was continued without a reenforcement of this sort and while still holding on to the Verdun pivot, the right wing would come up directly against Paris with insufficient forces. How was it then proposed to deal with that great fortress? Now this was precisely the case which actually occurred.

Finally, there was a case which, by a remarkable oversight, was not at all foreseen in the instructions of August 27; the enemy, resting upon his fortresses and the strong sectors of terrain, would be weakened on his defensive wing on the Moselle front, but would be strengthened in the region of Paris by utilizing his railways leading toward the capital and would there form a powerful offensive wing with which he would attack us by surprise. Then instead of being surrounded, he would attempt to surround us, while our Sixth and Seventh Armies remained held up in front of the Moselle and the left wing of our Fifth Army before Verdun. The defective distribution of our forces at the time of the concentration thus continued to make itself felt up to the end of the Marne campaign.

The question arises, whether the displacement of our forces, which was not begun on the 23rd, would still have been possible on the 27th when the instructions of the High Command were issued. The reconstruction of the Belgian railways was not yet sufficiently advanced to make possible large-scale rail movements through Belgium. Moreover, it was too late to transport the troops by rail to Aix-la-Chapelle and to march them the rest of the way. But the corps could have been transported by rail to Luxemburg and marched from that point. It was not necessary to bring them directly to the extreme right wing. The reenforcement of the right wing could have been secured by shoving troops toward the right inside the front of the armies, intercalating at the proper place the corps thus brought up.

Today it will be willingly admitted that a procedure of this sort on the 27th or even the 30th of August, when the impossibility of breaking through the upper Moselle front was beginning to be realized, would have been preferable to the decision actually taken.

Only a few days after their despatch, the instructions of August 27 became obsolete. Though they had not been countermanded, the German army obeyed a natural necessity and wheeled of its own accord toward the south.

The order of the High Command on the 27th again directed the armies to work in mutual understanding. The importance attached to the French fortresses in this order is worth noting. It was held to be necessary to adopt measures against Maubeuge, La Fère, Laon, Hirson, Verdun, Nancy, Toul, and Epinal.

To realize the impression necessarily made by the order of the 27th upon the command of the First army, it is necessary to leave out of account any knowledge of what had occurred. The circumstances seemed to require that the enemy, who was everywhere falling back, should be pursued rapidly without regard to other considerations, so as not to allow him time to halt. While we were striving to reach the lower Seine to surround the enemy, we could expect, according to the instructions, that our left wing would cross the upper Moselle. The enemy could thus be encircled by both wings at the same time. No discussion had taken place with the High Command. From the conversation which we had with the bearer of the instructions, an elderly staff officer of the High Command, it appeared that the latter was imperfectly informed regarding the events which had occurred in connection with the First and Second, Armies. If the same thing held with regard to the other armies, some doubts were justified as to whether the instructions of the 27th rested upon sufficiently firm foundations.

August 30 – The first Army Changes Front toward the Oise River. The Right flank of the German Army Takes the Southerly Direction

On the evening of August 29, after the arrival of the instructions of the High Command of August 27, the command of the First Army-was of the opinion that it should first repel the French forces which had turned up on its right flank before continuing its march in the southwesterly direction as it had just been order to do. It was at this time of the evening that it received the call for support from the Second Army, which was to draw the First Army in the opposite direction.[5]

The situation there seemed serious. On the evening of the 29th the importance of the victory won by the II Corps at Proyart over the French VII Corps was not yet fully known at Péronne. We were confronted with a very difficult question. We could not know to what extent the Second Army was in need of our support. Perhaps it was not so urgent. Thelonger and more vigorous the resistance met by the Second Army on the Upper Oise, the better the chances of the First Army, by continuing its march to the west of the Oise, in the approximate direction of Montdidier – Noyon, to fall upon the flank and rear of the enemy. Such a maneuver was likely to be much more effective than any direct tactical support. General von Kluck consequently considered that it was preferable to hold his forces concentrated and to keep on for the present in the direction hitherto followed. Only the 17th Division, which had been delayed in front of Maubeuge and which was now behind the left wing of the army, was put at the disposal of the Second Army.

The latter in its haste had already applied directly to the IX Corps which was nearest to it and had requested it to direct the 17th Division upon Origny-Sainte Benoite (near Mt. d'Origny 14 km. E. of St. Quentin) by way of St. Quentin and to put the 18th Division at its disposal at the approaches to that city. The 17th Division was immediately called out and got under way by the IX Corps, but a telephone call from the First Army prevented the despatch of the 18th Division.

---

[5] See pages 112-113.

It was not until 11:45 at night that the order of the operations of the First Army for the day of the 30th could be issued at Péronne. In this order General von Kluck directed that the enemy should be held in front and surrounded on his two wings. The army was to march toward the Avre along a broad front extending from the point where this river enters the Somme up to the south of Roye.[6] North of the Somme the IV Reserve Corps was marching from Albert upon Amiens. The II Cavalry Corps was sent to the left wing: setting out from the region south of Chaulnes it marched via Roye in the southerly direction. It maybe questioned whether this employment of the cavalry corps was a judicious one. It would have been desirable and in accordance with the rule to move it to the outer right wing, north of Amiens. In advancing upon the Avre before the front of the army, it would in all probability have advanced but slowly. On the left wing there was a considerable gap between the First and Second Armies. The situation on the Oise was very uncertain. An enemy attack might very well proceed from that direction as Noyon was reported as occupied. It was there especially that the cavalry corps might have found a vast field of action in case of victory by the Second Army. It was in this direction also that the further course of the operations seemed likely to lead the First Army. It was for this reason that the command of the First Army decided in favor of the direction of Roye. Our cavalry was unquestionably too weak: all the necessary tasks could not have been met. As has been stated, it would perhaps after all have been better to leave one cavalry division on the extreme right wing.[7]

The command of the First Army remained at Péronne on August 30. In the course of the day the situation changed continually, demanding ever new decisions.

The army command, on the morning of the 30th, first learned that the II Corps had won a complete victory at Proyart and that it had routed the French VII Corps. The enemy had also fallen back

---

[6] See Sketch 6.

[7] See pages 111-112.

before the front of the IV Reserve Corps. Also it could be taken for granted that on the rest of the front the enemy would not hold after the numerous defeats which he had suffered. Experience up to that time had shown that, apart from one regular division of the VII Corps, there was no need for overestimating the adversary. To pursue him too far beyond the Avre was to turn us aside from our path and deprive us of the possibility of cooperating strategically with the Second Army if occasion arose to attack in the flank and rear the forces by which it was confronted. To take possession of the region of Roye – Montdidier and of the lower Avre was to suffice. Hence the thing to do was to halt the First Army in time and prepare it for an oblique toward the south.

It was no easy matter to execute this movement while the army was still under way. We had telephone connection with only one corps, the IX. The only way by which we could get the new orders to the other corps was by means of liaison officers sent in all haste at 9:30 in the morning These orders were to the effect that in case the enemy fell back behind the line: Montdidier – lower Avre, the army would slip to the left in the direction of Montdidier – Roye and form in echelon to the left.

But a new turn soon intervened, in which our telephone connection with the IX Corps stood us in good stead. In the course of a telephone conversation with an officer of this corps we received, at 11 a.m., the following information having its source in a communication of the Second Army to the IX Corps:

> The second Army was attacked yesterday afternoon by ten French divisions at the least, on a front extending from west of Vervins to the region of La Fère. The struggle was a bitter one, but the enemy offensive failed. From the papers of a French corps chief of staff it was learned that the French had intended to attack St. Quentin while the German First Army was to be held frontally by the English and French. At Noyon there is an enemy force of one and one-half brigades. General von Bülow regrets that the First Army did not turn facing the Oise in accordance with his expressed desire. The 17th Division will soon be put back under the orders of its army. The enemy seems to be falling back.

Thus it appeared that the time had come to have the center and left wing of the army execute the (already prepared) turn toward the south, so as to be ready to exploit a success of the Second Army. New orders were therefore issued, and the IV, III and IX Corps were arranged in such a way as to enable them to advance from the neighborhood of Roye in the direction of the Oise.

In the afternoon we had on hand at Péronne a great mass of information, upon which the decision for the next day, the 31st, was formed.

First of all, there was a radio message from the Second Army (dated 5:10 p.m. and received at 5:55 p.m.), as follows: "Enemy beaten today in a decisive manner. Large contingents are falling back upon La Fère."

Our radio station also heard the following radio message, apparently from the Third Army: "In front of the Fourth Army, enemy in retreat to the southwest. Third Army will advance on the 30th beyond Chateau Porcien – Attigny."

At 6:35 p.m. arrived a second radio message from the Second Army: "With view to thorough exploitation of the success, it is urgently desirable that the First Army turn facing La Fère – Laon around Chauny as pivot. The 17th Division this evening will take road: Origny – Saint Quentin, and tomorrow will rejoin IX Corps. Army headquarters Saint Quentin. Thanks for assistance rendered."

So the situation was clarified: The Second and Fourth Armies were victorious; in front of the Second Army the enemy was falling back, directing a considerable portion of his forces upon La Fère; the Third Army was advancing upon the rear of the enemy forces retreating in front of the Fourth Army. In these conditions there was no need to assume that the enemy would hold on the Avre in front of the First Army. He was everywhere routed or in retreat. In the region of Amiens – apparently territorial troops – he had fallen back toward the southwest. Before the front of the army he had fallen back behind the Avre. In the afternoon, air reports announced that on the route: Montdidier – Saint Just en Chaussee the enemy was retreating in disorder. Also in front of the II Corps the enemy was falling back through Moreuil. The danger to the flank seemed to have passed; the march to the southward now seemed possible.

As regards the enemy forces on the Oise, our aviators

announced in the evening that a division was falling back from Bailly [10 km. S. of Noyon] and Carlepont (south of Noyon)in the direction of Attichy. The I Cavalry Corps reached Noyon. The English appeared to be in retreat toward the south.

In which direction was the First Army now to turn? The decision to be adopted was one of great moment. It was destined to exercise an influence upon the whole further movement of the German forces. It was assumed that the Second Army would pursue the enemy toward the south. The Third Army, also, was pushing in that direction. The success had to be exploited. The First Army was well situated for this task, on the evening of the 30th, in the region of Roye, while cover was afforded by the II Corps at Moreuil and the IV Reserve Corps facing Amiens. In the exalted feeling that great victories had been won, the decision was reached in the afternoon to march toward the Oise. The direction of the lower Seine was abandoned.

But it was quite impossible to comply with the urgent request of the second Army to oblique upon Laon – La Fère. Before we could have reached that region, the English and French would have escaped toward the south. The First and Second Armies would have piled up behind them. The idea of cooperating in the attack on the fortifications of Laon and La Fère, fortifications without military value and which in our opinion would perhaps not even be seriously defended, was rejected. Hence the only way by which we could exploit the success of the Second Army was by carrying outa sweeping pursuittoward the south, starting from the line: Moreuil – Roye – Guiscard. The army was not, as at Maubeuge, to let itself be drawn too closely to the Second Army to serve it as a tactical support. It was necessary to keep informed as to the further course of the operations.

In the evening, Captain Bührmann, sent by the First Army to the staff of the Second Army, returned to Péronne with the announcement that the Second Army would halt on the 31st and rest. General von Bülow had informed him that the state of the troops, unfortunately, would not permit him, after the long marches and heavy fighting which they had been through, to undertake the pursuit at once with all his forces. Now as for us, we had been counting absolutely on a pursuit. After this it appeared to us impossible to push the first army alone in a too markedly southerly direction. The interval which separated us from the Second Army was becoming too great; we were left in the air.

Army orders for the day of August 31 were issued on this basis at 9:30 in the evening. General von Kluck decided to take the direction: Compiegne – Noyon. An attempt would be made, by forced marches, to strike again in the flank the enemy forces which were falling back in front of the Second Army in the general direction: Laon – La Fère. The IX Corps was ordered to advance through Guiscard – Quierzy upon Coucy le Chateau, the III Corps as far as Bailly and Cuts, the IV Corps up to the region of Mareuil, the II Corps as far as the neighborhood of Tricot, the IV Reserve Corps via Amiens upon Ailly. The II Cavalry Corps was to advance above Compiegne against the French left wing in the direction of Soissons. The I Cavalry Corps was urged to cooperate by way of Noyon. All preparations were made for rapidly taking possession of the crossings of the Oise or establishing them.

In the matter of new enemy forces, Moroccans had been identified, on the 29th and 30th, in the region of Rosieres (west of Chaulnes) by the II Cavalry Corps and the III Corps.

At 10:30 p.m. the following report was addressed to the High Command: "First Army has wheeled in the direction of the Oise and will advance on 31st upon Compiegne – Noyon to exploit success of Second Army. IV Reserve Corps is moving southward via Amiens to cover right flank of army." This report was communicated to the Second Army.

An important change had been effected in the operations. Whether it was advisable or not, remained to be seen.

The report addressed to the High Command was not exact. Only the III Corps and half of the IX crossed the Oise on the 31st. The IV and II Corps, the IV Reserve Corps and half of the IX Corps were still on the evening of the 31st to the west of the Oise and arranged in such manner that if so ordered they would have been able to continue advancing in the direction prescribed by the High Command, namely, the lower Seine, by marching north of the Oise. Lieutenant-Colonel Hentsch, of the staff of the High Command, told me a little later that our report had led the High Command to believe that the whole army had already wheeled toward the Oise and that the Command had let itself be influenced by this belief in its further dispositions. However that may be, the reply of the High Command arrived by radio in the course of the same night, the 31st, at 2:13 a.m.: "Third Army has wheeled facing south toward the Aisne. It is attacking beyond Rethel – Semuy and will pursue in southerly direction. The movements initiated by the First and Second Armies conform with the designs of the High Command. Cooperate with the Third Army. Left wing of the Second Army in approximate direction of Reims."

The High Command had moved on the 30th from Coblenz to Luxembourg. It still had the opportunity to modify in time the measures adopted by the First and Second Armies if they did not meet with its approval. But the orders issued by these latter conformed to the situation of the other armies. The whole right wing of the German forces (First, Second and Third, Armies) was wheeling southward.

In his "*Report on the Battle of the Marne,*" General von Bülow has observed, with reference to the urgent request for changing front addressed on the 31st to the First Army, that he had, in mind only a momentary tactical support and not a complete change in the strategical direction of march; that he was still quite unaware at that time of the presence of considerable forces before the front and on the flank of the First Army and that the High Command also, when it gave its approval, probably knew nothing of the detrainments which had taken place as early as August 29 at Amiens, Montdidier, Moreuil, and Roye and of the powerful attack at Villers-Bretonneux against the right wing.[8]

In addition to the presence of territorial divisions, the command of the First Army had announced to the High Command since the 29th, in accordance with the information received, the appearance of the French cavalry corps on the Somme, the engagements of the Gist and 62nd Reserve Divisions with the II Corps, and later the advance of the enemy forces coming from Amiens – Moreuil, the appearance of the reserve Alpine chasseurs and the advance of the VII Corps. This last report had gone from

---

[8] *Bericht zue Marneschlacht.*

Péronne on the 30th at 1:10 in the mornnig. On the 30th at10:30 in the evening we had reported that the enemy (VII Corps) had been repulsed, that Moroccans had also been identified and that at Amiens the territorial divisions had fallen back in the southwesterly direction. This information had been transmitted at the same time as the report announcing that the army was wheeling toward the Oise – the report to which the High Command had replied on the morning of the 31st with its approval. Hence the High Command was perfectly informed.

Good liaison with the Second Army had been assured in the course of these days by the despatch of officers back and forth. Captain Bührmann, sent by us on the 30th to the Second Army,[9] had been taken with him, as was usually the case, written instructions dated August 30, 2 p.m. which he delivered, according to an annotation, at 4:35 p.m. These instructions read:

> Yesterday detrainments were announced all along the line: Amiens – Moreuil – Montdidier – Roye; at Noyon one and one-half brigades. Important enemy forces have attacked from the direction of Amiens. In addition to the troops previously announced (61st and 62nd Reserve Divisions, four territorial divisions, 3rd and 5th Cavalry Divisions, important new units formed at the depots), there have been identified: the VII Corps, the division of reserve Alpine chasseurs, one division of cavalry, Moroccans, and English (at Noyon). Today the army with its right wing threw the enemy back beyond the Avre; it has wheeled with its left wing upon Guiscard, with its center into the region of Roye, ready to intervene in case of need, by a night march, in direction of Ham, Jussy, Chauny, Noyon, Compiegne, according to the position in which the Second Army is engaged. While the enemy was being thrown back today, the center and the left wing were already wheeling toward the Oise and are now available. The right wing (IV Reserve Corps and II Corps) will still be required for covering the right flank facing Amiens – Avre. An enemy corps is assembling this afternoon at Amiens.
>
> For the army:
> VON KUHL.

[9] See page 130.

In the records of the Second Army there is a general table, formed on the basis of the foregoing instructions, of the enemy forces identified on the 29th and 30th before the front of the First and Second Armies.

As for the possibility of a change of front of the First Army against Noyon – Compiegne or even upon Laon – La Fère merely in the form of a momentary tactical support, that must be doubted. It would necessarily assume a decisive strategical importance.

Remarks

General Maurice thinks that on August 31 General von Kluck made the same mistake as on the 27th when, instead of pursuing the English, he marched toward the southwest; for on the later date also, he got contact with the French forces on the Avre (it was really the Sixth Army in process of being formed, under Maunoury), but then turned toward the southeast.

In fact, the commander in chief of the First Army had to choose between the two following decisions: either to continue the pursuit of the enemy met with on the Avre and in the direction followed up to that time and thus keep on in the direction of the lower Seine as prescribed by the High Command, or to face about toward the Oise in order to exploit the success of the Second Army, which for the second time had announced a decisive victory, and surround the left wing of the main body of the French forces. In the first case it was impossible to obtain decisive results. While the retreating enemy was being pursued beyond the Avre, the main body of the French forces could continue falling back unimpeded by way of La Fère, for the Second Army wished to rest on the 31st. But if the First Army faced about toward the Oise and turned away from the enemy forces encountered on the Avre, there would be a certain danger, or at least a certain insecurity, on the right flank. Even today I am unable to find a solution which is not open to criticism. The German army lacked a rear echelon. I still think, however, that the decision arrived at was the best. All that was needed was not to lose contact with the enemy forces hitherto encountered, although they were in large. part of little value, beaten and in retreat. They nevertheless remained in our flank and might be reinforced. We assumed, it is true, that due to our victorious attacks the enemy was gripped all along the front of the German Army to such a degree that it was impossible for him to undertake any important displacement of forces. Still it would have been well to have one division of the cavalry corps follow the enemy to the west of the Oise, in order to cover the flank of the army against surprise, however important and promising might be the advance by way of Compiegne and Soissons against the flank of the main body of the French forces. The operations of this period show daily the importance of a strong cavalry force in the war of movement.

When, during the night of the 30-31st, the High Command approved our decision, its instructions of the 27th, which reached us on the evening of the 28th, were completely invalidated. The First Army, which was supposed to march toward the lower Seine, was advancing by way of Compiegne – Noyon beyond the Oise. The Second Army was moving in the direction of Reims instead of Paris, the Third Army in the direction of Rethel instead of Chateau-Thierry. Why this change? It is explained in part by the violent enemy reaction, but especially by the fact that the enemy was holding out on the upper Moselle and at Verdun. If the Fifth, Sixth, and Seventh Armies were held up here, it was impossible for us to spread out with the right wing as far as the lower Seine. Thus there gradually took form the new decision of the High Command, with which we shall become acquainted in the order of September 2 and according to which the whole right wing of the German Army was to face about to the left and drive the enemy back from Paris.

In any case, after the brief radiogram of the High Command on the night of the 30-31st approving our decision, the situation demanded at once a new order and an understanding regarding the further plans.

August 31 and September 1 – The First Army loses Contact with the French and the English

The staff of the First Army had reached Lassigny at noon of the 31st. The aviation reports received in the course of the afternoon showed that the region of the Oise between Noyon, Chauny, Coucy le Chateau, and Carlepont was clear of enemy troops but that on the other hand strong columns were on the march from Vic toward the south (approximately one corps) and from Compiegnein the direction of Verberie (approximately one division), both probably English, while a column marching from Coucy le Chateau upon Soissons was manifestly French. The corps at Lassigny were therefore directed, at 2 o'clock in the afternoon, to push as far as possible in the direction of Soissons – Verberie in order to make contact again with the retreating enemy. Cavalry detachments, supported by artillery and infantry on motor trucks, were to be pushed forward in advance. The I Cavalry Corps was directed to move upon Soissons, the II Cavalry Corps was to advance in the direction of Villers-Cotterets.

Army headquarters was transferred in the afternoon to Noyon. In the course of the afternoon the heads of the columns of the army's left wing (half of the IX Corps and the III Corps) passed through Vezaponin (northwest of Soissons), Vic, Attichy and, with its right wing, Moreuil – Lamotte – Maignelay; the IV Reserve Corps got as far as Ailly. The troops of the left wing negotiated a march of 50 kilometers. Considering that since the launching of the forward movement the army had been marching and fighting without a day of rest, this performance of the 31st must be described as astonishing. The troops were inspired by the thought that the enemy wing was to be reached and defeated.

After strong pressure on our part, the Lepel brigade of the IV Reserve Corps, then at Brussels, was finally yielded to us by the governor of that city and directed upon Péronne. We learned of the brilliant victory at Tannenberg. All forces were tense with the determination to win a great success on the Oise as well.

In accordance with its army order of the 30th for the day of the 31st ("The army will halt tomorrow and rest") – an order which had been communicated to us – the Second army had remained in place on that day and had made its preparations for the attack on La Fère. This operation was assigned to the right wing of the army (VII Corps and X Reserve Corps), which in the course of the day pushed forward toward the fortress detachments of infantry under the protection of which the pioneers and artillerists madereconnaissances. The place was to be taken under fire on September 1. On the evening of the 31st, Captain Brinckmann of the staff of the Second Army arrived at Noyon. According to my notes, he declared that after the battle of St. Quentin the Second Army was exhausted and unable to pursue, that it intended to get under way on September 1 but that it wished first to attack La Fère. I insisted that these fortifications were of no value and that the place was perhaps not even armed, that the Second Army would be delayed and remain in the rear, that the French were falling back with their left wing by way of Soissons, the English from the Oise line: Noyon – Verberie toward the south, and that the French would get away from us. We could not accede to the desire of the Second Army that we should support the attack on La Fère with the heavy artillery of our IX and III Corps. Such a course would have deprivedustoo long of our artillery, of which we had urgent need for the fighting soon to take place, and we considered it useless to execute an artillery attack against La Fère.

General von Kluck decided to continue on September 1, by the most extreme marching efforts, his attempt to overtake the enemy. The English were supposed to be in retreat from Noyon – Verberie toward the line: Senlis – Crépy en Valois – Villers-Cotterets, and the French left wing from Soissons toward the south. After violent combats with enemy rear guards at Verberie, Gilocourt, and Villers-Cotterets, the German forces succeeded in reaching, on the afternoon of the 1st, the region: Verberie – Crépy en Valois – Villers-Cotterets – eastern edge of the forest of this latter name. This time it was the marching performances of the right wing which must be admired (the IV Corps covered upward of 40 kilometers in a straight line). The IV Corps got all the way to the north of Saint Just en Chaussee, the 17th Division hastily pushed to the northwest of Coucy le Chateau in the direction of its corps. The II Cavalry Corps was to advance south of Villers-Cotterets toward the east against the French flank, the I Cavalry Corps to the south of Soissons. But the II Cavalry Corps was stopped at Verberie; south of this point one of its divisions fell into a difficult situation.

On the evening of the 31st, report was made to the High Command that the enemy forces around Amiens had fallen back toward the southwest. On September 1, . inferior French forces fell back before the IV Reserve Corps and the II Corps by way of Clermont toward the southwest. On the evening of the 1st, it was necessary to report to the High Command that the army was no longer successful in reaching the French left wing and that its plan was to form on the 2nd along the line: Verberie – La Ferté Milon so as to be ready for further employment.

According to my notes of that day the situation was judged as follows at the staff of the First Army: "In the region Douai – Cambrai – Amiens there is no further danger; the enemy there has been dispersed. It is hardly possible any more to reach the French again; they have escaped without being pursued. It is also difficult to overtake the English. To continue marching in the direction hitherto followed is out of the question, for the right wing would be menaced by Paris. Hence a halt is required in order to group the army with a view to further operations, according as we are ordered to march once more toward the south, while covering toward Paris, or toward the lower Seine below Paris. If we continue, marching toward the south and the French decide to defend the Marne, we shall certainly have to reckon with a flank attack from Paris."

Thus arose the decision to close up for the present, September 2, only as far as the line: Rully (south of Verberie) – Crépy en Valois – La Ferté Milon – Neuilly Saint Front. The exhaustion of the troops rendered a halt extremely urgent; the cavalry was now advancing only with difficulty. At 8 o'clock in the evening General von Kluck had already reached a decision to this effect, when the liaison officer of the III Corps brought in some English orders found on a cyclist. It was the order of the English I Corps to come to rest. It appeared from this that the whole English Army was still close in front of us and that it had wished to come to rest at noon south of the line: La Ferté Milon – Crépy en Valois – Verberie. Mentioned in the order were the 1st, 2nd, 3rd and 5th Divisions, the III Corps, the 3rd and 5th Cavalry Brigades.[10] In spite of its exhaustion, it was necessary once more to send the army to the attack as long as there was a chance of overtaking the enemy.

Scarcely was the decision formed and the new order in course of preparation when a radiogram was intercepted stating that the Second Army was obliquing toward the south in order to "hasten to the rescue of the Third Army." The phrase had an ominous tone; the situation of the Third Army must have been critical. Was it the duty of the First Army to remain in place and wait for the situation at the Second and Third Armies to clarify? It was not impossible that that situation would take a bad turn. It was our duty, then, to be in a position to go into action, that is to say, to have full freedom of movement. That did not appear to us assured while we remained in place, covering toward the English. It was necessary to throw them back. Hence the decision to attack was maintained, even when other intercepted radiograms announced that the enemy was in retreat in front of the Third Army. It was impossible to obtain a clear view of the situation in the face of these conflicting radiograms.

The new order could not be issued until 10:15 p.m. According to this order, the line: Verberie – Villers-Cotterets was to be crossed on September 2 at 8o'clock in the morning; the IX Corps was to advance at 3 a.m. to the east of the forest of Villers-Cotterets [N. of La Ferté Milon] in order to surround the enemy; the IV Reserve Corps was to be brought up toward Creil by a night march; the II Cavalry Corps was to support the attack on the right wing. It was necessary to send to the High Command a new report: "Three English corps identified immediately in front of the First Army. The army will attack tomorrow beyond Creil – La Ferté Milon so as to be ready for further employment after throwing back the enemy." We intimated by this that we were awaiting new directions.

The blow missed. The English had got away by falling back in good time and could no longer be overtaken. We should have

[10] In fact, on the evening of September 1 the English were on the line: La Ferté Milon – Betz – Nanteuil le Haudouin.

started during the night. It is quite clear, however, that that was impossible after the marching performances previously accomplished.

After having rested on the 31st, the Second Army was to attack La Fère on September 1 with its right wing (VII Corps and X Reserve Corps) and advance with its left wing (X Corps and Guard Corps) onto the Serre [River] sector. As early as noon, it was observed that La Fère had been evacuated by the enemy. Hehad not defended it at all.

The Second Army then desired to advance in the general direction of Laon beyond the Serre while the First Army would reconnoiter beyond Soissons in the direction of Chateau-Thierry – Reims; but at 2:30 p.m. there came an order from the High Command: "Third, Fourth and Fifth Armies are engaged in heavy fighting against superior forces. Right wing of the Third Army near Chateau-Porcien on the Aisne. It is urgently desirable that the left wing of the Second Army advance in that direction and come into action with cavalry today if still possible. One enemy cavalry division has been seen to the west of Chateau-Porcien." General von Bülow at once turned his left wing to face in the southeasterly direction while his right wing was to cover the movement and take possession of Laon on September 2. At 6:15 p.m. he received a communication from the Third Army stating that it did not need the support: "Enemy in retreat in front of the Third Army. We are pursuing to the right as far as Aussonce." The left wing could now be turned again facing south in order to resume the pursuit of the enemy retreating past and close to the west ofReims. But it was now too late. The day of rest on the 31st, the loss of time caused by La Fère, the movementsimposed on. the army on September 1 by the action of the High Command, had enabled the enemy to get a long start. Only the First Army might still perhaps have been able to reach him in the flank.

The second Army got under way again on September 1 toward the Aisne sector: Soissons – Pontavert, after Laon also had been carried without resistance. Its intention was to advance on the 2nd beyond the Vesle up to the line: Noyant (south of Soissons) – Poilly (southeast of Fismes).

According to the account of General von Hausen, the

intervention of the Second Army for supporting the Third Army was not requested by the latter, but ordered by the High Command in view of the general situation. The Third Army had got underway on August 30, headed southward upon Chateau-Porcien – Rethel – Attigny, in order to cut off the retreat of the enemy forces falling back in front of the Fourth Army.[11] On being questioned regarding this measure, the High Command declared that it had its approval. Here also, then, the operations took the southerly direction of themselves. On the 30th and 31st, the Third Army met with strong resistance on the Aisne, and again on the 31st the left wing failed to cross the river at Attigny – Semuy.

On the evening of the 31st, the Third Army received the following radiogram from the High Command: "Highly urgent that Third and Fourth Armies move forward without halt in conjunction with Fifth Army, as Fifth Army is engaged in heavy fighting to cross the Meuse."

The long negotiations entered upon by the Third and Fourth Armies in the matter of the mutual support to be rendered by their inside wings in order to cross the Aisne led, as frequently occurs in such cases, to no result. The higher order was lacking.

The right wing of the Fifth Army having meanwhile crossed the Meuse, the advance of the Third Army no longer appeared so urgently necessary. It now wished to give its troops a day of rest, of which they were in great need, and not to continue its attack until September 2. On September 1 it received a telegram from the High Command stating that it was urgently desirable that "the Third Army should continue to attack in the southerly direction without delay and regardless of cost, for the success of the day depends on it." The attack was then continued, and the left wing also crossed the Aisne on September 1.

On September 1 the Fourth Army arrived at the line: Grivy (French map Grivy-Loisy) – Thenorgues; the Fifth Army to the line: Buzancy – Aincreville – Dannevoux, after having forced the passage of the Meuse in the region of Dun in the course of the heavy fighting of the last few days. Its left wing covered east of the

---

[11] See page 129.

Meuse toward Verdun.

In the course of these days, the embarrassment again presented by the French fortresses, to the advance of the German army is worthy of note. Givet, a small outer fort with elevated superstructures and whose walls were visible from afar, capitulated on August 31. The Third Army had been obliged to employ the 24th Reserve Division for the attack. The transfer of the siege batteries of Namur to Givet gave rise to much friction. After two days of bombardment, the fortress surrendered. On September 2, the 24th Reserve Division, which had now become available, had got only as far as Rocroi when it was assigned the task of attacking Hirson. On the 3rd, the Third Army learned that the fortress had already fallen without a fight into the hands of the Second Army. The result was that on September 4, the 24th Reserve Division had only arrived as far as Chaumont-Porcien when the Third Army, which now embraced but two and one-half corps, was already crossing the Marne.

The stop which La Fère occasioned to the Second Army has already been mentioned.

September 2 – Advance of the First Army upon Chateau-Thierry against the French Left Wing

As has been stated the projected attack of September 2 by the First Army against the English did not succeed.

At noon the command of the First Army arrived at Compiegne. We installed ourselves in the superb chateau.

The II Corps came up against the enemy at Senlis and threw him back.[12] The attack had been supported by the II Cavalry Corps. In the afternoon fighting occurred in the streets of Senlis. According to the report of the II Corps, the enemy forces comprised one French division, reserve Alpine chasseurs, Moroccans and, at Nery, an English cavalry brigade. A later report of September 3 stated that the French division was the 56th

---

[12] See Sketch 7.

Reserve Division which had been detrained at Montdidier. A new unit, then.

According to an air report (received at 12:50 p.m.), a long enemy column had been observed in the afternoon on the right flank of the army, marching along the road from Beauvais to Gisors (southwest of Beauvais). The roads leading from Beauvais toward the northeast, north, and northwest were clear of enemy forces.

The IV Reserve Corps reached Creil by way of Clermont and there came up against the enemy. On the left wing of the army, events took an important turn. The commander of the IX Corps had realized early in the forenoon of September 2 that the English could no longer lie overtaken. During a two-hour halt near Les Vallées de Nadon (north of Neuilly Saint Front), he received a precise and important air report (sent from Neuilly Saint Front at 8:45 a.m.) according to which enemy columns were in retreat from the line: Braisne – Fismes, in a southerly direction toward the bridges of Mont Saint Pere and Jaulgonne (between Chateau-Thierry and Dormans). They were estimated at three corps.

The commander of the corps, General von Quast, decided to attack these forces the same day by way of Chateau-Thierry, and he set out at 1 o'clock in the afternoon from Neuilly Saint Front with the 18th Division in order to march on Chateau-Thierry by way of Bonnes. The 17th Division was brought up in the direction of Oulchy le Chateau by way of Soissons. The I Cavalry Corps was urged to attack the enemy in the rear by way of Fere-en-Tardenois; the III Corps was invited by a liaison officer sent by automobile from Neuilly Saint Front at 12:45 p.m. and who arrived at 2:05, to support the attack by advancing in the direction of Charly – Nogent l'Artaud. The commander of the IX Corps was thus endeavoring, by a bold and independent decision and with the utmost energy, to attain a goal of which the army command had given up hope.

General von Quast had first made an attempt to obtain in advance the assent of the commander of the First Army, and to this end he had sent a staff officer to Compiegne; but he decided later not to await his return, so as not to lose time. Meanwhile the staff officer arrived at Compiegne; the command of the First Army approved the plan, and at 1:45 p.m. dictated to him an order directing that the corps advance in the direction of Chateau-Thierry into the left flank of the enemy. It was only the confirmation of the decision already in course of execution.

At 2 p.m. the command took account of the newly formed situation by despatching an army order. According to this order, the IV Corps was to advance as far as the Therouane [river] in the region: Oisserie – Fosse Martin; the III Corps was to advance in the course of the same day as far as possible in the direction of Chateau-Thierry. The II Cavalry Corps was to remain on the right flank in order to reconnoiter toward Paris and the Marne below Paris as well as in the direction of Pontoise – Beauvais.

From information received in the course of the day with reference to the English it appeared that they had fallen back behind the line of the Marne between Meaux and La Ferté-sous-Jouarre. At Meaux great bivouacs had been observed. It no longer appeared possible to overtake the English. On the other hand, there was still a possibility of stopping the French north of the Marne by a flank attack while waiting for the arrival of the Second Army. Once they had got behind the Marne they could no longer be reached.

The command of the First Army considered also the possibility of crossing the Marne somewhere between La Ferté-sous-Jouarre and Chateau-Thierry in order to render more effective the blow delivered against the enemy flank. , but rejected the idea. We were not strong enough. General von Kluck, as my notes bear witness, was thoroughly opposed to it.

A detailed report was addressed to the High Command at 8 p.m.:

> On September 1 and 2, advance guards of First Army, in conjunction with cavalry corps, threw back English advance guards in the course of violent fighting. Main body of forces retired on Dammartin – Meaux. II Corps has beaten a French infantry division and the English cavalry division east of Senlis. Large masses of French troops retreating by way of Fere-en-Tardenois and to the east indirection: Chateau-Thierry – Dormans. IX Corps has turned facing this direction to strike the enemy flank. III Corps following in echelon on Crouy; result still unknown. Aviators also announce concentrations of troops south of Marne line: La Ferté [S. Jouarre] – Meaux. IV Reserve

> Corps, vicinity of Creil, II Corps east of Senlis, cover toward Paris. IV Corps in liaison east of Nanteuil [le Handouin]. Marne line: Chateau-Thierry – La Ferté [Jouarre] clear to the present time. *Attempt of First army to cross the Marne on September 3 would, however, be rather risky.*

We were informed, by the Second Army at 7:30 p.m. that the enemy in front of it was in full retreat and that it wished to have its advance guards reach the Marne on the 3rd.

The IX Corps after a double march reached Chateau-Thierry before the close of the day of September 2 with the 18th Division;[13] the 17th Division followed in haste as far as Oulchy le Chateau. The III Corps, which again had been ordered to advance as far as possible in the direction of Chateau-Thierry, was unable to execute that order because of the lateness of the hour at which the order reached it. It had come to rest in the region of La Ferté Milon. The IV Corps reached the region southeast of Nanteuil-le-Haudouin, the II Corps the region south of Senlis, the IV Reserve Corps Creil, the cavalry corps the region of Nanteuil-le-Haudouin.

At 9:45 p.m. the order for the day of September 3 was dictated to the liaison officers of the army. Among the communications received there must still be mentioned one, to the effect that, in addition to the columns which had fallen back toward Meaux, other enemy columns coming from the direction of Nanteuil-le-Haudouin had fallen back on Dammartin. The IX Corps, from which no report had yet been received at that time, was to continue on the 3rd to attack the flank of the French forces falling back in front of the Second Army upon Chateau-Thierry by way of Fere-en-Tardenois. The III Corps, to the south of the IX, was to take the direction of Chateau-Thierry "to attack the enemy on crossing the Marne." "In case the enemy is no longer reached, the two corps will clear toward the west the road: Soissons – Chateau-Thierry on which the right wing of the Second Army is marching." The IV Corps, covering its right flank toward Paris, was to advance into the region of Crouy. The II Corps was to slip to the left upon Nanteuille-Haudouin, the IV Reserve Corps was to follow it

---

[13] See Sketch 7.

toward the region east of Senlis. The cavalry corps remained in. the region of Nanteuil-le-Haudouin. The cavalry absolutely needed a day of rest.

The situation and plans of the command were explained to the liaison officers of the corps. They were informed that on the following day another attempt would be made to stop the enemy forces which were falling back in front of the Second Army by attacking them in the flank with the left wing of the army while the center and right wing would take measures to assure cover toward Paris – Meaux."Crossing of the Marne is not regarded as likely and will be considered only in exceptionally favorable circumstances; if, for example, under strong pressure from the Second Army, the French should pass the Marne in great disorder and if the crossings might at the same time be seized by us."

The Second Army had continued its forward movement on September 2 and had advanced beyond the Vesle up to the region: Noyant – Cuiry House – Chery – Poilly. Army headquarters at Fismes.[14]

The Third Army, marching toward the south, and fighting the while, reached the line: Isles[15] – Nauroy – Saint Souplet – Sainte Marie a Py. It had made some important observations, which, however, were not known to the command of the First Army. In front of it, the enemy was in full retreat toward the south. Detrainments of troops took place in the situations of Suippes, Somme-Tourbe, Cuperly, etc. Hence the enemy was withdrawing forces from his front and transporting them, it appeared, by way of Chalons-sur-Marne and Arcis-sur-Aube, while covering by means of rear guards. The High Command, regarding it as likely that "the enemy would make attempts to retreat toward the southwest," urged the Fourth and particularly the Third Army to advance vigorously in the general southerly direction.[16]

On September 3 the Second Army wished to "continue the

---

[14] See Sketch 7.

[15] Shown on general map as Jsles – an error.

[16] Radiogram of September 2, 4:40 a.m.

pursuit in full force. Its aim was, by treading ceaselessly upon the heels of the enemy, who already seemed to be badly shaken, to further the process of disintegration. The great quantities of equipment and ammunition abandoned along the line of march and in the evacuated battery positions were rightly regarded as evidence of that disintegration."[17] The High Command approved this plan and added: "Reach the south bank of the Marne."

If the First Army did not succeed on September 3 in striking the enemy in the flank, neither was the Second Army able to prevent him from crossing the Marne because of the distance which separated the two adversaries. Behind this sector, it was an easy matter for the French to throw off their pursuers.

The Fourth Army arrived on September 2 as far as Somme Py – Manre – Sechault – Autry. The enemy was retreating upon Chalons, Sainte Menehould, and Clermont.

The Fifth Army, also, met with strong resistance after crossing the Meuse. Its situation was not an easy one, for its advance was being effected through the difficult region of the Argonne, with Verdun and the forts of the Meuse on its flank. It was consequently obliged in the course of its further march to cover toward Verdun. On the right bank of the Meuse the V Corps was preparing an attack against the forts of Troyon and Paroches while the general reserve of Metz was taking charge of the cover toward Toul – Nancy.

Orders of the High Command of September 2. Change of Front toward the Southeast

During the night of September 2-3 the following momentous order of the High Command arrived at Compiegne: "*The plan of the High Command is to drive the French back from Paris in a southeasterly direction. The First Army will follow the Second in echelon and will protect the flank of the German forces.*" Another radiogram from the High Command read: "It is desired that the

---

[17] Von Bülow.

army cavalry appear before Paris and destroy all railways leading to the capital."

The narrative up to the present time has shown how the broad enveloping movement of the right wing of the German army had gradually led to a change of front in the southerly direction up to the day of September 2 when the order of the High Command directing a turn to the southeast was issued.[18] The enemy was still holding out on the upper Moselle. At the beginning of September the High Command had decided to continue the attack in the direction of Nancy – Bayon in order to break through or at least to hold the enemy. All along the rest of the front the armies were advancing victoriously. No certain information was at hand to indicate important displacements of enemy forces. The observations made by the Third Army on September 2[19] were not yet known. As for the enemy, forces which had revealed themselves up to that time in the right flank of the First Army, the High Command was perfectly well informed on the matter by our reports. It was thought that these forces as well as the fortress of Paris could be dealt with by forming the First Army in echelon.

But the High Command knew that the First Army was in advance of the Second, even though our report of the evening of September 2 had not yet reached it. The second Army, in fact, had remained at rest on the 31st and had advanced on the 1st toward the Aisne, while on that same date the First Army had already arrived at Crépy en Valois and Villers-Cotterets and, according to its report, it wished to attack on the 2nd by way of Creil – La Ferté Milon. Hence the High Command should not have directed that "the First Army will follow in echelon," but "the First Army will halt, cover toward Paris and later follow in echelon."

The plan of the High Command proved erroneous. It was hoped to surround and encircle the enemy not only on the right but also on the left beyond the upper Moselle. The right wing turned out to be too weak, the cover toward Paris was insufficient, the left

---

[18] See pages 134-135.

[19] See page 146.

wing was unable to cross the Moselle.

About the same time Joffre had decided to get the French army away from the envelopment by which it was menaced, by falling back toward the south behind the Seine and the Aube, while at the same time reenforcing the newly formed Sixth Army in the region of Paris. The offensive was then to betaken at the favorable moment.

In the further course of the narrative, after obtaining knowledge of the events, we shall come to the conclusion that the German army ought to have halted on the Marne in order, to regroup its forces and to strengthen its right wing at the expense of the left. That would, to be sure, have required time the enemy might have displaced his forces more rapidly than we. The continuation of the operations would not have been easy, and a quick decision definitely out of the question. But even if our offensive had been stopped, our situation would have been incomparably better than the one which actually came about. If we had succeeded in holding out on the Marne facing Paris and on the lower Seine, our position would have been much nearer and much more menacing for the enemy than the line on which we remained into the year 1918, a line starting from Soissons, passing in front of Lille and extending all the way to the coast near Nieuport. Above all, the Channel ports would have been in our hands.

September 3 – The first army crosses the Marne. The Second and Third Armies reach the Marne

On the morning of September 3 the command of the First Army moved from Compiegne to La Ferté Milon. There it heard the surprising news that the IX Corps on the previous evening had seized the bridges of Chezy-sur-Marne[20] and Chateau-Thierry and that now, the 3rd, it wished to advance to the attack beyond the Marne. The attack at Chateau-Thierry had taken the enemy completely by surprise. The IX Corps had there, on the evening of

---

[20] Chezy on general map.

the 2nd, fallen in with a French infantry column which was marching toward this point without a misgiving, engaged in singing.

From aviation reports received it appeared that at noon enemy columns were falling back on both sides of the Marne, from Meaux toward the south, and that certain elements also seemed to be moving in the direction of Coulommiers. At 10 a.m. a combat had been observed on the heights southeast of Chateau-Thierry and detachments belonging to our own troops seemed to be passing through that city. To the south of the field of battle the road from Chateau-Thierry to Montmirail was clear of enemy troops. At 10:30 a.m. large bivouacs had been seen to the south and southeast of Montmirail. Large columns were marching from Montmirail upon Montenils [5 km. SW. of Montmirail] Large columns had also been observed on the roads from Mezy to Condé-en-Brie and from Condé-en-Brie to Artonges and Verdun. The Mezy bridge had not been destroyed, while that of Dormans had ben blown up at 10:50 in the forenoon.

The IX Corps had acted on its own initiative. Was it now to be drawn back or should the army follow it? The army command decided, not without some hesitation, to adopt the latter course. At 1 p.m. the army order was issued. On receipt of the communication from the IX Corps announcing that it was going to attack beyond the Marne by way of Chateau-Thierry, the III Corps had obliqued in the forenoon upon Charly and Nogentl'Artaud. It was now to push beyond the Marne by way of Villeneuve (east of Rebais), while the IV Corps, marching in the direction of La Ferté-sous-Jouarre, would advance up to the Marne, seize the bridges, push advance guards over the river and cover toward Coulommiers. The II Corps, IV Reserve Corps and II Cavalry Corps remained in place facing Paris.

The information received in the course of the afternoon indicated that the enemy had fallen back before the II Corps and the IV Reserve Corps upon Paris. Approximately one reenforced brigade was noted marching upon Dammartin by way of Nanteuil-le-Haudouin. One division coming from the northwestwas reported to have arrived in the afternoon at Precy (southwest of Creil on the Oise).

The chief of staff of the cavalry corps reported that the rest given the troops had had a good effect and that the cavalry corps would be able to resume its movement the following day; only the 4th Cavalry Division, which had suffered heavily on September 1, was not yet completely assembled. In the course of the day the IX Corps drove the enemy back in the southeasterly direction and rested in the evening on the heights carried north of Courbein. The III and IV Corps reached the Marne in the vicinity of Charly and La Ferté-sous-Jouarre, while the II Corps, the IV Reserve Corps and the II Cavalry Corps remained to the north of the Marne in the region of Nanteuil-le-Haudouin facing Paris. The army was, to be sure, strongly distributed toward the right; but in relation to the Second Army, at least with its left wing, as General von Bülow remarks, forward rather than backward.

At 9:45 p.m. General von Kluck ordered that the march beyond the Marne should be continued on the 4th in order to drive the French back toward the east. Any English forces that might be met with were to be thrown back. The IX Corps was ordered to take the direction of Montmirail, the III Corps the direction of Saint-Barthelemy and Montolivet, the IV Corps the direction of Rebais. The II Corps was also brought up and was to reach the region east of Meaux with its advance guards. The covering of the right flank facing Paris remained confided to the IV Reserve Corps in the region of Nanteuil-le-Haudouin. The 4th Cavalry Division was placed under its orders, while the II Cavalry Corps with its two other divisions was to march upon La Ferté-sous-Jouarre. As for the I Cavalry Corps, it was known that it was to advance on September 4th from Chateau-Thierry in the direction of Montmirail.

Two reports were sent that day (September 3) by the First army to the High Command. The first went out in the afternoon, when the decision had been reached to follow the IX Corps beyond the Marne: "First Army is driving back the French with its left wing and crossing the Marne at Chateau-Thierry and westward. It is pushing its center upon La Ferté-sous-Jouarre and covering the right flank in the region of Nanteuil with the II and IV Reserve Corps. Signs of disintegration in certain enemy units: they will be exploited to the limit." At 10:30 p.m. a second report was sent:

"First Army has crossed (September 3) the Marne line: La Ferté – Chateau-Thierry with its foremost units; the French were changing front toward their eastern wing. English north of Coulommiers. First Army will continue its movement on the 4th by way of Rebais – Montmirail." The remark concerning the French change of front related to the fact that the IX Corps had met with powerful enemy forces south of Chateau-Thierry.

The High Command took no position during the following days with regard to the announced designs of the First Army. It was assumed that they meet with its approval.

On the evening of September 3 the Second Army communicated to us the following: "The army has closely pursued the enemy today LIP to and beyond the Marne. Enemy also pouring back south of the river in complete disorder. Marne bridges in part destroyed." The opinion which the Second Army had already formed on September 2 regarding the enemy (page 137) was thus more clearly expressed again on the 3rd. The Second Army reached the Marne on the 3rd, between Chateau-Thierry and Binson, but it could no longer overtake the enemy. In its army order on the evening of the 3rd was the following: "Enemy also beyond the Marne retreating in disorder toward the south and southeast. Only certain detachments are still holding this evening in front of the X Corps. Pursuit being continued beyond the Marne."

The Third Army, which had advanced that day toward the Marne in the direction of Tours – Chalons in order to seize the fords with advance guards, was unable to cross the river. It met with strong resistance and settled down at the end of the day to the north of, Tours – Chalons, approximately on the line Bouzy – Cuperly. It was not until the 4th that it was able to cross the Marne. The 23rd Reserve Division had to be left behind to assure cover toward the eastern front of Reims. It took possession of the works on this front without anyfighting, but was nevertheless held up a whole day. The command of the Third Army had the impression that the enemy was falling back on its front but that he was displacing large forces to the left bank of the Marne from Chalons westward. Heavy traffic was observed on the railways running west and south. Naturally these observation were not yet known to the First Army.

The Fourth Army took the direction: Vitry-le-Francois – Revigny and with its right wing reached the region of La Cheppe on September 3.

The right wing of the Fifth Army got as far as Varennes – Montfaucon. After the incessant fighting of the past two weeks, the army desired to give its troops a day of rest on the 4th, but on the 3rd it received the following orders from the High Command: "General situation, particularly as concerns the Sixth and Seventh Armies, urgently requires that the Fifth Army continue advancing September 4 in the southerly direction while investing also the west front of Verdun. A halt of the Fifth Army on September 4 would. seriously interfere with the unity of the whole of the operations."

Critique of the First Army's Decision to Cross the Marne

The considerations already set forth[21] had led the command of the First Army, as early as September 1, to the idea that the operations could no longer be continued in the form followed up to that time. Once more there was a fortress which exercised a restricting and hemming opposition to the forward movement of the army: the gigantic fortress of Paris. To go around it to the west over the lower Seine had been proved impracticable. Now our right wing was pressing directly up against it.

The importance of Paris did not lie particularly in its fortifications. It is true that they impeded our movements, but due to their small strength and mediocre armament they had no great strength of resistance. Paris was, however, the center to which converged the French network of railways. It was easy to assemble there, to the south, the west and the north, powerful masses of troops in menacing proximity to our flank.

It was for these reasons that the First Army believed, on September 1, that it must make a halt. It was not until September

---

[21] See pages 137-138.

2, when an opportunity presented itself to strike the French troops in the flank, that the command of the First Army decided to continue its forward movement, but only up to the Marne. Crossing the Marne it held to be impracticable. Then in the night of September 2-3, arrived the order of the High Command according to which the right-wing armies were nevertheless to cross the Marne. The brief radiogram of the High Command offered no information regarding the reasons for this order or regarding the general situation. We tried to figure it out for ourselves. We imagined that the enemy, beaten, was in retreat all along the front and that the German army was doubtless advancing against his right flank beyond the Moselle. The enemy army might in that case be surrounded, if his left wing could also be enveloped.

Hence it was necessary to drive him back toward the southeast. The First Army was the only one in a position to do that, for the Second Army, even granting that it reached the enemy, could only come upon him frontally. But according to the order of the High Command, the First Army was to follow the Second in echelon. To that end, it would have had to stop for two or three days in order to let the Second Army get a sufficient start. But by that time it would have been too late to drive the French back toward the southeast and the whole operation would have been doomed to failure.

Now the IX Corps had, of its own accord, already crossed the Marne as early as September 3and had compelled the French left wing to fight. According to information furnished by the Second Army, the enemy was hurled back in complete disorder. Was it not the duty of the First army to profit by its situation as an advanced echelon? Were we to neglect the last opportunity of overtaking the enemy, let escape the reward of our unspeakable efforts?

But in crossing the Marne the army went contrary to the letter of the order of the High Command. It was perfectly aware of the fact. The right flank was to be covered toward Paris by its own echelon formation. Such a measure promised to be sufficient against the enemy forces beaten on the Somme and on the Avre. On the part of the English, there was scarcely any offensive to be feared. There still remained, however, a danger to the right flank. We took this chance in order to strive for a great goal which seemed possible of attainment.

It was a bold decision at which the command of the army had arrived. The dice were thrown, the Rubicon was crossed.

September 4 – Continuation of the Movement. The Second and Third Armies cross the Marne

In the first army, the IX Corps continued in the course of the day of September 4 to throw back the enemy in the direction of Montmirail. At the end of the daythis locality was still in the enemy's hands. He was putting up stubborn resistance. The command of the corps did not have the impression of being confronted with an enemy in flight. There were no indications whatever of a precipitate retreat, such as gunsthrown away, abandoned cannon and vehicles. The III Corps came up against the resistance of rear guards, which it broke. It attained its march objective, namely, the region of Saint Barthelemy – Montolivet. The IV Corps got as far as the region of Rebais, without fighting. The II Corps came to rest in the afternoon in the elbow of the Marne to the northeast of Meaux. The bridges of Meaux and La Ferté-sous-Jouarre were blown up. The IV Reserve Corps reached the region of Nanteuil-le-Haudouin, the II Cavalry Corps La Ferté-sous-Jouarre.

From information received in the course of the day it appeared that the enemy was continuing his retreat from Montmirail upon Esternay and from Coulommiers – Rebais toward the south. Dammartin was occupied by enemy infantry.

The army command began to *entertain doubts regarding the further progress of the operations*. The farther the army pushed toward the south, the more difficult become the covering of the flank toward Paris. The forces of the army were not large enough. The army command had counted on sufficient forces being brought up into the second line behind the right wing of the German Army. I knew that was an important point in the Schlieffen plan and that the replacement divisions, among others, were kept in mind for that task. But the awaited echelon failed to arrive and the general situation of the German forces was not clear to us. We experienced doubts regarding the decisive victories of the other armies. These considerations gave rise to the following radiogram sent on the morning of September 4 to the High Command: "First Army requests information regarding the situation of the other armies whose announcements of decisive victories have been followed on numerous occasions by requests for support. With the continual heavy fighting in the course of the marches imposed upon it, the First Army has reach the limit of its endurance. It was only in this manner that it succeeded in opening the passage of the Marne for the other armies and compelling the enemy to continue his retreat. In this connection the IX Corps has given a splendid account of itself by the boldness of its operations. We now hope to be able to exploit the success. Instructions No. 2220 of the High Command directing the First Army to follow the Second Army in echelon[22] could not be followed in these conditions. The plan of throwing the enemy back toward the southeast and cutting him off from Paris can be executed only in case the First Army moves forward. The necessity of covering the right flank weakens the army's offensive force. It is highly urgent that the right wing be reenforced soon by other units (III or VII Reserve Corps). In view of the incessant changes in the situation, the First Army will not be in a position to form important decisions unless it is permanently kept informed regarding the situation of the other armies which seem to be farther in the rear. Liaison with Second Army regularly maintained."

The objections and requests of the First Army were justified. It would have been preferable, it is true, that the command of the First Army had set forth its grounds for concern no later than September 3. If the High Command had not yet got reenforcements under way, it would then be too late for them to arrive in time. Furthermore, our radiogram was late in reaching the High Command, and then the latter had already reached another decision and sent an officer to bring us detailed instructions. The above radiogram reveals the great uncertainty in which the command of the First Army found itself, and the meagerness of the information

---

[22] Anweisung O.H.L. 2220.

which it possessed regarding the general situation.

In spite of the doubts which it had expressed, the First Army Command believed that it could still continue its movement one day longer in accordance with its plans up to this time. The IX Corps was to advance on the 5th into the region of Esternay. As a consequence the Second Army found itself hemmed in and with its left wing pushed back upon the road Montmirail – Sezanne. The III Corps was to reach the region of Sancy, the IV Corps Choisy. Protection toward the northeast front of Paris fell, north of the Marne, to the IV Reserve Corps and in the region of Marcilly – Chambry (north of the Meaux) to the 4th Cavalry Division, and south of the Marne, facing the northeast front of Paris, to the II Corps which also was then pushed south of the Marne toward the region of Coulommiers. The cavalry corps was ordered to advance into the region of Provins in order, if possible, later to attack the French right[23] wing at the passage of the Seine.

The following report was addressed in the evening to the High Command: "Left wing of First Army has thrown the French back upon Montmirail. English in the region of Coulommiers seem to be retreating toward the south and southwest. The army will move forward on the 5th. Enemy will be attacked wherever encountered. IX Corps at Esternay, III at Sancy, IV at Choisy, II at Coulommiers, IV Reserve Corps north of Meaux, II Corps and IV Reserve Corps assure cover of right flank with the 4th Cavalry Division II Cavalry Corps with the 2nd and 9th Cavalry Divisions at Provins. Army headquarters: Rebais."

The Second Army crossed the Marne on September 4 and reached the line: Pargny la Dhuis – Mareuil en Brie – Epernay without encountering the enemy.[24]

The Third Army, also, succeeded on the 4th in crossing the line of the Marne between Athis (east of Epernay) and Chalons-sur-Marne. Its troops were thoroughly worn out. A day of rest was therefore prescribed for the 5th.

---

[23] This evidently an error. It should be the left wing. – Editor's Note.

[24] See Sketch 8.

The Fourth Army reached the region between the Moivre and Valmy.

The Fifth Army got as far as the line: Sainte Menehould – Clermont – Recicourt and covered toward Verdun, in the region of Forges on the left bank, and by means of the V Corps on the right bank.

September 5 – Change in the Operations. The First and Second Armies are Directed to Change Direction Toward Paris. The German Left Flank Continues its Offensive. Beginning of the Battle of the Ourcq

At 7 o'clock in the morning there arrived at First Army Headquarters at La Ferté-Milon a *radiogram from the High Command*, sent on the preceding evening, which set before the First and Second Armies a quite new task and brought about a complete change in the operations: "The First and Second Armies will remain facing the eastern front of Paris, First Army between the Oise and the Marne holding the bridges of the Marne to the west of Chateau-Thierry, Second Army between the Marne and the Seine holding the passages of the Seine between Nogent [l'Artaud] and Mery, incl. Third Army line of march: Troyes and eastward."

Thus the instructions issued a short time previously by the High Command were again countermanded. The reasons for this modification were unknown to us. We were unable to form an exact picture of the situation, for we could not get a general view of the relations existing at the center and on the left wing of the German forces. The idea of throwing the French back toward the southeast had been abandoned. The great enveloping movement through Belgium had not succeeded in surrounding the French: *the Schlieffen plan had failed.*

The First Army was obliged to let go of the enemy, all its efforts had been in vain. We could not "remain" between the Oise and the Marne, we could only go back. The First Army Command was unable to comprehend that expression of the High Command, for we assumed that it must have known exactly the arrangement of our army from our reports.

The High Command itself, had probably come to experience doubts, similar to those which he had expressed in the radiogram of the morning of the 4th. The German right wing was too weak to march past Paris. Was a special danger menacing us in that region? We had no information to indicate new displacements of French forces. The closer we held on to the French all along the front, the more securely were such displacements prevented.

In these conditions the command of the First Army thought it advisable to propose to the High Command that as soon as the Marne was crossed we should continue pursuing the French for a small distance, up to the Seine, and not to invest Paris until later. Once the French had been thrown back behind the Seine, the French forces which had appeared in our right flank to the north of Paris would be obliged to fall back also. The following radiogram was sent to the High Command: "In accordance with previous instructions of the High Command, the army is marching by way of Rebais – Montmirail toward the Seine. The corps covering toward Paris on both sides of the Marne. At Coulommiers, fighting contact with approximately three English divisions, at Montmirail with the left wing of the French. The latter resisting vigorously with rear guards; they would suffer seriously if the pursuit were continued up to the Seine. As yet they have only been pushed back frontally and are still to be reckoned with. They are retreating upon Nogent. If the prescribed investment of Paris takes place, the enemy will have all freedom of action toward Troyes. At Paris large enemy forces are probably only in process of concentration. Portions of the field army are no doubt being brought up in that direction, but that will require time. It seems to me that to let go of an army which is still in good fighting condition and to displace the First and Second Armies atthis time is rather ill advised. I propose that the pursuit be continued up to the Seine and to leave the investment of Paris until later." This proposal was a logical outgrowth of the reasoning heretofore employed by the command, of the First Army, but it rested upon an insufficient knowledge of the situation.

Regardless of this proposal, measures were taken at once for putting into effect the orders of the High Command. The prescribed change of front was difficult from the technical marching point of view, and time-consuming, now that the army had advanced so far toward the Seine. At the very least it appeared necessary first to throw back the enemy forces that had been noted directly in front of the army at Coulommiers and Montmirail. It was also necessary to come to an understanding with the Second Army. A staff officer, furnished with written instructions, was sent to the Second Army for the purpose of acquainting it with the viewpoint of the First Army and with the proposal which it had made to the High Command. This officer was also to call the Second Army's attention to the fact that the enemy forces in front of it were by no means beaten in. a decisive manner, in the opinion of the First Army Command, but were still in perfect fighting condition and had put up a vigorous resistance at Chateau-Thierry. He was also to state that the Second Army could not cross the line Esternay – Montmirail until it had been evacuated by the First Army and that the latter's movement could not be halted before the end of the day.

The Army Command did not attempt to halt more than the IV Reserve Corps and the II Cavalry Corps. The first was located nearby, the second could be reached by radio. The IV Reserve Corps was ordered to halt at whatever point it had reached when the order was received. But the order did not reach it until noon, when it had already attained its marching objective. As for the II Cavalry Corps, it was to avoid getting away from us by continuing its march toward the south. With the other corps we had at the time no liaison; officers were not assigned to the duty of coming for orders until after Rebais, to which place we were to move at noon. We considered that it was not possible to reach the staffs of the corps at the proper time, in view of their distance from La Ferté-Milon, nor to halt the corps, some of which had only a short march to make, without giving rise to friction.

Since the prescribed movement was to begin early on the 6th, preparation was made for the measures to be taken.

On reaching Rebais at noon, the First Army Command was presented with reports to the effect that the enemy was falling back through Sezanne, Esternay, and Provins in a southerly direction the Montmirail bivouacs had been evacuated, a long column had been seen marching to the southwest upon Brie Comte Robert (southeast of Paris).

The III Corps drove back a strong cavalry detachment supported by artillery and small units of infantry. The IV Corps in the course of its movement got contact with the enemy, but the latter retired after a few shots had been fired. At Montmirail the IX Corps again came up against enemy forces which were falling back upon Sezanne. In the evening the following report from the IV Reserve Corps was received: "The enemy forces near Dammartin seem to be quite small but still in place." In front of the II Corps the enemy was falling back to the south and southwest. In the afternoon the II Cavalry Corps transmitted the following: "The enemy forces from Coulommiers did not fall back toward the south until 6 o'clock in the morning." Hence the enemy was in full retreat all along the front from Coulommiers up to Montmirail. There was nothing to indicate the existence of danger to the right flank north of the Marne.

The center and left wing of the army reached their marching objectives in the region of Coulommiers – Esternay.

In the afternoon Lieutenant Colonel Hentsch of the High Command came to apprise us of the situation. At the same time we received very detailed written instructions through another officer of the High Command.

These instructions of September 5 for the First to Seventh Armies, inclusive, were as follows:

> The enemy has evaded the enveloping attack of the First and Second Armies and has succeeded with part of his forces in getting connection with Paris. Reports from the front and trustworthy information supplied by secret agents make it possible also to conclude that forces coming from the line: Toul – Belfort, are being transported toward the west and, furthermore, that forces are being withdrawn from in front of our Third, Fourth, and Fifth Armies. Hence it is not longer possible to throw the whole French army back toward the Swiss frontier in a southeasterly direction. Rather it is to be expected that the enemy will bring together large forces in the region of Paris and bring up new units in order to protect his capital and to menace the right flank of the German forces.
>
> The First and Second Armies will therefore remain in place before the east front of Paris. Their task will be to take the offensive

against any enemy undertaking from the region of Paris and to lend each other mutual support in these operations.

The fourth and Fifth Armies are still in contact with important enemy forces. It will be their duty to drive these forces back without a halt in a southeasterly direction, a move which will have the further effect of opening the passage of the Moselle between Toul and Epinal to the Sixth Army. It is still impossible to say whether this operation, in conjunction with the activities of the Sixth and Seventh Armies, will succeed in throwing important enemy forces back upon the Swiss frontier.

The task of the Sixth and Seventh Armies is still, for the present, to seize any enemy forces appearing before their front. They will advance as soon as possible to the attack on the Moselle line between Toul and Epinal, covering toward these places.

The third Army will march upon Troyes – Vendeuvre. It will be employed either in supporting the First and Second Armies beyond the Seine in the westerly direction or in taking part, in the southerly and southeasterly directions, in the combats waged by our left wing, according as the situation may require.

His Majesty therefore orders:

1. The First and Second Armies will continue facing the east front of Paris so as to take the offensive against any enemy undertaking from that direction. First Army between the Oise and the Marne. The crossings of the Marne below Chateau-Thierry will be held in order to permit passage from one bank to the other. Second Army between Marne and Seine. Seizure of the passages of the Seine between Nogent [Sur Seine] and Mery is very important. Both armies are recommended to keep the main body of their forces far enough away from Paris so that they can retain a sufficient freedom of action for their operations. The II Cavalry Corps will remain under the orders of the First Army and will transfer one division to the I Cavalry Corps. The I Cavalry Corps will remain under the orders of the Second Army and will transfer one division to the Third Army.

The task of the II Cavalry Corps will be to observe the north front of Paris between the Marne and the lower Seine and to reconnoiter between the Somme and the lower Seine up to the coast. Distant reconnoitering beyond the line: Lille – Amiens, in the direction of the coast will be assured by the air forces of the First Army.

The I Cavalry Corps will observe the south front of Paris between the Marne and the Seine below Paris; it will reconnoiter in the directions [see insert on general map No. 1] Caen, Alencon, Le Mans,

Tours, and Bourges and shall receive the air forces necessary to that effect.

The two cavalry corps will destroy the railways leading to Paris as near to the capital as possible.

2. The Third Army will march upon Troyes – Vendeuvre. A division of cavalry will be assigned to it by the I Cavalry Corps. Reconnoitering toward the line: Nevers – Le Creusot; air forces to be assigned.

3. The Fourth and Fifth Armies, by advancing resolutely in the southeasterly direction, will open the passage of the Moselle to the Sixth and Seventh Armies. Right wing of Fourth Army through Vitry-le-Francois and Montierender; right wing of Fifth Army through Revigny – Stainville – Morlaix. The Fifth Army will cover with its left wing toward the works of the Meuseand will carry the forts of Troyon, Les Paroches, and Camp des Romains. The IV Cavalry Corps will remain under the orders of the Fifth Army, and will reconnoiter before the front of the Fourth and Fifth Armies toward the line: Dijon – Besancon – Belfort. Reports will be sent also to the Fourth Army.

4. The task of the Sixth and Seventh Armies remains unchanged.

Signed: VON MOLTKE.

According to my notes, Lieutenant-Colonel Hentsch verbally supplemented these instructions in the following tenor: "The situation is bad. Our left wing is held up in front of Nancy – Epinal and, in spite of heavy losses, is not progressing a single step. Verdun is cut off. To the west of Verdun, the Fourth and Fifth Armies are executing a sweeping movement in order to deliver a flank attack upon the French stationed behind the front: Verdun – Toul. There, too, the advance is very slow. Troop movements seem to have taken place from the right wing of the French army toward Paris. Something seems to be under way also farther north, approximately in the direction of Lille. Fresh English troops are reported to be disembarking, perhaps at Ostende. It is possible that Antwerp will be supported by the English."

The First Army was now confronted with an entirely new situation. There was no further thought of our breakthrough on the upper Moselle, on which we had been counting. The French were by no means being held everywhere; large displacements of troops were in progress. The danger on our right flank was increasing, though it did not yet appear to be quite imminent. The plan which we had formed in the morning, of first throwing the French back over the Seine, was discarded. We informed Lieutenant-Colonel Hentsch of the measures which we had already taken for falling back and facing Paris and how this movement was to be executed beginning the 6th. He declared these measures to be in conformity with the designs of the High Command and emphasized several times, in the presence of the senior staff officer of the staff of the First Army, Lieutenant-Colonel Grautoff, that the movement was to be carried out calmly and that there was no particular hurry. The statement of General Tappen,[25] according to which the order of the High Command had not been completely carried out on the right wing in the haste of moving forward, requires then, in the light of the foregoing, to be proved.

It must not be forgotten, in judging these events, that neither the High Command nor the command of the First Army had the faintest notion of the imminence of a general offensive of the whole French army such as was actually in course of preparation. It was absolutely taken for granted that the French army would continue its retreat. The only question was of a danger from the direction of Paris and menacing our flank. Otherwise, a movement such as that of the right oblique of the Second Army could never have been ordered.

Meanwhile we received also from the Second Army at Rebais an appraisal of the situation which was in complete conformity with the data contained in the instructions of the High Command.

It was 11 o'clock at night before the army order for the day of September 6th could be issued. In the course of the evening we received another air report, stating that in the afternoon an enemy corps had been seen partly bivouacked at Tournan (southeast of 'Paris) and partly still moving in that direction, and that a division had also been perceived bivouacked at Rozoy. On September 6, the II Corps was to advance into the region northeast of Meaux, the IV Corps in the direction of La Ferté-sous-Jouarre as far as Doue, the III Corps up to La Ferté Gaucher, while the IX Corps was to remain in place. The idea was to establish our new front by means

---

[25] Loc. cit. , page 23.

of a counter march and a right turn in the course of which the various corps would preserve the same order, the IX Corps consequently remaining on the left flank. To this end, the movement was to begin with the left flank and proceed by echelons. The army might also have been required to make a half turn and then execute a change of front to the left; the corps would then have been in inverse order, the IX Corps on the right wing. This, however, would have necessitated a displacement of the columns and trains, the movement of which was already sufficiently difficult. It had to be regulated daily by the staff.

The II Cavalry Corps was to mask the movement in rear and to the right of the army, facing the southeast front of Paris and the lower Seine, by advancing into the region: Lumigny – Rozoy. All the necessary measures for crossing the Marne in good order were taken.

Since the Third Army remained in place on the Marne and rested that day (September 5) the Second Army executed only a short march up to the line: Montmirail – Vertus; then, after the arrival of the instructions of the High Command, it initiated its new movement by an oblique onto the line: Montmirail – Morains le Petit. On the 6th it was to continue the oblique up to the line: Montmirail – Marigny le Grand. Here the execution of the movements presented itself in a much simpler form than to the First Army, which was obliged to execute the prescribed oblique in the course of the backward march.

The Third Army proposed to continue its movement toward the south on the following day.

The Fourth Army reached (September 5) the line: Vitry le Francois – Heiltz l'Eveque – Saint Mard sur le Mont.

The Fifth Army covering toward Verdun, reached with its center and right wing Villers en Argonne – Fleury.

The day of September 6 passed otherwise than we had expected at the staff of the First Army. As early as the afternoon of the 5th, cannon thundered to our right flank. The protection of the flank was confided in this region to the commander of the IV Reserve Corps, General von Gronau. The first report, stating that the IV Reserve Corps had met with a superior enemy force at Dammartin and had fallen back at an advanced hour of the evening behind the Thérouane sector, reached us too late in the evening at Rebais, long after the order for the day of the 6th had been despatched. This report was received through a conversation of the II Corps with the senior officer of the staff of the First Army, Lieutenant-Colonel Grautoff.

The Battle of the Ourcq had begun. It was the curtain-raiser for the gigantic Battle of the Marne. The enemy attack was striking in the German right wing in an unfavorable situation, for the First Army had advanced too far. The great French offensive, executed along the whole front, took us completely by surprise. No suggestion, no statement of prisoners, no newspaper item had announced it. The enemy had not decided upon it until the last moment. We were confronted with a serious crisis.

Was the First Army capable of surmounting it? The troops were exhausted. Ever since the launching of the forward movement, they had marched continuously, without a single day of rest. Greater and greater marching efforts were required of them with the object of still overtaking the enemy. The IV Reserve Corps had not been at all inferior to the regular corps. From August 17, the day on which it crossed the frontier, to September 4 it had covered 480 kilometers, or an average of 27 kilometers [about 17 miles] per day for 18 days, most of the time on a single road, and up to August 26, behind another corps. From August 31 to September 2 it had marched 90 kilometers in three days. As for the astonishing performances of the regular corps, I have referred to them a number of times. Nowhere in military history, so far as I am aware, is it possible to find a single example of marching performances such as those of the First Army. But now the troops were nearly exhausted, and the plaints of the corps commanders were daily becoming more pressing. On September 4, the commander of the III Corps, General von Lochow, addressed to the first Army a letter in which he referred to the exhaustion of his troops in consequence of the unheard-of marching performance which they had accomplished and the serious effects on their discipline and fighting capacity.

It was in this condition that the First Army entered the battle of the Marne. The worst was still ahead, and the troops showed themselves equal to that also. The various corps, hastening up to the field of battle, accomplished marches surpassing all that was done before. Only such a splendid army as that with which we entered the field in 1914 was capable of such exploits.

Critique of the Army order of September 4

The order of the High Command of September 4 was manifestly based on the hypothesis that the First Army was not so far forward as was actually the case. Otherwise the order would not have stated: the First Army will remain between the Oise and the Marne. How can that be explained? The reportof the First army dated the afternoon of September 3, and stating that the Marne was going to be crossed, did not reach General Headquarters until 5:20 p.m. of the 4th; the report of the evening of September 3 arrived a little later. It was clear that they had not yet been presented when, at 7 p.m., the radiogram from the High Command to the First army was sent. The great distance at which the General Headquarters was located and the inadequacy of the connections were here revealed as constituting a great disadvantage. It was impossible to direct the operations in such conditions.[26] The First Army, on the evening of September 2, had reported that the IX Corps had obliqued upon Chateau-Thierry in order to attack the flank of the retreating French and that the III Corps had followed it in echelon to the east of Crouy. Therefore, as the Second Army on that day was still only crossing the Vesle, it might at least have been inferred that the First Army was very far in advance. Thus we find in the files of the High Command a radiogram from the First Army of the afternoon of September 3, addressed to the Second and Third Armies, picked up at Luxembourg and remitted to the High Command at 2:19 a.m. of September 4th, as follows: "First Army today crossing the Marne at Chateau-Thierry and westward." It bears an annotation in pencil by Lieutenant-Colonel Tappen which shows that it came to his attention. On September 5, Lieutenant-Colonel Hentsch had supposed that the staff of the First Army was still at La Ferté-

[26] See pages 41-42.

Milon. A staff officer of the IV Corps while looking for the Headquarters of the First Army, met Lieutenant-Colonel Hentsch in the afternoon. The latter expressed astonishment to learn that the IV Corps was so far south and declared that he had assumed it to befarther north.

The order of the High Command was based upon the following plan: *to form on the right wing a defensive front against which the attack to be expected from Paris would break in vain, while the left wing would continue the offensive.* The Schlieffen plan had been transformed into its opposite! Instead of the crushing offensive on the west wing, we were attacking the fortified front in the east, the very thing that was to be avoided.

The prospects of a successful defense toward Paris were certainly sufficient, on condition, however, that the new front could be established at the proper time by the First and Second Armies. The High Command believed. that there was enough time for this. That belief is apparent, moreover, from the whole form of the order. But the great danger lay in the fact that the enemy was able to call out far superior forces, thanks to his excellent network of railways ending at Paris, and also assemble them farther north for the purpose of surrounding us, once we had settled down to the defensive east of Paris and had given him full freedom of action.

The results to be expected from the offensive of our left wing were very doubtful. Up to that time we had not succeeded in breaking through between Toul and Epinal. Perhaps the prospects had become more favorable since the enemy was withdrawing troops from that region. But, precisely on September 5, we, too, began to take troops from the front of the Sixth and Seventh Armies and place them on the right wing. It was evident that by continuing the offensive on the Moselle it was only desired to hold the enemy; while on the west of the Meuse the Fourth and Fifth Armies would continue their march in the southerly direction and fall upon his rear. But the success of that maneuver was doubtful. We have already noted the difficult situation of the Fifth Army. It could scarcely be hoped that a concentric attack of the Fourth, Fifth, Sixth, and Seventh Armies would succeed in encircling the enemy or throwing him back toward Switzerland. The best that could be expected was that we might throw the enemy far, back into the interior of the country.

The plan contained no great, inspiring idea. The impression created by it was that of a maneuver resorted to in embarrassing circumstances.

Looking backward at events it is easy to criticize. What should have been done? The unfortunate attempt to break through on the Moselle should have been abandoned at last and the left wing placed on the defensive.

To the extent that the circumstances allowed, the omissions and errors of the past should have been remedied, and the largest possible number of troops should have been transported from the left to the right wing. It is true that the enemy had already anticipated us in the matter of the displacement of forces and was provided with better railways.

Hanotaux believes that Joffre, in a similar case, would have fallen back. There was no reason whatever for falling back; it would not have bettered our situation.

In the order of the High Command, as well as in the information furnished by Lieutenant-Colonel Hentsch, one finds a certain anxiety with regard to enemy undertakings proceeding from the coast, either from Ostende or through Lille. The English had, in fact, planned to execute an attack, starting from the sea, for the purpose of disengaging the English army. But there were available for that purpose only a few marine battalions, some 3000 men. They were disembarked at Ostende on August 27 and 28, and their task was rather to protect that port against a German undertaking. Ostende was, in fact, to be kept from falling into the hands of the Germans as long as the English transports were directed to Le Havre. When the English base, as we shall see later, was moved to Saint Nazaire, the occupation of Ostende lost its importance. The English marines were reembarked on August 31. Consideration had also been given for a time to landing at Ostende and Zeebrugge the 16,000 Belgians which had arrived at Le Havre from Namur, but instead, they were transported to Antwerp.

When the order of September 5 reached the armies, it was already overtaken by the events. *On the morning of the 6th, the Franco-English attack began unexpectedly all along the front.*

Chapter VII – The French and English Operations from the August Battles to the Battle of the Marne

Beginning of the Retreat (August 24)

On the evening of August 24 the French offensive had failed along the whole front. At that time the armies stood as follows:[1]

The Lorraine Army east of the Meuse facing Metz, left wing at Spincourt.

The Third Army, in liaison with the preceding, on the Othain, through Marville up to a point southwest of Virton. The Fourth Army on the line: north of Montmedy – Carignan – south of Sedan – north of Mézières.

The Fifth Army retreating through Mariembourg – Avesnes.

The English at Bavai.

On the evening of the 25th the situation was as follows:

The Lorraine Army was on the Orne at Conflans – Etain. It was disbanded on the evening of the 25th, two divisions were sent to the Somme, four remained on the Meuse heights south of

---

[1] See Sketch 9.

Verdun.

The Third Army was in the region Azannes – Dun.

The Fourth Army was on the line Stenay – Mézières.

The Fifth Army was on the front Rocroi – Hirson – west of Avesnes.

The English was at Landrecies – Le Cateau.

The effect of the great August battles – Lorraine, Longwy-Longuyon, Neufchateau, Namur, and Mons – was considerable. The Allies in retreat abandoned the northeast portion of France, the most important industrial region, whose loss involved the greatest consequences to them. The defeats suffered by all the armies weighed heavily upon the troops. The events of 1870 were called to mind. The French accounts indicate clearly the powerful impression created by the fighting from August 20 to 25. A marked discouragement became manifest in certain corps.[2] With reference to certain units of the Fifth Army, it is stated that the masses flowed back in indescribable disorder. Palat takes a decided stand against the account of Hanotaux, who tries to minimize the importance of the August battles. Palat declares that as a result of the retreat the French forces were south of the Marne on September 5 and that the command had resigned itself to falling back behind the Seine; that Paris was without sufficient protection and that the government had retired to Bordeaux. We shall see later how the effect of the retreat continued to grow and attained an alarming height. "If the Battle of the Marne had been lost, everything would have been over one month after the opening of hostilities. Any recovery would have been impossible."[3]

General Lanrezac depicts as follows the situation of the French Army after the August battles: "The whole French army is then in the most dismal situation. It was not only the Fifth Army which suffered a serious defeat: de Langle's was beaten north of the Semoy and found itself forced to retire toward the Meuse. Ruffey's army had little better success between Arlon and Thoinville and

---

[2] Palat, loc. cit., Vol. III, pages 241 and 314.

[3] Le Gros: "*La Genèse de la Bataille de la Marne*," page 19.

was obliged to fall back upon Verdun. The armies of Castelnau and Dubail were forced to retreat toward the fortified position of Nancy and behind the Mortagne. We had been defeated everywhere, from the Sambre up to the Vosges. All out armies had been badly handled, and had nothing left to do but retreat in all haste and thus avoid total destruction."[4]

Joffre's Order to Retreat (August 25)

The headquarters of the French commander in chief on August 25 was at Vitry-le-Frangois. The chief of the general staff was General Belin, with General Berthelot as chief of the operations section. The staff of the French High Command is entitled to credit for not losing its head after the heavy defeats and for conducting the retreat in a sensible manner. Joffre himself was indefatigable in his efforts to raise the fallen morale of the French forces, to coordinate the movements of the various armies, and to heighten the power of resistance and the offensive spirit of his troops.

The basic order was issued on August 25 at 10 p.m. Palat thinks that the text hitherto known is apparently not quite accurate. The order reads as follows:[5]

> 1. Since the planned offensive could not be executed, the further operations will be regulated in such a way as to constitute on our left, by the junction of the Fourth and Fifth Armies, of the English army and of new forces withdrawn from the eastern section, a mass capable of resuming the offensive, while the other armies will hold up the enemy effort for such time as may be necessary.
>
> 2. During their backward movement, the Third, Fourth and Fifth Armies will each take account of the movements of the adjoining armies, with which they will remain in liaison.
>
> The movement will be covered by rear guards left on favorable sectors of the terrain in such manner as to utilize all the obstacles in

---

[4] *Le Plan de Campagne Francaise et le Premier mois de la Guerre*, 1920, pages 185 ff.

[5] See Sketch 10.

order to arrest, by short and violent counterattacks of which the main element will be the artillery, the march of the enemy or at least to retard it.

3. Limits of the zones of action between the different armies:

Army W (British): to the northeast of the line: Le Cateau – Vermand – Nesle, inclusive.

Fourth and Fifth Armies: between and not including the preceding line on the west and the line: Stenay – Grand Pre – Suippes – Condé (sur Marne) on the east (inclusive).

Third Army, includingthe Army of Lorraine: between the line: Sassey – Fléyille – Ville-sur-Tourbe (23 km. NE. of Somme Tourbe) – Vitry-le-Francois (inclusive) on the west and the line: Vigneulles – Void – Gondrecourt (inclusive) on the east.

4. On the extreme left between Picquigny and the sea a barrage will be kept on the Somme by the territorial divisions of the north, with the 61st and 62nd Reserve Divisions as a reserve.

5. The cavalry corps on the Authie will be ready to follow the movement of the extreme left.

6. In front of Amiens, between Domart en Ponthieu and Corbie, or in rear of the Somme between Picquigny and Villers-Bretonneux, a new grouping of forces, composed of elements transported by rail (VII Corps, 4 reserve divisions and perhaps a regular army corps) will be formed between August 27 and September 2.

This group will be ready to take the offensive in the general direction of St. Pol – Arrasor Arras – Bapaume.

7. Army W (British) in rear of the Somme, from Bray-sur-Somme to Ham, will be ready to push either toward the north upon Bertincourt or toward the east upon Le Catelet.

8. The Fifth Army will have the main body of its forces in the region: Vermand – St. Quentin – Moy (offensive front) so as to set out in the general direction of Bohain, its right holding the line La Fère – Laon – Craonne – St. Erme.

9. The Fourth Army: in rear of the Aisne, on the front: Guignicourt – Vouziers, or in case that proves impracticable, on the front: Berry. au Bac – Reims – Montagne de Reims (30 km S. of Reims), while always reserving the means of taking the offensive facing north.

10. The Third Army: resting its right on the fortress of Verdun and its left on the gap of Grand Pré or on Varennes – St. Menehould.

11. All the above-mentioned positions shall be organized with the greatest care so as to be able to offer the maximum resistance to the enemy. We shall start out from this situation for the offensive

movement.

12. The First and Second Armies will continue to hold the enemy forces opposed to them. In case of a forced retirement, their zones of action will be:

Second Army: between the road: Frouard – Toul – Vaucouleurs (inclusive) and the road: Bayon – Charmes – Mirecourt--Vittel – Clefmont (inclusive).

First Army: to the north of the road: Chatel – Dompaire – Lamarche – Montignyle Roi (inclusive).

Signed: JOFFRE.

One has to recognize in this order the will to resume the offensive quickly. The decisive direction in which the offensive is to be taken, that of the German outer right wing, is also indicated. Finally, the fact that the forces required for this maneuver may be withdrawn, from the French eastern front, because of the confidence entertained in the strength of the French fortified sector, it also correctly recognized.

The main body of the forces was to be brought back onto the general line: Verdun – Rethel or Reims – Laon-St. Quentin – Péronne, while a new army was being assembled at Amiens. The retreat was being conducted, then. , in the general direction of Paris; the army was to be arranged in a straight line from Verdun to Amiens, while resting upon the fortifications of Verdun, Reims, Laon, La Fère, and upon the obstacles presented by the Aisne and Somme, and be covered on its right flank by the fortified line: Epinal – Verdun. The attack was confided to the new group constituted toward Amiens, to the English, and to the left wing of the Fifth Army. The Fourth Army was to join in the attack, while the Third Army was given a defensive task. The reenforcements for the left wing at Amiens were to be taken from the eastern front.

Count Schlieffen had foreseen this arrangement. The German left wing was to march in this case upon Abbeville. But in 1914 this was out of the question because of the distribution of forces resulting from our concentration. Swiftness had to take the place of what we lacked in the way of forces on the right wing. The operations of the First Army, particularly, had been directed according to this idea. Its role was to spread out toward the right as far as cohesion of the whole of the German forces permitted. The fact that the German First Army, after the battle of Le Cateau, did not follow the English in the southerly direction, as General Maurice thinks would have been advisable, but struck out in the direction of Péronne, Proved thereafter to be extremely effective. The English were not in a position to take the sector: Bray – Ham which was assigned them in the new battle front, but were obliged to fall back ceaselessly, day and night, by way of La Fère and Noyon in front of the enveloping movement by which they were menaced. On the 28th, the German First Army had already crossed the Somme on either side of Péronne; on the 30th its right wing was in front of Amiens before the placement of the new French army could be effected. All the units of this French army which were already in this region, or which arrived there gradually, were separately beaten and dispersed. The swiftness of our advance thus found its reward. Just as at the beginning it had dislocated the concentration in common of the Belgian, English, and French left wing, so now it was overthrowing the whole plan of Joffre. Instead of falling back behind the Aisne and the Somme, he was obliged to continue on behind the Marne.

If Joffre had succeeded in carrying out his plan, the First Army, which according to the instructions of August 27 was to push forward north of the Oise, would have come up against powerful forces at Amiens and Péronne. General Tappen states that the High Command several times considered making a halt before forcing the difficult obstacles in order to enable the troops to close up, but that the idea was abandoned. And quite rightly. If we had stopped, for example, in front of the strong position contemplated by Joffre, our offensive would have come to standstill. Whether this would have been the beginning of position warfare, we will not venture to say. But the continuance of the operations would certainly have been very difficult, and an envelopment of the French left wing impossible.

Joffre's order loses sight of what was possible of accomplishment. How could the new army, assembled as late as the period of August 27 to September 2, still hope to be able to attack in the direction of Arras or even of St. Pol? It could not be expected that the Germans, who were already in front of Solesmes on the 25th, would leave that army time to assemble up to

September 2.

The plan of executing a heavy attack against the German right flank is not formally mentioned in the order, which deals in rather general terms with the manner of resuming the offensive. It has been maintained in France that the plan of attacking was not to betaken very seriously anyhow and that it had been expressed more with the object of calming the country. This allegation comes from the partisans of Gallieni, who wish to attribute to him the principal merit of the later attack on the Marne. We shall come back to this question. Palat, also, thinks that the governing idea does not appear with sufficient clarity in Joffre's order, perhaps because it had not yet been formulated in Joffre's own mind.

The French army could not keep on in the southwesterly direction assigned to it. Even if contact was still maintained on the right with Verdun, the army was pulled apart by the great extent of the front toward the left. Furthermore, it was to be very difficult for the English to fall back north of the line: Le Cateau – Nesle by filing past obliquely in front of the enemy. The French forces, of their own accord, took a more southerly direction, as we had done, while the English army was pushed back behind the Oise and the new French army dispersed.

August 27-30 – The Concentration of the Sixth Army in the Vicinity of Amiens did not Materialize

General Maunoury, hitherto commander of the Army of Lorraine, was designated to lead the new Sixth Army which was to be formed at Amiens. According to Joffre's plans, his first task was to disengage the English who were badly menaced with being enveloped by the German First Army. In case the other armies resumed the general offensive, he was to move against the German right flank. In case of necessity, he was to fall back upon Paris and cooperate in the defense of the capital. It was intended to have the army assemble during the period August 27 to September 2 in the region of Amiens. General Maunoury left Verdun on August 28 and proceeded to Montdidier, where he set up his headquarters. The Sixth Army was to be formed from the following units:

1. The VII Corps, composed of the 14th Division and the 63rd Reserve Division, under General Vautier. This corps came from Alsace, where the Army of Alsace had been disbanded[6] and was to be detrained on August 28 in the vicinity of Amiens.

2. The 5th Group, composed of the 55th and 56th Reserve Divisions under General Lamaze. These divisions had hitherto belonged to the Army of Lorraine and had fought in Lorraine. They were embarked, beginning August 27, on the Meuse at St. Mihiel and Dieue and disembarked up to August 29-30 at Tricot and Estrées Saint Denis (south of Montdidier).

3. A native brigade (Moroccans), under General Ditte.

4. The 6th Group, composed of the 61st and 62nd Reserve Divisions, under General Ebener. Belonging originally to the garrison of Paris, they had been transferred on August 25 to the army detachment d'Amade.[7] After their defeat they had become so dispersed that it had been necessary to draw them back upon Paris where they had been placed under the orders of the governor of Paris. It was not until September 7 that they rejoined the Sixth Army.

5. The Sordet cavalry corps. Its condition was such that its still utilizable elements were formed into a division of 18 squadrons under General Cornulier-Lucinière. On August 29, this division stood on the Avre, with the cavalry corps in rear, to the west of Montdidier. It remained for a time with Maunoury's army, but was later drawn back upon Versailles.

The army which General Maunoury was going to have at his disposal was not, then, very important. There was aprospect ofreenforcements (IV Corps and 45th Division), but it proved impossible to concentrate them in time.

At Montdidier, Maunoury found reports announcing that German columns were marching upon Péronne. The Germans occupied this city on the 28th. Maunoury intended at first to go

---

[6] See pages 80-81.

[7] See page 103.

forward to meet them, but later preferred to remain for the present on the defensive, until his troops were reassembled, and then to make a surprise attack. On the center, in the locality: Corbie – Bray – Chaulnes, the VII Corps was to cover Amiens and the road to Paris. On the left wing, the Sordet cavalry was to maintain liaison with the d'Amade group on the lower Somme. On the right wing, at Curchy – Nesle, the reserve divisions of General Lamaze were to cover the region: Roye – Lassigny, and keep in touch with the English. The cavalry division of General Cornulier-Lucinière moved to the right wing. The plans of General Maunoury were, however, upset by the German advance.

General d'Amade tried to reform his divisions, which had suffered heavily from the disconnected operations in. the north. Portions of the 81st and 82nd Territorial Divisions called up from Abbeville and Picquigny upon Amiens, but were still in great disorder. Nothing much could be expected from d'Amade's troops. In an interview with Joffre at St. Quentin, General d'Amade declared that "the territorials had scattered as soon as they saw the German cavalry."[8]

The 55th Reserve Division had scarcely been disembarked and started forward when it was attacked by superior forces. At this same time the English army was falling back behind the line: Noyon – Chauny – La Fère. The right wing of the Sixth Army followed this movement and-wheeled toward Roye while covering the flank of the VII Corps which was to turn facing Chaulnes – Bray, that is, to the east. It was hard for Maunoury's army to cover both Amiens and Paris at the same time and to maintain liaison with both the English and d'Amade without spreading out too much.[9]

The VII Corps also, shortly after detraining, came up against the German right wing and after a violent combat near Proyart on August 29 was beaten and thrown back beyond Villers-

---

[8] Lanrezac, loc. cit., page 208.

[9] See Sketch 4.

Bretonneux.[10] According to certain French accounts, it fell back still farther (20 kilometers) during the night. The German attack had struck the best troops of the new Sixth Army, the 14th Division. The VII Corps fell back beyond the Avre while maintaining liaison to the right, at Guerbigny, with the 55th Reserve Division which was to defend Roye in order to keep contact with the English. The 56th Reserve Division had not yet finished detraining.

On August 30, Maunoury learned that the English were falling back upon Compiegne – Soissons. His army was left in the air. He retreated upon Clermont. On hearing of the German advance upon Amiens by way of Albert, the d'Amade group, whose fighting value was very slight, was pushed forward, August 30, from lower Somme upon Rouen.

General von Kluck was therefore right when, at that time, he attached no great importance to the French troops which had appeared in his flank and been beaten, and when he assumed that a rapid German advance toward the south would compel them to beat a precipitate retreat or else lose all contact with the French army. As for acting upon the German flank, the French were not for the moment in a condition for that. The situation remained unchanged until Maunoury's army was able to assemble later under the protection of Paris, inject some order into its units, and bring up reenforcements.

The Retreat of the Third, Fourth, and Fifth Armies up to September 2. The Battle of St. Quentin. Fighting of the Third and Fourth Armies on the Meuse

After the Battle of Namur, the Fifth Army had fallen back upon Avesnes – Mariembourg and on August 25 had reached the line: Maroilles – Avesnes – Fourmies – Regniowez, and on the 27th the Oise on the line: Guise – Rumigny. Its marching objective was the region of Laon – La Fère.

---

[10] See page 110.

On August 27, Joffre reached the decision to execute a counteroffensive with his left wing. The reason given for this decision was the design of disengaging the English from the pressure to which they were being subjected by the German right wing. Marshal French asserts that on the one hand they had learned of the displacement of large German forces and that on the other, it was desired particularly to cover Paris. As regards the displacement of German troops, in reality nothing was heard of that until August 29. However that may be, Joffre's plan was broadened in the sense that the Sixth Army and the English were to cooperate in the action, so that the armies of von Kluck and von Bülow would be attacked from Amiens, St. Quentin, and Guise.

The thrust of the Fifth Army was to take place, according to Joffre's idea, in the direction of St. Quentin, covering to the north facing Guise, while the English would move forward with their left wing from La Fère upon St. Quentin and the Sixth Army would set out from Amiens. The Fifth Army, which was exhausted and falling back toward the south, was to be regrouped facing west for this attack. Lanrezac, according to his own statements, had expressed objections to the attack in the direction of St. Quentin. He feared, he says, that in this case he would be attacked in his right flank and that the gap which already existed between the Fifth and Fourth Armies would also become widened, but that Joffre held to his decision to attack.

In spite of Joffre's insistence, the attack could not take place before the morning of the 29th. But meanwhile the English had fallen back behind the Oise upon La Fère – Noyon, thus abandoning the Somme and facing to the northeast instead of north. Joffre's visit to French to persuade him to cooperate in the action in any manner whatever, was in vain; French, pleading exhaustion of his troops, declared himself obliged to continue his retreat upon Soissons – Compiegne.

Hence the attack had to be launched on the morning of the 29th without the aid of the English. The III and XVIII Corps were to attack in the direction of St. Quentin by way of the Origny-Sainte-Benoite [near Mt. d'Origny] and Ribemont while the X Corps would assure cover to the north facing Guise. The I Corps on the center was held in reserve at the disposal of General Lanrezac. On the left wing, the reserve divisions of Valabregue had to be used in the place of the English, so that the most important part of the attack fell to the reserve troops. But meanwhile the German Second Army had seized the passages near Guise on the afternoon of the 28th and on the 29th delivered an attack starting from the line: Guise – Etréaupont.[11]

General Lanrezac got into a difficult situation. In whatever direction he turned with the main body of his forces, whether upon Guise or upon St. Quentin, he was always attacked in the flank from the other direction. For an operation on the interior line, space was lacking. On his left the English were slipping away, on his right there was a great gap. For the second time, he was in danger of being annihilated. He decided to break off the attack on St. Quentin and with the III, I, and X Corps to throw back beyond the Oise the enemy forces which were advancing at Guise and to the east, while the XVIII Corps and the reserve divisions would avoid any decisive combat against superior forces. At 5 p.m. the French attacked all along the front extending from Origny to Vervins and, according to their own account, threw the Germans (Guard and X Corps) back Upon the Oise, although, as Palat admits, the success was not converted into a victory. The Germans held on to the crossings of the Oise. Meanwhile, the XVIII Corps and the reserve divisions were thrown back upon the Oise, and the St. Quentin offensive had failed.

Larenzac's position became untenable. His retreat was menaced by the defeat at St. Quentin. The German Third Army which was coming from the direction of Rocroi might slip into the gap existing between his army and the Fourth Army. Therefore, General Joffre, at 10:30 p.m. on the 29th, ordered the Fifth Army to retreat. On the 30th, this army crossed the Serre between Marle and La Fère, on the 31st it reached the locality: Premontre – Montcornet (on either side of Laon), and on September 1, it arrived in great haste by a night march, behind the Aisne between Soissons

[11] See Sketch 4.

and Guignicourt[12] to escape the envelopment with which it was menaced on both sides.

The battle of St. Quentin is extremely interesting from the tactical point of view and merits detailed study. Its strategical effect was the failure of Joffre's plan of August 25. The French army could no longer take a stand on the line: Verdun – Amiens. But this battle had an equally important influence on the German operations. The Second Army was held up and had to rest on the 31st while the First Army was led to make a change of front upon Compiegne – Noyon to exploit the success. The first army thus gained an advance on the Second Army and remained ahead of it for a while. Thus gradually arose the idea of the High Command to cut the French off from Paris.

Although he had recognized the great difficulties of his situation, General Lanrezac, according to his own statements, intended on the evening of the 29th to continue his attack on the 30th in order to exploit the success which he had obtained in the direction of Guise and throw the enemy back beyond the Oise. He did not wish to break off the offensive which Joffre had prescribed in spite of his own objections, without a formal order from Joffre. This order arrived, as we have already stated. One can only regret that Lanrezac did not carry out his plans. The day of the 30th would have been fatal to him, even with a new success at Guise, grantingthat he had obtained it. We should have been presented with brilliant prospects for a Cannae maneuver if, on our side, we had had a single command which would have made an effort to support the Second Army, not by directly bringing up the adjoining armies, but by executing a sweeping pursuit. The Third Army was in a position to win a great success by continuing its march in the direction of Chateau-Porcien.[13] Unfortunately, it was dragged about right and left by the appeals of its neighbors.

On August 26 the French Third Army crossed the Meuse on the line north of Verdun – Dun; the Fourth Army at Stenay –

---

[12] See Sketch 6.

[13] See page 113.

Mézières. The two armies vigorously resisted the crossing of the Meuse by the German troops. The Fourth Army in particular executed, on the. 27-28th, a powerful counteroffensive. But their measures were very much influenced by the attitude of the Fifth Army. This latter had brought its right wing upon Vervins before the Battle of St. Quentin, with the result that on the 28th there was a great gap between the Fifth Army and the left wing of the Fourth which had fallen back upon Launois. Into this gap the German Third Army, advancing by way of Rocroi, threatened to slip. Consequently, on the 29th, the Fourth Army ceased its resistance on the Meuse and fell back the same and following day upon the Aisne. On the 29th, the Foch army detachment was formed by taking the left wing from the Fourth Army. Hence it was not composed of units which had just been called out. This breaking up of the strong Fourth Army into two parts was destined to facilitate the maintenance of liaison between the Fourth and Fifth Armies. August 30 and 31, the Foch army detachment succeeded by hard fighting in holding on behind the Aisne, on the line: Attigny – Rethel – Chateau-Porcien, in stopping up the hole between the Fourth and Fifth Armies and in barring the road: Rethel – Paris. On the 30th, the Fourth Army crossed the Aisne on either side of Vouziers. On the same day the Fifth Army began to retreat beyond the Serre in the direction of Laon.

In the course of the following days the Fourth Army and the Foch army detachment continued their retreat; on Sept. 1 they reached the region between Reims and Aisne, while the Fifth Army arrived on the Aisne between Soissons and Guignicourt. The Fifth Army then adopted Dormans as its general direction of march, the Foch army detachment and the Fourth Army the region on either side of Chalons.

Meanwhile, and up to September 1, the Third Army had defended the Meuse in the vicinity of Dun; it then wheeled gradually to the rear and to the left around Verdun as a pivot and on September 2 stood on the line: Apremont – Montfaucon. On the 30th, General Sarrail succeeded Ruffey as commander of the Third Army. The IV Corps was withdrawn from the front of the army, embarked at Vienne-la Ville and transported to the new Sixth Army of Maunoury.

Retreat of the English behind the Marne August 28 to September 3. Intervention of Kitchener

After the battle of Le Cateau, the English had fallen back from Landrecies and Le Cateau upon La Fère and Noyon. On the evening of the 28th their I Corps stood south of La Fère between the Oise and the forest of St. Gobain, their II Corps at Noyon. On the 29th the army rested. Since the German First Army with its left wing took the direction: Le Cateau – north of St. Quentin, it lost. contact for the present with the English army. The latter became effectually disengaged through the battles of St. Quentin and Guise on August 29 and 30.

General Maurice reproaches General von Kluck with not having pursued the English immediately after the battle of Le Cateau[14] and with having taken a southwesterly direction instead.[15] He declares that if the English II Corps had been closely pursued and compelled again to engage in combat with superior forces, it would have been destroyed; while as a matter of fact, von Kluck turned on the 27th against the French and marched in the direction of Péronne, so that the English army escaped. General Maurice is of the opinion that General von Kluck should have pursued the English on the 27th with the main body of his forces, beaten them or driven them back to the south of Paris, and sent to the Somme only the forces required to prevent the French from taking part in the action. He would then have been able to prevent the French from utilizing the network of railways centering at Paris; the troops of General Maunoury and General d'Amade would have been cut off from the main body of the French army; Maunoury would not have been able in this case to hold out near Amiens.

The reasons by which General von Kluck was led to take the direction of Péronne after the battle of Le Cateau have already been discussed, as well as the circumstances which delayed the

[14] Loc. cit.

[15] See pages 109-110.

pursuit of the enemy by the second Army. It was assumed that the English would fall back toward the southwest so as not to lose their connection with the ports. That is why it appeared necessary to execute a sweeping pursuit. If the First Army had followed the English from Le Cateau toward the south, it would have left Maunoury at full liberty to assemble his army while the English would have been able to slip off toward the south. A menacing group of forces would then have been able to form in our right flank, while a premature oblique toward the south on the part of the First Army would have embarrassed the movement of the other armies.

For the English, the prime objective, according to their own account, was that of reforming their army. The fatigue occasioned by the retreat was, as General Maurice says, enormous. The men had no time to prepare warmmeals. The heat of the sun was crushing. Whenever a halt was made, the men fell down from exhaustion. During the continuous retreat, they sniffed danger everywhere. Palat, plainly on the basis of a description furnished by an eye witness who had observed the English on the 28th while they were passing through Noyon, gives in his work an impressive picture of the condition in which the English army found itself during its retreat: "The troops followed each other through Noyon in a continuous stream. A mixture of horse without riders, of riders Without horses, of isolated Scotchmen whose knees shone under the plaid, artillerymen, infantrymen, lightly wounded men on vehicles, – all pressing forward in disorder and feverish haste."[16]

The headquarters of General French was located at Compiegne from the 28th to the 30th. As his heavy losses had still not been replaced, he held it necessary to continue the retreat in the direction of Compiegne – Soissons. On the 29th occurred the interview with Joffre at Compiegne to which reference has already been made.[17] In this interview he insisted that the English army could not take part in an offensive for several days but was obliged

[16] Vol. V, page 178.

[17] See page 180.

to rest and await reenforcements. He considered it preferable to draw the Germans to a great distance behind him and not to halt until he was south of the Marne between the Marne and the Seine. Joffre was consequently obliged to content himself with urging on French at least to be good enough not to retire completely from the front and to fill the gap between the Fifth and Sixth Armies.

The morale which prevailed in the English army is shown by the fact that in the course of a conference between the commander-in-chief and his generals, following the meeting with Joffre on the 29th, General Smith-Dorrien, in command of the II Corps, expressed the view that there was nothing left to do but return to the base, embark the troops and go back to England. Though French rejected this idea, the proposition, none the less, as Palat remarks, throws a "sad light on the moral state of the English High Command."[18]

The communications with Le Havre being menaced by the further retreat, a beginning was made to move them to St. Nazaire and Nantes with an advanced base at Le Mans. Ever since the retreat which followed the battle of Mons, the ports of Le Havre and Boulogne had Appeared in danger. As early as August 24 transportation to these ports had been stopped. The War Office had wished to organize a new base at Cherbourg. French at that time had held, however, that it was not yet necessary to transfer the base from Le Havre and that it sufficed to abandon Boulogne. But on the 29th he declared that the change of base from Le Havre was necessary at once. It was decided to shift from the Channel to the open sea coast and to organize the new base at St. Nazaire, on the Loire, although the matter involved great difficulties. Up to this time it had only been necessary to assure the safety of the convoys in the Channel and on short voyages; now it had to be done along great stretches on the open sea. The great depots of Le Havre had to be transferred to St. Nazaire, where the 6th Division was later disembarked.

But in moving the base from the Channel, it was not designed to abandon the Channel ports. These latter were of decisive

---

[18] Loc. cit. Vol. V, page 220.

importance for naval warfare, and their loss would have involved the most serious consequences. The greatest importance was attached to the defense of Dunkirk, Calais, and Boulogne; arrangements to that effect were made with the French government.

On August 30 the English army continued its retreat toward the Aisne in the direction of Compiegne – Soissons. Marshal French learned that, according to the instructions of General Joffre, the Fifth Army was to fall back behind the Serre, the left wing at La Fère; the Fourth Army behind the Aisne in the vicinity of Rethel; the Sixth in the direction of Compiegne – Clermont, the cavalry corps on the left wing. French himself was expected to halt, and fill the gap between Compiegne and La Fère, it cannot be determined with certainty. Whether Joffre really intended to accept battle on the line indicated, now that the general offensive of the left wing, planned on the 27th,[19] had been executed but incompletely and without success, cannot be now determined. Count Schlieffen had considered the possibility that the French would be able to constitute a great defensive flank behind the Oise on the line: La Fère – Paris. He wished in this case to attack the position frontally – go around it to the westand south of Paris.[20]

But the French, according to his account held on August 30, to his previous view and declared that he could neither change front nor fight for several days yet; adding, however, that he was ready to hold his place between the Fifth and Sixth Armies in case the retreat was continued Slowly and cautiously. He referred in this connection to the general instructions he had received from his government.

On August 31 the English crossed the Aisne and reached the locality: Nery – Crépy en Valois – Villers-Cotterets. At his new headquarters at Dammartin, French had received another communication from Joffre urging him to halt and accept combat. Marshal French reports that at that moment Lanrezac was on the

---

[19] See page 179.

[20] See Sketch 4.

point of drawing his left wing farther back and enlarging the gap between the two armies: "I was firmly convinced that if I had yielded to that pressing demand, the whole Allied army would have been thrown back in disorder onto the Marne and that Paris would have become an easy prey to the enemy. It is impossible to exaggerate the danger of the situation at that moment. Neither on that day nor on the following days did I receive a man, a cannon, a horse or a, machine gun to compensate my losses. Consequently I refused." The mutual complaints of the French and English were renewed throughout the retreat. The Fifth Army and the French General Headquarters declare that the precipitate retreat of the English gave rise to the failure of all their plans, while the English, on the other hand, refer to the retreat of the French Fifth Army and the insufficient protection of their left flank by the Sixth Army. This dispute came to the surface also after the war, in the historical accounts. It must be granted to French, however, that if he had remained in place he would have been subjected on September 1 to an enveloping attack from the First Army.[21]

Regarding the depressed morale of the English commander in chief we are more accurately informed by his telegrams and his correspondence with Lord Kitchener. It appears from these that French wanted to fall back behind the Seine, a matter which he neglected to state in his book. On the morning of August 31 a telegram from French was received at London, according to which he had informed Joffre as follows: "I told him plainly that in view of the present condition of my troops I found it absolutely impossible to remain in the front line, since he has now started the retreat. I have decided to start retreating early tomorrow behind the Seine in a southwesterly direction passing close to the west of Paris. That means a week's march, approximately, at a considerable distance from the enemy and without fatiguing the troops. ...I am not satisfied with Joffre's plan. My desire was that a vigorous offensive be taken from the very beginning and I so stated. In reply he referred to the present incapacity of the English army to advance as an excuse for effecting the retreat and gaining

---

[21] See Sketch 6.

time. Naturally, if he has in mind the advance of the Russians, he may be right. My designs have been misunderstood. I haven't the least idea of carrying on a prolonged and final retreat."

According to that, Joffre wished to await the effect of the Russian advance. French, himself, wants to appear as favoring the offensive. But he is also planning to fall back behind the Seine, and leaves it to the French to execute a "vigorous offensive." An easy proposition. How was Joffre to carry it out?

A few hours after the foregoing telegram had been deciphered, there arrived at London a not very reassuring letter from French dated from Compeigne on August 30:

> I can't say that I look forward with much confidence to the further course of the campaign in France. ...My confidence in the capacity of the leaders of the French Army to continue this campaign to a successful issue is diminishing rapidly. That is the real reason for the decision which I have reached to retire so far with the British forces.
>
> It is announced this evening that the French Fourth Army has been drawn back on Rethel. Anyhow that was the line assigned to it in the new orders of Joffre. The rumor that it was thrown back may therefore not be correct. But it is none the less very disquieting.
>
> I am thoroughly convinced of the necessity of maintaining the most complete independence of action and of being in a position to fall back on my base whenever the circumstances make such action necessary. A great deal of pressure has been exerted to have me continue on the front in spite of my infirm situation. But I have absolutely refused, and I hope that you will approve my course. It is not only in accord with the spirit and letter of your instructions, but it is also dictated by common sense. Knowing what I do of the fighting qualities of the French soldier and of the care, the energy, the skill and the time which have been lavished for years in perfecting his instruction and training, I can only attribute these persistent defeats to defective leadership.

Kitchener was a strong character. His great foresight had led him to realize that they were faced with a war of long duration. England required time to become a great military power. She had no right to leave her ally in the lurch, now that Paris was menaced. French's desire to withdraw from the front line might have disastrous consequences. As the question was one of considerable political importance, the cabinet was hastily convoked. But Kitchener meanwhile telegraphed to French: "I am surprised at your decision to fall back behind the Seine. Let me know, if you can, all your reasons. What will be the effect of such a decision on our relations with the French Army and on the general military situation? Will your retreat leave a gap in the French line, and may it not give rise among the Allies to a discouragement from which the Germans will be able to derive advantage for executing their plan: namely, first, to crush the French so as to be able then to turn against Russia? It was announced here yesterday that 32 trains of German troops were on the way from the western front to meet the Russians."

According to the account of Sir George Arthur, Kitchener then explained to the cabinet the serious danger of a gap being formed between the French and English armies. He declared that the liaison with Joffre had to be maintained and that the retreat behind the Seine might lead to losing the war. The cabinet shared his view. Kitchener telegraphed French on August 31: "Your telegram No. 162 submitted to cabinet. The government is very much afraid that you will no longer be in a condition to cooperate very closely with our Allies and to furnish them continuous support if you withdraw your troops so far back from the front just at this moment of the campaign. The government expects that you will conform as strictly as possible to the designs of General Joffre for the conduct of the campaign. It awaits the reply which you have doubtless made to my telegram of this morning. It is assured that you will have all confidence in your troops and in yourself."

The reply of the English commander in chief arrived around midnight. The French, he said, were retiring to right and left of him, without keeping him informed. If they continued in this way and abandoned all idea of offense, the gap existing in the French front would remain. They would have to put up with the consequences. "All that I can say is that it will be hard for my army, in its present condition, to resist a violent attack, even a single German corps. If by reason of the Russian pressure, the German retreat becomes a reality, it will be easy for me to interrupt my retreat and reform my troops north of Paris." And he added that the French could now, by means of an offensive, bring their inside wings closer together and fill the gap. "But as they fail to take advantage of such an opportunity, I don't see why I should be asked to run the risk of a complete disaster in order to rescue them once more. I can't believe that you realize the state of disorganization of my II Corps and how this situation paralyses my offensive capacity."

Kitchener could not endure it any longer in London. He betook himself in haste to Paris on September 1; and in the afternoon, at the English embassy, a conference took place which was attended by the president of the council, Viviani, and the minister of war, Millerand. Meanwhile the military situation had improved. The German First army no longer appeared to be pursuing Maunoury, but to be turning against the left wing of the French forces. The pressure which was being exerted upon Maunoury and the English thus disappeared. The English army was able to rest, Maunoury could be reenforced. French declared himself ready to accede to the demands made upon him. Kitchener summed up in writing the result of the conference: "French's troops are now on the battle line. He will remain there and conform to the movements of the French army, acting with care, however, to avoid having his flanks uncovered at any point."

French, in his account, skips over the events just narrated. But, in view of the published documents there can be no doubt regarding their accuracy. These events are of great importance to any one who wishes to form a, judgment regarding the events of the Marne. The hopeless discouragement of the English commander and the shattered condition of the English troops are indisputable. The successes obtained by the First Army in pursuing the enemy without repose and by stretching to the limit the forces of men and beasts were still greater than had been assumed. The confidence of the English in the French leadership had disappeared. The English losses from Mons up to the Marne were reckoned at 20,000 men. It was due exclusively to the intervention of Kitchener that the English army did not retire behind the Marne without further ado. During the battle of the Marne, the First Army took it for granted that French would not pass all at once from a long retreat to a violent offensive. And is was not mistaken.

On the evening of September 1, the English army stood in the region: La Ferté-Milon – Betz – Nanteuil-le-Haudouin. Rather important rear-guard fighting had taken place at Verberie, Nery, and Villers-Cotterets.

On September 2 it reached the Marne at Lagny and Meaux; only the 4th Division was still in rear at Dammartin. On September 3rd, the Marne was crossed.[22]

On the evening of September 1, French had returned to his headquarters at Dammartin. It was transferred in the night to Lagny [sur Marne], where important new instructions of Joffre arrived on September 2.

Retreat of the Sixth Army upon, Paris, August 31 to September 3

Maunoury, who had begun to retreat on August 30 upon Clermont,[23] installed himself on the 31st in a defensive position to the northeast of that city. Ditte's Moroccan brigade remained in reserve at Creil, Sordet's cavalry corps was at Beauvais, the cavalry division of Cornulier-Lucinière at Pont Sainte Maxence on the Oise. It is reported to have observed already that the Germans were taking the direction, of Compiegne. Maunoury, fearing for his right flank, advanced on September 1 into the region of Senlis – Creilin order to take up a position nearer the English left wing, which in the evening was at Nanteuil le Haudouin.[24]

Since on September 2 the English continued their retreat upon Meaux – Lagny, Maunoury turned off first into the region south of the forest of Chantilly [just SE. of Chantilly]. In order that his army might not be cut off, it was decided that it should take up a position inside the radius of the fortress of Paris and cover the capital. The 56th Reserve Division and the Ditte brigade were

---

[22] See Sketch 7.

[23] See page 179.

[24] See Sketch 6.

again engaged, on September 2, in violent fighting near Senlis.[25]

The Sixth Army arrived in the advanced zone of the fortress of Paris during the night of September 2-3, at a time when the English were getting ready to cross the Marne.

According to the French accounts, Maunoury's troops were in a state of extreme exhaustion, succumbing under the fatigue resulting from the long marches, the heat, the privations, the fighting and all the difficulties which may put a newly formed army to the test.[26] According to Palat, it was especially in the reserve divisions of Lamaze that signs of disorganization were visible. These considerations have their importance in forming a judgment regarding the success of the German operations up to that time and the prospectsfor thefuture.

On the morning of September 3the Sixth Army was selected to defend Paris and assumed the name of the Army of Paris. It was drawn up in front of the capital in the region of Dammartin and to the northwest.

The Ebener group (61st and 62nd Reserve Divisions) had been drawn back upon Paris, as already stated. Both divisions were "badly shaken." Joffre wrote on the 3rd to General Gallieni, governor of Paris: "I hope that the reserve divisions will soon show some cohesion again." Sordet's cavalry corps was to rest at Versailles and came under the orders of the governor of Paris.

As reinforcements, General Maunoury had been given some assurance of receiving the 45th Division and the IV Corps.

The garrison of Paris comprised: five territorial divisions, one portion of which stood on the northeast front of Paris, and the other south of the Marne on the east and southeast front; a brigade of marines, ten companies of zouaves, Gillet's cavalry brigade, and three groups of sortie artillery.

Hanotaux estimates the total strength of Maunoury's army and of the garrison of Paris at more than 140,000 men, but a large portion was inferior or used up.

---

[25] See Sketch 7.

[26] Hanotaux.

The Retreat of the French. Fifth Army behind the Marne on September 2 and 3

The events which occurred in connection with the French Fifth Army on September 2 and 3possess a special importance. They serve to clarify the whole strategic situation. It is accordingly necessary to enter here into the tactical details (Sketch 7).

After crossing the Aisne, the Fifth Army arrived on September 2 as far as the region of Oulchy le Chateau – Fere en Tardenois – Courtagnon (southwest of Reims). On the left wing were the two divisions of the Valabregue group which, according to the account of General Lanrezac, were in an "alarming condition." "As General Valabreuge pictures the situation, most of the units were exhausted and demoralized to such a degree that if they had had to engage in serious fighting there would have been danger of their disintegrating and creating confusion and disorder in the neighboring corps." It had been planned originally to get these two divisions under way at 9 o'clock in the morning and to have them cross the Marne at Chateau-Thierry. Conneau's cavalry corps, recently formed, was concentrated by rail, September 2-3, in the vicinity of Epernay and was to be pushed from there upon Chateau-Thierry. The 8th Cavalry Division, the first division to be detrained, advanced, on September 2, along the south bank of the Marne and by way of Dormans upon Chateau-Thierry in order to hold this locality, but by evening found itself confronted by the enemy and was unable to make its way out of the city. It occupied the bridge, where a detachment of territorials was already stationed, but fell back later upon Essises (south of Chateau-Thierry). During the night the French forces were further increased by a brigade of the 10th Cavalry Division, while the other units of the division advanced from Epernay upon Montmirail.

Lanrezac was of the opinion that the only German troops at Chateau-Thierry were cavalry. In spite of the disquieting conditions of the Valabregue divisions, he planned to have them march on the 3rd upon Chateau-Thierry. To bear farther toward the east appeared impossible because the XVIII Corps, which was marching in that region, had only one road at its disposal. The

Valabregue divisions were to attack Chateau-Thierry from the north, while portions of the XVIII Corps, pushed forward and crossing the Marne farther east, would attack it on the south. But late in the night of the 2-3rd, a report was received to the effect that a German infantry division was in front of Chateau-Thierry. Lanrezac's plan was becoming impracticable. He was then obliged to decide to have the Valabregue divisions and the XVIII Corps cross the Marne farther east. The movements began on September 3 at 2 o'clock in the morning. The XVIII Corps was pushed to the left wing south of the Marne, with the reserve divisions on its right. Meanwhile, during the night, the Germans had seized the city and bridge of Chateau-Thierry. The territorials had fallen back before the bridge could be destroyed.

The Fifth Army arrived behind the Marne in the early morning of the 3rd. The left-wing division, which was pushed forward south of the Marne in the direction of Chateau-Thierry for the purposes of cover, fall back upon Condé-en-Brie, "upon the mere threat of an attack, when it was fired on at a great distance by the enemy heavy howitzers."

There can be no doubt thatLanrezac'sarmy would have fallen into a most difficult situation if it had been overtaken on September 2 and 3 by the German Second Army at the passage of the Marne while the IX Corps attacked it in the flank. The great strategical importance of this thrust and the scope of the independent decision ofGeneral von Quast are quite manifest. This was the correct point for our entrance into action for the purpose of seizing the French left wing before coming into the radius of action of the fortress of Paris. The right wing of the First Army was still in a position to assure cover toward Maunoury's army, which had been beaten, and toward the English, who were still in retreat. The closer we go to Paris later, the less was it possible for the First Army to fulfill all these tasks at the same time without an echelon following in rear. It can only be regretted that the bold action of the IX Corps was not crowned with a decisive success on September 2.

Joffre's Decision to Retire Behind the Seine. Army Orders of

September 1 and 2

His previous plans having failed, Joffre was meanwhile obliged to adopt a new decision. The relief which was expected from the Russian offensive appeared, however, to have become a reality. According to Palat it was announced from Antwerp on August 29 that 160 trains had passed in the northeasterly direction through Belgium on the 28th and during the night of the 28-29th.[27] A telegram from Copenhagen announced on the 28th that railway traffic was blocked in Germany by reason of the transportation toward the east. Another report stated that approximately two corps had been transported from the region of Courtrai toward the Russian front. Kitchener, also, in his telegram of August 31 to French speaks of German displacements toward the Russian front.[28] As a matter of fact, the two German corps in question had marched to Aix-la-Chapelle, Malmedy and St Vith and had not been embarked there until August 30.[29] As regards the exact effect of these reports on Joffre's design to retire behind the Seine, that is a doubtful matter.

On September 1 and 2 new orders were issued by Joffre.[30] The "General Instructions No. 4" of September 1 read:

> 1. In spite of the tactical successes obtained by the Third, Fourth, and Fifth Armies in the region of the Meuse and at Guise, the encircling movement of the enemy against the left wing of the Fifth Army makes it imperative that the whole of our forces pivot around our right wing.
>
> As soon as the Fifth Army has escaped the decided menace of envelopment on its left, the whole of the Third, Fourth, and Fifth Armies will resume the offensive.
>
> 2. This rearward evolution may lead the armies to retire for a time in the general direction of north-south.

---

[27] Loc. cit. Vol. V, page 151.

[28] See page 190.

[29] See page 120.

[30] See Sketch 11.

The Fifth Army on the marching wing must in no case permit the enemy to seize its left; the other armies, less hurried in the execution of their movement, will be able to halt, face the enemy and seize any favorable opportunity to oppose his advance.

The movement of each army must, nevertheless, be such that it does not uncover the neighboring armies, and it shall be the duty of the army commands to communicate to each other regularly their intentions, their movements, and their information.

3. The lines separating the zones of march of the different armies shall be as follows:

Between the Fifth and Fourth Army (Foch detachment) the road: Reims – Epernay (to the Fourth Army), road: Montmort – Sezanne – Romilly (to the Fifth Army).

Between the Fourth and Third Army the road: Grand Pré – St. Menehould – Revigny (to the Fourth Army).

In the zone assigned to the Fourth Army, the army detachment of General Foch shall keep in constant touch with the Fifth Army, the interval between this detachment and the main body of the Fourth Army being observed by the 7th and 9th Cavalry Divisions from the Fourth Army and supported by detachments of infantry furnished by this army.

The Third Army will effect its movement under cover of the Meuse Heights (Hauts de Meuse).

4. As the limit of the backward movement, and without implying that such limit must necessarily be arrived at, we may contemplate the moment when the armies are in the following situation:

One of the newly formed cavalry corps in rear of the Seine, to the south of Bray;

Fifth Army in rear of the Seine, to the south of Nogent-sur-Seine;

Fourth Army (Foch detachment) in rear of the Aube, to the south of Arcis-sur-Aube, the main body behind the Ornain to the south of Vitry le Francois;

Fourth Army behind the Ornain to the east of Vitry;

Third Army to the south of Barle Due.

The Third Army would then be reenforced by the reserve divisions leaving the Meuse Heights to take part in the offensive movement.

If the circumstances permit, portions of the First and Second Armies would be called upon in due time to participate in the offensive; and finally, the mobile troops of the fortified camp of Paris might also take part in the general action.

JOFFRE.

On September 2 a secret note was sent to the army commands:

> The general plan of operations which gave rise to the despatch of Instructions No. 4 embraces the following points:
>
> (a) To withdraw the armies from the enemy pressure and lead them to organize and fortify themselves in the zone in which they are established at the end of the movement.
>
> (b) To establish the whole of our forces on a general line marked by Pont-sur-Yonne, Nogent-sur-Seine, Arcissur-Aube, Brienne le Chateau, Joinville, and on which their ranks will be filled by the despatch of the depots troops.
>
> (c) Reenforcement of the left-wing army by. two corps drawn from the armies of Nancy and Epinal.
>
> (d) At that moment, the taking of the offensive all along the front.
>
> (e) Covering of our left wing byall the cavalry available between Montereau and Melun.
>
> (f) To ask the English army to take part in the maneuver:
>
> 1. by holding the Seine from Melun to Juvisy,
> 2. by making a sortie on the same front whenever the Fifth Army proceeds to the attack.
>
> (g) Simultaneously, the garrison of Paris would act in the direction of Meaux.
>
> JOFFRE.

The significance of these orders is hotly contested in France. While some see in them the basis of the subsequent victorious offensive, others maintain that Joffre wished above all to get away from the encircling movement which menaced him by a distant retreat behind the Seine and that the circumstance that a battle took place behind the Marne was due to Gallieni, governor of Paris. The closer the Germans advanced, the more the personality of Gallieni came into the foreground. There appears to have been a certain jealousy between Gallieni and Joffre. During the battle of the Ourcq, Joffre informed the governor of Paris, September 7, that he, Joffre would send his orders directly to the Sixth Army. At the same time, Joffre requested him not to send to the government any information regarding the operations, saying that that was exclusively his (Joffre's) own affair and that he was in abetter position to judge of what might be communicated to the government on this point.[31]

The question of whether the principal city of the country, as a fortress, was to be defended or abandoned and in the former case the part to be played by the fortress in the operations of the field army, naturally occupied a large place in the considerations of the commander in chief and of the governor of Paris. General Gallieni had been appointed governor of Paris on August 28. On August 28, the government had reached the decision to abandon the capital as an "open city," but changed its mind on the 30th in response to the representations of the local authorities and of several cabinet members. On September 2, at the request of Joffre, the fortress of Paris was embraced by the Ministry of War in the zone of operations of the armies and thus placed under the orders of Joffre. an the same day the government retired to Bordeaux.

Gallieni believed that the defensive capacity of Paris was low by reason of its small and inferior garrison, and because its defensive organizations were mediocre and very much exposed to bombardment, and also because of itsantiquated armament. Hewroteto the commanderin chiefon September 2: "Unless you furnish reenforcements, at least three corps, Paris is quite unable to offer resistance." In a letter of September 8 to the Ministry of War, he makes the following remarks: "Paris can not be defended longeven underfavorable conditions. It is therefore absolutely necessary, whatever happens, that it be defended by the regular army...Paris must be constantly covered by the army." During the brieftime which he had available, General Gallieni tried in every way to increase the defensive capacity of Paris. We have already listed the troops at his disposal,[32] in addition to the Sixth Army placed directly under his orders.

The point which is given most prominence in Joffre's ordersisthat of withdrawing the army from the enveloping movement by a march toward the south. The design of taking the offensive is, to be sure, equally emphasized; but once the army had

---

[31] From September 3 to September 7 the VI Army was directly under Gallieni's command – Editor's Note.

[32] See page 193.

arrived behind the Seine and the Aube, this offensive became very difficult, for it had to be carried beyond these streams. Now there is no mention whatever of bridge heads in that order. The whole of the cavalry, also, wasdrawn back behind the Seine.

The attack was to be carried out mainly by the Third, Fourth, and Fifth Armies, hence essentially from the front. The idea of a strong flank attack is as little evident in the order of September 2 as in that of August 25.[33] The main emphasis would, inversely have had to have been placed on the flank attack launched from Paris with superior forces, while, if necessary, the strong Seine sector could have been held with smaller forces.

That is why it had been maintained in France that Joffre first thought especially of a defense behind the Seine and the Aube and of gaining time until the Russians successes had produced their effects.[34] Le Gros declares that the offensive was postponed to an indeterminate date, that it was mentioned in the orders, as on August 25, rather to reassure public opinion, and that the abandonment of Paris is further evidence that Joffre desired above all to retreat. He even says that Joffre formed the plan of continuing the retreat up to the line: Briaire – Morvan – Dijon – Besançon[35] in case the Russian offensive had to be waited for: "It has been ascertained that this line was contemplated in case of necessity."[36] Nothing further is known on this matter. The orders and the other data fail to reveal such a design.

I think that these allegations are being carried too far. The hope that the Russian victories would bring relief to the French front may very well have played a part in Joffre's decision. He himself, moreover, advanced this idea to French, as appears from the

---

[33] See page 175.

[34] For example: Le Gros, loc. cit. page 50 ff.

[35] See General Map No. 1.

[36] Le Gros, loc. cit. page 45.

latter's communication to Kitchener.[37] However, the intention of taking the offensive is expressed in the orders. As for saying that Paris was to be abandoned, that is out of the question. Although the capital could not hold out long before the modern means of attack, still there is no doubt that it could be held for a certain length of time, the more so as the Sixth Army was placed at the disposal of the defense. There is one point which remains obscure: was Verdun to be comprised in the front of the army? If the French fell back on the line: Brienne le Chateau – Joinville, it would have had to be left to its fate. In any case, however, the right wing of the French forces, the Third Army, was to maintain contact with the fortified front of the Meuse and Moselle.

The decision on the French side was henceforth provisionally arrived at: the retreat behind the Seine was decided upon. Joffre expressly refused to accept combat on the Marne. French, who originally had striven to get behind the Seine, declares that it was he who at that time proposed to fight on the Marne and advised that a strong left wing be formed to that end. From Joffre's written reply it appears that Joffre held that French's plan was impracticable because of the situation of the Fifth Army. He declared, in fact, that the English army was not assured of having effective support on its right wing, but that the English were covered on their left wing by Maunoury's army which was to defend the northeast front of Paris, hence that French might well hold out for sometime on the Marne but that he was then to fall back upon the left bank of the Seine in the direction of Melun – Juvisy. He added that the object of the instructions just issued was to put the army in a situation from which it would be possible shortly to take the offensive and that the moment for that offensive would be made known in due time so that the English army might take part in the general attack.

Assuming that the German concentration in August 1914 had been effected wholly according to the designs of Count Schlieffen, it would be possible to paint a brilliant picture of the operations. If, at the beginning of September, we had arrived in front of Paris

---

[37] See page 189.

with a very strong right wing, followed in echelon by other forces, there would have been the best possible chances of carrying out the Schlieffen campaign plan. The essence of this plan consisted, as we have already said, in throwing the French back in the easterly direction against their fortresses on the Moselle and attacking them in the left flank. Joffre was about to facilitate in an unexpected manner the execution of this very design by desiring to rest the main body of his forces to the right on the fortified front of the east and to arrange his army south of the line: Bar le Duc – Nogent-sur-Seine with a front facing almost northwest. That the Sixth Army could then have been locked up in Paris, if it had not fallen back in all haste; that the English would have been beaten or thrown back and the left wing surrounded at Nogent-sur-Seine: all that was quite within the realm of possibilities and can not be denominated as a chimera.

September 3 – The Retreat Continues. Gallieni Perceives that the Germans are Abandoning the Direction of Paris and Obliquing toward the Southeast

On September 3 the British army crossed the Marne and reached the locality south of Lagny and southeast of Meaux. In the afternoon the first reports were received indicating that the German right wing was giving up the idea of marching directly upon Paris. Powerful columns were mentioned as marching toward the southeast and east. The locality immediately in front of the English army north of the Marne was said to be clear of enemy troops; at least four corps were marching toward the Marne, in the direction of Chateau-Thierry and farther east; The Fifth Army was already engaged in combat. It was soon announced that Chateau-Thierry was carried by the Germansand that the French were falling back.[38]

In the course of September 3 Gallieni also learned through his air forces that the enemy columns which up to that time'had been marching upon Paris seemed to be obliquing toward the southeast.

---

[38] See Sketch 7.

Officers of his staff on observation duty at the out-posts of the north front of Paris confirmed the report. On the preceding evening several reports had already drawn attention to this point. Gallieni then ordered the troops of the Sixth Army to "conceal their presencefrom the enemy air reconnaissances and to avoid any encounter not absolutely necessary to the defense of the fortress." The order contained the statement: "A German corps, most likely the II, has advanced from Senlis toward the south, but did not continue its movement upon Paris and seems to have obliqued toward the southeast. Generally speaking, the German troops which were stationed in front of the Sixth Army seem to have taken the southeasterly direction." Gallieni at once notified Joffre to this effect by telephone. In reading the French accounts, one has a clear perception of the great weight of care removed from the shoulders of the General Headquarters when the danger to Paris disappeared. They breathed again. But Gallieni is said to have pointed out at once the opportunity which was arising for shoving the Sixth Army to the attack on the north bank of the Marne.

Gallieni tried also to exert influence upon the English High Command with a view to inducing it to attack. French replied that he had received his first reenforcements and that these had to be distributed on the 4th between the various units; that for the time being he could make no move, but that he might perhaps be able to advance on the evening of the 4th in the easterly direction, particularly if the Sixth Army, which now appeared to have no enemy force in front of it, also advanced to his left wing. He also expressed the desire that the detrainment of the French IV Corps, announced as coming to reenforce the Sixth Army, should be effected in such manner that there might be formed with the English as strong an army as possible. French thus adopts, as usual, a wary attitude and lets himself be pushed. Gallieni, on the contrary, acts with decision and circumspection.

Meanwhile the first reenforcements, of which a hope had been held out, began to arrive at the Sixth Army.

The French IV Corps, under General Boelle, was taken from the Third Army. Its transportation began on September 2. The 7th Division was to be detrained at Noisy le Sec, while the 8th Division was first designed to assure liaison at Lagny with the

English. It was very likely that the corps would not be able to enter into action before September 7.

The 45th Division, under General Drude, arrived from Algeria as early as September 3. On the 2nd it passed through Paris toward the region north of Le Bourget.

The other displacements of forces which Joffre had announced in his order of September 2 were also under way. The XXI Corps of the First Army was transported, September 4-6, from Joinville and Vassy and passed to the Fourth Army. On September 3, the XV Corps left the Second Army and passed by way of Vaucouleurs and Gondrecourt to the Third Army, where it arrived on the 8th.

On September 3 the Fifth Army had reached the region south of the Marne between Chateau-Thierry and Epernay. General Lanrezac was concerned about his left wing. He wished to bear more toward the east in order to get away from the encircling movement, but then increased the distance between himself and the English. As it was, liaison with the English army was already very lax. The new cavalry corps of Conneau which had been pushed into the gap was unable to fill it sufficiently. General Lanrezac was replaced that day in the command of the Fifth Army by General Franchet d'Esperey.[39]

The Foch army detachment on September 3 reached the locality northwest of Chalons, astride the Marne.

The Fourth Army continued its march in the direction of Vitry le Francois.

The Third Army continued its retreat between the Meuse and the Aire up to the region comprised between Varennes and Verdun.

September 4 – Gallieni Persuades Joffre to take the Offensive

September 4 was the decisive day, the turning point of the campaign.[40]

---

[39] See Sketch 7.

[40] See Sketch 8.

Early in the morning, Gallieni proceeded with his chief of staff to the outposts of the northeast front of Paris and there received confirmation of the report that the enemy columns had taken the southeasterly direction. He was also informed that the Germans had crossed the Marne at Trilport. He then became convinced that the Sixth Army should be pushed forward to attack the German flank. Although he had, as yet, received no reply from Joffre with regard to his suggestion of the day before, he nevertheless took all dispositions and at 9 o'clock in the morning issued the following order to Maunoury:

> In view of the movement of the German armies which seem to be slipping past our front in the southeasterly direction, I propose to push your army forward into their flank, that is to say, in the easterly direction in liaison with the English troops.
>
> I shall advise you of your direction of march when I learn that of the English army. But begin at once to make your dispositions, so that your troops may be ready to march this afternoon and to undertake tomorrow a general movement east of the entrenched camp.
>
> Push cavalry patrols forthwith into the whole sector between the road to Chantilly and the Marne.
>
> I am herewith placing the 45th Division under your command.
>
> Come and speak to me personally as soon as possible.
>
> Signed: GALLIENI.

An isolated attack of the Sixth Army was, however, impossible. The backward movement of the whole French army had to be stopped and the attack launched all along the front. Gallieni again got in touch with Joffre. There was no interview between them, but three telephone conversations. The first ended with a refusal on the part of the commander in chief. Joffre is said to have complained to the government that Gallieni was driving him into a premature offensive. Gallieni continued to exert pressure, until Joffre at last gave his consent, "to the salvation of France," thinks Le Gros. Bonnal declares that this recital of the events was made to him personally by Gallieni.

Without waiting for a written, order from Joffre, Gallieni then despatched at 8:30 p.m. the following order:

> 1. All the reports concur to demonstrate that the mass of the German First Army which has been facing the Sixth Army has struck out toward the southeast. Important columns were mentioned yesterday evening as bearing upon the Marne with a view to crossing it between La Ferté-sous-Jouarre and Chateau-Thierry. The movement clearly appears to be directed against the English right and the left of the French Fifth Army.
>
> In these conditions, Paris being no longer menaced, all the mobile forces of the army of Paris will maneuver in such manner as to maintain contact with the German army and to follow it so as to be in readiness to take part in the prospective battle.
>
> 2. The Sixth Army will push cavalry patrols in the directions of Chantilly, Senlis, Nanteuil-le-Haudouin, Meaux, and Lizy-sur-Ourcq. Measures have been taken for reenforcing the cavalry of the Sixth Army with all available elements.
>
> 3. Tomorrow the Sixth Army will set out in the easterly direction, keeping to the right (north) bank of the Marne, in such manner as to bring its front on a level with Meaux and to be ready to attack, on the morning of the 6th, in conjunction with the English army which will attack the front: Coulommiers – Changis.
>
> 4. In view of this march toward the east, the Sixth Army will be reenforced successively by the following units:
>
> The 45th Division passes at once under the command of General Maunoury.
>
> The IV Corps will hold itself ready to follow the movement of the Sixth Army, one division at a time, as soon as a whole division has been detrained. Their placement under the command of General Maunoury will be regulated by special orders.

Paragraphs 5 to 7 of the order contained directions regarding the safety of Paris, the defensive organizations and the headquarters.

At midnight Gallieni received the final orders of Joffre. His dispositions required no change.

Everything depended upon the British army joining in the offensive. Otherwise the whole plan collapsed. On the 3rd, French was still little inclined to it, and preferred to continue his retreat. At noon of the 4th, Gallieni visited the English headquarters at Melun, but found only the chief of staff, General Wilson, who wished to hold to the decision to retreat. Meanwhile French had gone to see the commander of the I Corps, General Douglas Haig, at Coulommiers. The state of the troops furnished cause for concern, they had the most urgent need of rest. On returning in the evening to Melun, French learned that Gallieni had been there and had made known Joffre's new plan, according to which the English army was to fill the gap between the right wing of the Sixth Army on the Marne and the left wing of the Fifth Army at Provins. French found that gap disturbing. He therefore ordered, according to his account, that the army should continue to fall back in order to facilitate the arrival of reenforcements and provisions. During the night of September 4 and 5 the English army fell back behind the forest of Crecy, into the locality: Rozoy – Tournan. The spirit of enterprise was not a characteristic of the English leader.

Joffre's Orders of September 4 and 5 for the Attack

It was a serious moment when General Joffre was obliged to reach a decision at Bar-sur-Aube on the evening of September 4. The final reports had come from Paris by telephone. General Berthelot is said to have favored retreating behind the Seine in order to let the German First Army run completely into the trap. Joffre, on the contrary, wanted to seize at once the favorable moment."Well, gentlemen, we're going to fight on the Marne!" he decided at last. The orders were given.

We shall have to admit that he was right. In truth, the French success would have become much greater if the Germans had pushed into the arc of the Seine near Melun and had been blocked up in front of that mighty stream, while the Sixth Army, receiving new reenforcements and methodically assembled, had debouched from Paris and to the north and hurled itself into the flank and upon the rear of the Germans. But it was not at all certain that the Germans would fall into the trap. At any rate, the events have demonstrated the correctness of General Joffre. In fact, on that same evening when it was decided to take the offensive, the German High Command, which had been informed of the French transports, ordered its First and Second Armies to front toward Paris. General Berthelot's trap would have been set in vain.

However large one may reckon the influence of Gallieni upon Joffre's decision, one is still obliged to attribute the merit of this decision to him who bore the responsibility for it. He had, in fact, conducted the retreat of his armies in such manner, prescribed the displacements of troops and the reenforcements of the Sixth Army so opportunely, that the French army was in a position to respond at once to his call.

At 6 o'clock in the evening, the decisive order, the General Instructions No. 5, was issued.[41] It read as follows:

> 1. It is advisable to take advantage of the hazardous situation of the German First Army in order to concentrate upon it the efforts of the Allied Armies on the extreme left wing.
>
> All measures will be taken during the day of September 5 with a view to initiating the attack on the 6th.
>
> 2. The arrangement to be realized by the evening of September 5 will be:
>
> (a) All the available forces of the Sixth Army (Maunoury) to the northeast of Meaux will be ready to cross the Ourcq between Lizy-sur-Ourcq and May-en-Multien, in the direction of Chateau-Thierry. The nearby available elements of the cavalry corps will be placed under the orders of General Maunoury for this operation.
>
> (b) The English army will be established on the front: . Changis – Coulommiers, facing east, ready to attack in the general direction Of Montmirail.
>
> (c) The Fifth Army, closing up slightly on its left, will establish itself on the front: Courtacon – Esternay – Sezanne, ready to attack in the general direction south-north, the II Cavalry Corps assuring liaison between the British Army and the Fifth Army.
>
> (d) The Ninth Army will cover the right of the Fifth Army by holding the passes south of the swamp of St. Gond and shoving a part of its forces onto the plateau north of Sezanne.
>
> 3. The offensive of these different armies will begin September 6 in the morning.
>
> Signed: JOFFRE.

---

[41] See Sketch 12.

In the afternoon of September 5the Fourth and Third Armies also received their orders:

Fourth Army (General Langle de Cary): "Tomorrow, September 6, our armies of the left will attack in front and flank the German First and Second Armies. The Fourth Army, arresting its movement toward the south, will front the enemy, thus bringing its movement into harmony with that of the third Army which, debouching north of Revigny, takes the offensive by advancing toward the west."

Third Army (General Sarrail): "The Third Army, covering toward the northeast, will debouch toward the west in order to attack the left flank of the enemy forces which are marching west of the Argonne. It will bring its action into harmony with that of the Fourth Army, which has been ordered to front the enemy."

The First and Second Armies on the east front retained their defensive task and had no need of new orders. A telegram from Joffre on September 5 to the Minister of War sums up once more the reasons for his decision:

> The situation which determined me to refuse at first a general battle and to withdraw our armies toward the south has been modified in the following respect: The German First Army has abandoned the Paris direction and has obliqued toward the southeast in order to seek our left flank. Thanks to the dispositions taken, it has not been able to find that flank and the Fifth Army is now in position north of the Seine, ready to launch a frontal attack upon the German columns. On its left the English troops are assembled between the Seine and the Marne, ready to attack. These in turn will be supported and covered in the left flank by the mobile forces of the Paris garrison acting in the direction of Meaux in such manner as to assure them against any fear of being surrounded. Hence the strategical situation is excellent, and better conditions for our offensive can not be expected. That is why I have decided to take up the attack. The struggle which is about to begin may have decisive results, but may also have, in case of failure, the most serious consequences for the country. I am resolved to engage our troops to the limit and without reserve with a view to victory.

On the evening of September 5 Joffre transferred his headquarters from Bar-sur-Aube to Chatillon-sur-Seine. The reason for it is not apparent.

Critique of Joffre's Orders

The orders issued on the evening of September 4 at the French General Headquarters led to a struggle of worldwide significance, to a battle along the enormous front extending from Verdun to Paris. There can be no doubt that the French High Command seized the favorable opportunity and that it quickly adopted the necessary measures. There is no mistaking the grandeur of the dispositions taken for getting the operation under way. At first sight, one has the impression of a new Cannae in course of development. While the center (Ninth and Fourth Armies) were assigned a rather defensive task, the two wings were to execute an. encircling attack. But the conditions for a Cannae maneuver were by no means realized. The center might have been weaker, the left wing should have been much stronger, the right wing was not in a position to fulfill its task.

Maunoury's army was. not yet ready, his reenforcements had not yet all arrived. The offensive had been contemplated by Joffre only for a later date; now it had to be hurried up. The composition of the army was very unequal; by the side of good troops it comprised also the mediocre. They had all suffered more or less in the earlier fighting. The brunt of the battle was to be borne by the Sixth Army. Hence this army could not be too strong. It was to it and not to the Third and Fourth Armies that the two corps taken from the First and Second Armies should have been directed.[42] In view of the excellent communications by railways leading from all directions to Paris, they could still have been brought up at the proper time and decided the issue of the battle. It was also absolutely necessary to have more cavalry on that wing. Sordet's cavalry corps was exhausted.

The Third Army was strong enough, but the situation as a whole and the direction assigned to this army made its enveloping

---

[42] See page 204.

task more difficult. It was to push forward in the westerly direction to attack the left flank of the German troops advancing west of the Forest of Argonne. Now these troops were advancing not only west of the Argonne, but also over this plateau, and obliged the Third Army to front toward the north in order to face them. Furthermore, it was badly menaced in its rear. If the Germans should break through at any point to the south of Verdun, say toward St. Mihiel, and should cross the Meuse, the Third Army was lost. Hence the preliminary condition of its offensive was that it retain the line of the Meuse at Verdun and southward. "Verdun was the anchor on which hung the fate of France."[43] One may accordingly wonder whether it would not have been better to direct the Third Army to hold out on the defensive and to send to the left wing such corps as it could do without.

The frontal combats of the center armies were not likely to bring a decision. In the course of the retreat, the 5th Army had been displaced toward the left in order to bring it closer to the English army. The result was a dangerous gap between the Fourth and the Ninth Army. Liaison between the Fifth and the English army was nevertheless very lax. In attempting to execute an enveloping movement starting from Paris and to maintain liaison to the right with the fortified line of the Meuse, the army was torn asunder.

As to whether the English army would accomplish the task assigned to it in the fighting line by pushing determinedly forward, that was necessarily a very doubtful matter in view of the attitude which French had maintained up to that time. As a result of his ardent desire to get behind the Seine, he was left so far in the rear that when the battle began he could not reach the starting point assigned to him.

Hence the order of attack was vitiated by certain disadvantages which prevented obtaining a thorough success. The enveloping movement which was designed to bring about the decision failed. On the other hand, in the course of the battle, there was suddenly presented the possibility of a breakthrough. Just as on the German

---

[43] Hanotaux.

side, the different armies constituting the decisive wing were not conducted with the necessary cohesion; on both sides was the lack of an army-group command. On the French side, such command should have embraced the French Fifth and Sixth Armies as well as the English army. Just as with us, the General Headquarters kept much too far away from the decisive point.

A large number of the foregoing remarks have been made by the French themselves. But one is none the less obliged to recognize, on the whole, the leadership qualities of General Joffre. One fact which merits particular mention is that, confiding in the strength of the fortified front of the east, Joffre unhesitatingly withdrew from the First and Second Armies everything that could be spared.

Also of great importance for the battle was the utilization of the French fortresses of Paris, Verdun, and of the whole Meuse and Moselle front.

Placing the Armies in Readiness for the Attack of September 4 and 5

On September 3 and 4 the Third Army (Sarrail) had wheeled back between Verdun and Varerines into the general line: Souilly (southwest of Verdun) – Revigny, and on September 5 it stood in the vicinity of Vaubecourt, facing northwest, and forming and obtuse angle with the Fourth Army.[44] On the right wing it rested upon the fortress of Verdun and was in liaison with the advanced elements of the garrison; on its left wing, at Revigny, there was a gap between it and the Fourth Army, but this was to be filled on September 8 by the XV Corps coming from the Second Army in Lorraine.

On the evening of September 5, the Fourth Army (Langle de Cary) stood south of the Ornain on the line: Sermaize – Sompuis, facing Vitry le Francois. It was separated from the Ninth Army by a gap of 20 kilometers which the 9th Cavalry Division at Mailly

---

[44] See Sketch 12.

could not fill.

Its left wing formed contact with the former Foch army detachment, now the Ninth Army, which on the 4th had continued its retreat up to the region of Vertus and on the 5th stood facing the swamps of St. Gond on the line: Camp de Mailly [Mailly] – Sezanne. On September 4 the subordination of the Foch detachmentto the Fourth Army had been countermanded. It became independent in its quality of "Ninth Army" but still retained the samecomposition.

The Fifth Army on September 3 had reached, as we have already said, the region: south of Epernay – south Of Chateau-Thierry. The attack of the German IX Corps by way of Chateau-Thierry frightened it anew. In the night of the 3rd-4th its retreat was continued, its left wing marching from Condé-en-Brie upon Montolivet by way of Montmirail. The passage through Montmirail under enemy fire was particularly difficult. The Conneau cavalry corps was to retard the enemy march on the left wing. During the dayof the 4th this army attained the region: Etoges (north of St. Gond Swamp). – northeast of La Ferté-Gaucher; that is to say, that it stretched out toward the left to diminish the gap existing between it and the English army.

On September 5 the Fifth Army moved behind the line: Sezanne-Courtacon, which had been assigned to it as a base of departure for the attack, with Conneau's cavalry corps on its left wing.

General Lanrezac provides us with an account of the state of his army, which is of great importance for understanding the later events.[45] To escape being surrounded, the Fifth Army had marched day and night during the period of September 1 to 5. Many soldiers abandoned the colors under the pretext that they had lost their unit or that they were ill. They gradually got ahead of the marching columns, pillaging and terrifying the population by their tales. Disorder was increasing among the trains. They barred the way of the troopsso that the latter could not advance and remained standing day and night. The exhaustion became extreme. "I

[45] Loc. cit., page 256.

believe," writes General Lanrezac in his conclusion, "that no army has ever experienced such a painful situation as that of the Fifth Army in the period of August 30 to September 4." This description has been confirmed by Palat.

The same army, a few days later, threatened to break through the German front during the Battle of the Marne and exercised a decisive influence upon the course of events. This was owing not to its accomplishments but to the favorable situation presented to it. One can not avoid the impression that it was quite possible to seta bar in the way of its advance and that this bar would not have had to be very strong.

The British army, which was to fill the gap between the Sixth and Fifth Armies, had, as already stated, continued its retreat during the night of September 4-5 toward the region: Rozoy – Tournan, so that on the 5th it was far in rear of the line: Coulommiers – Changis which it had been assigned for attacking in the direction of Montmirail. Between the English and the Fifth Army there was no connection whatever. "Each army was marching on its own, without any understanding with the others."[46] Joffre arrived on September 5 at the English headquarters of Melun to talk about the operations with French. "Joffre was quite hopeful."[47]

On September 4, the Sixth Army remained essentially in place. As regards its condition, Palat gives the following description: "Its cohesion had suffered from its long and precipitate retreat. Gloomy, unfavorable news, with rumors of treason, increased the general discouragement."[48] The 55th Reserve Division, which had marched in all haste and without halt, did not present a fair spectacle. Numerous stragglers were seated on the vehicles and gun carriages. The division was in an indescribable state of disorder. The VII Corps also produced a dismal impression in the course of its passage.

---

[46] Palat, loc. cit., Vol. V, page 406.

[47] French, loc. cit.

[48] Loc. cit., Vol. V, page 407.

Such was the condition, on the eve of the Battle of the Marne, of the troops of the enemy left wing, charged with bringing about the decision. Its advantage consisted in the fact that it was in an incomparably better strategic position than that of the German right wing. It has to be granted, however, that the troops had it in them to pass at once from the retreat to the offensive. But one also acquires the conviction that a second great defeat would have broken their resistance for once and all. Joffre knew what he was talking about when he wrote to the Minister of War that the failure of the offensive would be attended by the most serious consequences to the country.[49] It remained to be seen in the great impending battle, whether the brilliant qualities of the German troops would be capable of changing to our advantage the unfavorable strategic situation and whether our leaders would have the grit to surmount the crisis.

---

[49] See page 209.

Chapter VIII – The Battle of the Marne

The 5th of September. Action of the IV Reserve Corps against the Sixth Army

On the morning of September 5the Sixth Army, made up of five and one-half divisions of infantry and one division of cavalry, set out from the line: Claye – Dammartin – southern edge of the forest of Ermenonville in order to move up, in accordance with the order of Gallieni, to the north bank of the Marne on a line with Meaux and take its dispositions for the offensive in the direction of Chateau-Thierry.[1] The offensive was to begin on the 6th.

On the right wing Ditte's native brigade (Moroccans) and the Lamaze group (55th and 56th Reserve Divisions), to which were attached Gillet's cavalry brigade and the two groups of sortie artillery, moved forward in three columns, namely, by way of Charny upon Penchard, by way of Le Plessis-aux-Bois upon Monthyon, and by way of Montgé upon St. Soupplets. The cavalry brigade reconnoitered in the direction of Meaux.

On their left, the VII Corps (14th Division and 63rd Reserve

---

[1] See General Map No. 2.

Division) marched first in the northerly direction, to proceed later toward the east and take up a position beside the Lamaze group by passing through Dammartin – Othis and northward.

On the right wing, between Claye and Thorigny, the composite cavalry, division of Cornulier-Lucinière was to maintain liaison with the English.

In the second line was the 45th Division (Drude) in the vicinity, of Mauregard (west of Dammartin). The IV Corps could not be detrained until September 6and 7. General Ebener's group of reserve divisions (61st and 62d Reserve Divisions) remained behind in the fortified camp of Paris.

Contrary to expectations, General Lamaze came up suddenly against the enemy. Violent fighting developed in the vicinity of Penchard, Monthyon, and St. Soupplets. According to the French account, it ended in the evening on the line: Charny – Villeroy – Le Plessis-aux-Bois – Cuisy – Montgé.

The enemy with whom the French had collided was the IV Reserve Corps. Reconnaissance by the French must have been very weak, though the Sixth Army was provided with sufficient cavalry. A curious thing was that it was concentrated entirely on the right wing, on the Marne. The aviation, too, seems to have been defective. The ill-advised advance of Maunoury was opposed to the intentions of Gallieni, who wished to conceal from his adversary the danger which menaced him.[2] For us, the fighting was of great importance: it revealed the enemy's hand.

The German IV Reserve Corps penetrated on the 4th by way of Creil – Senlis into the region southeast of Nanteuil-le-Haudouin. On the 5th, according to the army order, it was to"advance into the region: Marcilly – Chambry and take up the task, north of the Marne, of covering toward the northeast front of Paris." After receiving this order[3] the commander of the corps, General von Gronau, sent the following order, at 12:30 p.m., of the 5th, from Nanteuil-le-Haudouin:

---

[2] See pages 202-203.

[3] See page 157.

> 1. The enemy, apparently advanced troops of Paris, still at Dammartin. South of the Marne, enemy forces still reported at Coulommiers, apparently falling back toward the south and southwest. Reims has fallen.
>
> 2. The army continues its advance toward the Seine, covering toward Paris. The II Corps will advance beyond the Marne up to the lower Grand Morin below Coulommiers. It will cover the flank of the army toward the east front of Paris.
>
> 3. The IV Reserve Corps, to which is attached the 4th Cavalry Division, will advance into the region: Marcilly – Chambry (north of Meaux). It will cover north of the Marne toward the northeast front of Paris.

The 22nd Reserve Division was to advance at 4:30 in the morning from Villers Saint Genest by way of Bouillancy – Puisieux upon Chambry; the 7th Reserve Division at 6 a.m. from Sennevières by way of Chevreville – Bregy – La Ramee – Marcilly upon Barcy; the 4th Cavalry Division at 5:30a.m. from Droiselles by way of Silly le Long and Ognes, and then in echelon to the rear accompany the march of the 7th Reserve Division.

The course of events on September 5, according to the communications of General von Gronau and the war journal of the IV Reserve Corps,[4] was as follows:

Though the corps had ceaselessly endeavored to reconnoiter in the direction of Paris, the situation could not be clarified. Patrols were unable to penetrate the forest of Chantilly and Ermenonville, or to push toward the wooded heights of Dammartin, or to see what was taking place on the ground in the rear: Nor could the aviators sent out by the army determine whether important forces had been assembled at Paris or not.

Reports received up to the evening of September 4 showed that Dammartin was occupied by enemy cavalry and that small infantry elements stood in the rear. On September 5, the 4th Cavalry Division transmitted the same information at first; noting later that important infantry posts, established on the roads leading from Paris toward the northeast, prevented its own patrols from

---

[4] See Sketch 13.

advancing. It was also impossible for the patrols to advance toward the north front of Paris by making a detour, for the great forest located north of Senlis wasoccupied by enemy posts.

At 10 o'clock in the morning a report from the 4th Cavalry Division announced that-several columns of enemy cavalry were advancing through Dammartin, St. Mard, and Juilly; and the division had an impression that an attack upon it by one division of enemy cavalry was in process of development.

At the same time the army order from La Ferté-Milon arrived instructing the IV Reserve Corps to halt.[5] But the corps had already reached its march objective. The 7th Reserve Division had closed up on its front between Marcilly and Bercy, and the 22nd Reserve Division had done the same at Chambry.

The following hours, also, failed to bring any clarity. The cavalry division announced the advance of an enemy column from St. Mard upon Montgé.

In view of this situation the corps was unable to come to rest. It was necessary to know what was going on at Paris before the First Army could decide to march past the place. *Nothing but an attack could rend the veil.* At noon the commander of the corps said to his chief of staff, L. Col. von der Heyde: "Lieutenant Colonel, there is no help for it, we must attack!"

That was one of the great decisions which military history has to record.

General von Gronau issued the following order:

Barcy, September, 5, 12:15 p.m.

1. In the forest Montgé – Cuisy, is enemy cavalry which prevents our own from getting a view of the situation. Behind this forest, more enemy cavalry and infantry.

2. The 7th Reserve Division will advance to the attack in several columns by way of Cuisy – Montgé upon-St. Mard in order to drive the enemy back.

3. The 4th Cavalry Division will take part in the attack by advancing through Marchemoret in direction of Dammartin.

---

[5] See page 160

4. The 22d Reserve Division will be held in readiness between Barcy and Monthyon.

5. Corps staff with the 22nd Reserve Division.

VON GRONAU.

The 7th Reserve Division did not move forward in open formation as prescribed but in one column along the route Pringy – Monthyon. On the other side of Monthyon it collided with the enemy and passed to the attack. The 22nd Reserve Division which followed by way of Penchard entered the combat on its left. The cavalry division covered the right flank. Violent fighting took place in the region: St. Soupplets – Monthyon – Penchard and lasted into the night. The enemy was thrown back.

Meanwhile the 4th Cavalry Division had collided, in the course of its advance, with very powerful enemy forces. It was not possible to exploit in a decisive manner the success obtained. The enemy might take refuge inside the ring of forts; he might also received reenforcements, from Paris. The IV Reserve Corps had drawn upon its last forces. The goal was attained: powerful enemy forces had been identified. The task now was to prevent the enemy from advancing into the flank of the First Army. The corps could not remain where it was at the time. It might have become surrounded. Furthermore, the crossings of the Ourcq were to be kept open so that the First Army might, if it wished, send reenforcements. The commanding general consequently decided to fall back behind the Therouane sector. In the afternoon he issued the following order:

> The defeated enemy will not be pursued beyond the line: Cuisy – Iverny. At nightfall the corps will fall back behind the Therouane sector so as to avoid the danger of envelopment from the north and to get out of the radius of the fortress:
>
> The 7th Reserve Division from St. Soupplets to La Ram&and from Plessis-l'Eveque to west of Etrepilly.
>
> The 22nd Reserve Division from the line: Iverny – Penchard toward the line Etrepilly – Gue a Tresmes.
>
> The positions will be reenforced in the course of the night. Observation posts on the Therouane sector.
>
> 4th Cavalry Division at Bregy.

Corps H. Q. at Puisieux.

VON GRONAU.

In consequence of this order, the fighting gradually assumed a temporizing character on the line: Le Plessis l'Eveque – Iverny – Neufmoutiers. It only remained to take St. Soupplets in order to be able to withdraw the troops without embarrassment and also to wine a decisive victory on the right wing. To this end the last reserve of the corps command was put at the disposal of the 7th Reserve Division. At 7:45 p.m. St: Soupplets was taken by storm and the enemy thrown back upon the woodlands of Dammartin.

The further movements were effected by moonlight almost without incident. The only element which was obliged to remain in the rear and which fell into the hands of the enemy was a part of the main dressing station installed at Pringy with its untransportable wounded men. One must accord the greatest honor to the boldness of General von Gronau's decision to take up the attack, to the firmness with which the fighting was conducted, to the correctness of the time selected for the corps to fall back in order to avoid the menace of envelopment, and finally to the splendid conduct of the troops. The surprise planned by Joffre and Gallieni had failed. The great danger which menaced our flank had been recognized at the last moment, and General von Kluck could still adopt his measures that night.

The corps had waged a glorious struggle against considerably superior forces. It was still without the 43rd Reserve Brigade of Lepel, which had been left at Brussels. Each brigade had only one machine-gun company, each division a single regiment of artillery comprising six gun batteries. It had neither heavy artillery nor aviation.

On the French side, it was principally the Lamaze group and the Moroccan brigade which had been engaged. The VII Corps did not take part, for reasons unknown to us, although it was in a position to completely envelop the IV Reserve Corps. General Maunoury made no use whatever of his great numerical superiority otherwise, General von Gronau would have fallen into a critical situation. But luck favored the bold.

In the evening, General Maunoury was still far from the Ourcq, which he was to cross on the 6th in order to advance to the attack. An important part of the French plan of attack had become obsolete.

September 5 was the great day of the IV Reserve Corps in the war.

September 6

On the morning of September 6 the decisive struggle began all along the front from Verdun to Paris, to the complete surprise of the Germans. The French troops were enthused by an order from Joffre:

> At a time when a battle is in progress on which the salvation of the country depends, it is well to remind everyone that the time has passed for looking backward. All efforts must be expended in attacking and driving back the enemy. A body of troops which can no longer advance is obliged, at all cost, to hold the ground which has been gained and to die on the spot rather than retreat. In the present circumstances no weakness can be tolerated.

The first reports on the fighting of the IV Reserve Corps reached the headquarters of the First Army at Rebais in the night of September 5-6. In judging the situation it is necessary to clear one's mind of any a posteriori knowledge of what had occurred. On the morning of the 6th neither the First Army nor the High Command had the faintest suspicion of a general French offensive between Paris and Verdun. It was assumed that the enemy was in full retreat beyond the Seine and the Aube. As late as noon of the 6th, the Second Army, assuming that the enemy had already in large part crossed the Seine, issued an order for the pursuit. According to the statements made to us by Lt. Col. Hentsch and also according to the order of the High Command, a powerful French attack was to be expected against the right flank for the purpose of stopping our pursuit. It came sooner than the High Command had assumed.

In the night of the 5-6th, General von Kluck had a difficult decision to make. It was clear that action had to be taken with all speed. The different possibilities were briefly examined. Should the flank of the German forces be protected in a defensive manner or would it be better to stretch out on the flank and rear by attacking and throwing back the enemy? The High Command had ordered that an advance of the enemy forces making a sortie from Paris should be opposed offensively north of the Marne. There was no compelling reason whatever for confining ourselves to a defensive which in no case could offer sufficient protection-to the flank, The attack alone could relieve that flank. In view of the manner in which the situation was gauged on the morning-of the 6th at the headquarters of the first and Second Armies, it had to be assumed that the Second Army could oblique between the Seine and the Marne into the line prescribed for it.

General von Kluck decided in favor of the attack.

The army order had prescribed that the retiring movement, based on the order of the High Command, would take place on the 6th,[6] by echelon starting with the right wing – in the belief, shared by Lt. Col. Hentsch, that sufficient time was available.[7] But now the measures already adopted had been constructed; the complicated movement of the army was rendered more difficult by the need of bringing quick support to the IV Reserve Corps. The army command was obliged to maintain order in the rear zone, avoid blocking of the roads, and guarantee the supply of the army with provisions and ammunition by issuing precise orders for the marching columns and in particular to the parks and convoys of all the corps. As a matter of fact, the movements of the following days were effected without any great shocks or friction.

Around midnight, the II Corps received the order to advance, as soon as possible after receipt of the order, upon Lizy – Germiny in order to support the IV Reserve Corps.

In the forenoon of the 6th the staff of the First Army moved to Charly. The commander-in-chief went on ahead by automobile to the heights east of Lizy. Nothing was heard there of any fighting in

---

[6] See Sketch 14.

[7] See page 164.

connection with the IV Reserve Corps. It appeared that the enemy had given up the attack. We hoped to have the advantage of a lull and to be able to bring up reenforcements at the proper time. But once arrived at Charly, we soon learned from the quartermaster general, Col. von Bergmann, who had been sent to the IV Reserve Corps that this corps had been attacked in the direction: La Ramée – Trocy. So, at noon, the IV Corps, which was marching upon Doue, (NE. of Coulommiers) was ordered to send at once a regiment of field artillery to the II Corps under the protection of a cavalry escort.

At the IV Reserve Corps the night had passed quietly. On the 6th, at daybreak, General von Gronau explored the position on the Therouane. It hail been assigned to the troops only provisionally, for the night, because it was easy to indicate and attain. But it was not adapted to a stubborn defense against a superior enemy force. Even the course of the brook was unfavorable, for the right wing of the position formed a salient and was exposed to an enveloping movement. General von Gronau consequently established the 7th Reserve Division on the heights between Puisieux and Mahoeuvre, which were favorable to the defense, and the 22nd Reserve Division on its flank to the southeast as far as Gué à Tresmes. Since the enemy left wing was advancing by way of Bregy, the reserves had to be used to extend the position up to Acy en Multien. The extent of the front was too great; reserves could no longer be given off.

At 10 a.m. General von Linsingen, commander of the II Corps, arrived on the field of battle. The French, who had manifestly, not noticed the retirement of the IV Reserve Corps until after midnight, had advanced at dawn with great care. It was not until 9 o'clock in the morning that they collided with the outposts still in position on the Therouane. Violent fighting soon developed all along the front. By order of the army command, General von Linsingen was also given command of the IV Reserve Corps. At 12:30 p.m. he ordered the latter to hold its position; Vincy Manoeuvre – Gué à Tresmes, while the II Corps would come into action on its right and left, namely, with the 3rd Division by way of Varreddes, with the 4th Division by way of May en Multien – Vincy Manoeuvre. There thus arose from the very beginning a mixture of units which only increased during the course of the fighting. Once the II Corps had arrived, the attack was to be taken up all along the line.

The II Corps was brought up in the direction previously mentioned, because it was thought that the IV Reserve Corps had to be reenforced as quickly as possible. If it is desired to make *a posteriori* criticism based on knowledge of the events, one may say that it would have been better to move the whole II Corps to the right wing. In the course of the following days, the 3rd Division fell into an untenable position at Varreddes from which it had to be drawn back. The thin line of the IV Reserve Corps was able to hold firm until evening. The 4th Division advancing by way of Rosoy en Multien [Rosoy], executed, on the initiative of its leader, a more pronounced sweeping movement toward the north in the direction of Etavigny. The-II Corps, which had set out during the night, had to execute an extremely fatiguing march in the dust and heat. The 4th Division was unable to come into action until evening, but won another success over the French VII Corps to the north of Acy en Multien.

At 5:30 in the evening the IV Corps was ordered by the First Army Command to continue before the close of the day up to the region north of La Ferté-sous-Jouarre. The time and the direction of its coming into action to support the II Corps and IV Reserve Corps were to be stated later.

Meanwhile the events on the left wing of the army had in part gone counter to the plans of the command. There the IX Corps was for the present to remain in place, the III Corps to advance upon La Ferté-Gaucher – on the hypothesis, as already stated, that the enemy was still retreating. But on the morning of September 6, the advance guard of the 17th Division was suddenly taken under enemy fire. Aviators reported that enemy forces coming from the south were advancing upon Esternay. It is apparently a counter-attack of the enemy in retreat. The commander of the IX Corps, General von Quast, decided to take up the attack himself and asked the support of the III Corps as well as of the VII Corps which was on the right wing of the Second Army. The attack would facilitate the advance of the Second Army which was still engaged in hard fighting on the upper Petit Morin. Besides, as was stated in the request to the VII Corps, "the retirement of the III and IX Corps upon Paris was not regarded as possible until such time as the enemy was thrown back beyond the Seine."

The III Corps had already begun the retiring movement in accordance with previous orders when there arrived the request of the IX Corps. At the same moment its rear guards were attacked at Montceaux and Sancy. General von Lochow decided to front and accept combat. But naturally a rather long interval of time elapsed before his corps was deployed anew for fighting. Both corps held without difficulty. At the end of the day the combat situation was entirely favorable. On the right wing the I Cavalry Corps hurled back Conneau's cavalry corps at Courtaeon. The VII Corps provided effective support for the IX Corps by means of the artillery of the 13th Division which had been pushed forward.

In fact, the two corps had found themselves in a difficult situation. They had been engaged with the left wing and the center of the French Fifth Army. We were not aware of the fact. But we realized, none the less, that the situation was no longer in accord with the idea held up to that time. The right flank of the III Corps appeared to be in danger. So, at 5:45 p.m., the army command ordered the III Corps to cover the right flank of the IX Corps during the rest of the day, until a decision could be reached with regard to its further employment after the situation had had time to clarify.

Meanwhile the II Cavalry Corps had got contact with the English at Rozoy. The gap which had formed in the region of Coulommiers after the departure of the II and IV Corps required attention. The distance separating the III and IX Corps from the First Army was quite considerable. So long as they remained there, it seemed better to put them provisionally under the command of the Second Army. They as well as the Second Army were informed to this effect. In the afternoon the latter was also asked by radio to bring up the VII Corps and X Reserve Corps to the west of the III Corps for flank protection. But in the evening, Captain Brinkmann of the staff of the Second Army arrived at Charly and convinced the First Army command that it was impossible to comply with that request. He stated that one division of the VII Corps was already in action and that only one other was available behind the front. The First Army Command was then obliged to reach a decision regarding employment of the III and IX Corps. They could not remain where they were, and it could not yet be seen where they were most needed. According to the orders of the High Command, the whole First Army was to move onto the north bank of the Marne. There also the enemy flank attack had begun. The First Army command therefore decided in the afternoon to draw the two corps back for the present behind the Petit Morin, on the line: Montmirail – Boitron, but leave them still provisionally under the command of the Second Army. In the matter of issuing orders, we were here confronted with a lack of clarity which led to friction.

At 10:30 p.m., an order was despatched to the IV Corps directing it to move sufficiently forward during the night so that at daybreak it could attack beyond the line: Rosoy en Multien – Trocy, according to the more detailed instructions of the command of the II Corps.

Aviators had reported that enemy columns had set out at 6 p.m. from the line: Rosoy – Foret de Crecy (SW. of Crecy). It was decided that the II Cavalry Corps would cover in that direction in conjunction with the I Cavalry Corps and would fill the gap of Coulommiers in order to oppose the English advance which had now become manifest. The assent of the Second Army was requested to this end. It was a matter of the utmost necessity that all the cavalry be placed under a single higher command, and still more necessary to group the First and Second Armies under the orders of an army-group command. The First Army was pushing toward the Ourcq, the Second toward the Seine. And from September 5 to September 9 the High Command maintained silence.

On September 6 the two cavalry corps succeeded in holding up considerably the advance of the English toward the Grand Morin; the von der Marwitz corps in the region: Rozoy – Coulommiers, and Richthofen's corps from Courtacon.

In the evening the First Army Command received from the communications inspectorate (Etappeninspektion) disquieting information which increased the uncertainty of the situation: namely, that the vicinity of Lille was occupied by the French, perhaps also by the English. The railways and the communications to the rear appeared in danger. On the previous evening Lt. Col.

Hentsch, also, had spoken of concentrations of troops in the vicinity of Lille and of detrainments at Ostend,[8] adding that information of this sort had repeatedly reached the High Command.

The following report was addressed to the High Command at 10:45 p.m. "II Corps and IV Reserve Corps north of the Marne are engaged in violent fighting southwest of Crouy against powerful enemy forces come from Paris. IV Corps will come into action here tomorrow. III and IX Corps covering west of Montmirail the flank of the Second Army which to the east of this point is attacking powerful enemy forces toward the south." From this report the difficulty of the situation could be inferred.

The Second Army had wished to continue, on September 6, in compliance with the order of the High Command of September 5, to wheel around Montmirail, its left wing advancing from Morains le Petit upon Marigny le Grand, while the VII Corps would remain north of Montmirail. The Second Army Command, also, was going on the assumption that the enemy continued to retreat. It was still of that opinion at noon, when it issued an order to pursue:

> The French Fifth Army has already got the larger part of its forces behind the Seine. Non-contradictory reports indicate troop displacements from Romilly – Nogent sur Seine toward the west; only covering troops are left north of the Seine. Vigorous pursuit at all cost for the purpose of annihilating these forces and destroying the section of railway is required. Hence, continuation of the pursuit.

But in reality the Second Army collided with the advancing right wing of the Fifth Army and with the French Ninth Army. Its right wing, to the east of Montmirail, accordingly progressed but slowly and gained but little ground beyond the Petit Morin, while its left wing got as far as the northern edge of the swamps of St. Gond. The Second Army was not in an easy situation: the First Army was wheeling back toward the north, the Third Army had remained behind.

The Third Army, which had rested on September 5, advanced

[8] See page 163.

on the 6th in the southernly direction, assuming, like the others, that the only forces in front of it were rear guards. Along the way it received appeals for support from the second and Fourth Armies, both engaged in violent fighting, so that its right wing was drawn in the direction of Fère Champenoise, its left wing in the direction of Vitry le Francois, and in its center, in the vicinity of Sommesous and Soude [Soude St. Croix, 10 km. E. of Sommesous], facing Mailly, a gap was formed which could be filled later only by putting into line units drawn from the rear. As chance would have it, there was also a gap on the French side in the vicinity of Mailly. The evening wore away without the Third Army being able to take any effective action on the left wing of the Second.

The Fourth Army collided unexpectedly with powerful enemy forces on the Rhine-Marne canal between Vitry le Francois and Revigny. This region, cut by numerous streams, was extremely difficult to attack.

The Fifth Army advanced between Revigny and Verdun beyond the line: Laheycourt – Vaubecourt – St. Andre, while its left wing was investing Verdun. This army also met with stubborn resistance.

On the French side, the Sixth Army had continued its forward movement on September 6, and at 9 o'clock in the morning had reached the line: Chambry – Barcy – Forfry – Oissery; the Lamaze group on the right, and the VII Corps, which was to execute an enveloping movement, on the left. The cavalry division remained in the valley of the Marne; the Sordet cavalry corps, highly exhausted, was directed from Versailles and St. Cyr upon Nanteuil le Haudouin, partly by rail but mostly on foot, and is reported to have covered 70 kilometers with jaded horses.

According to the French account, a strong counterattack took place in the afternoon at Chambry – Barcy. No doubt the reference is to the intervention of the 3rd Division by way of Varreddes. The success of the 4th Division at Acy en Multien is not mentioned. In the evening the Sixth Army had arrived on the line: Chambry – Marcilly (Lamaze group) and Puisieux – west of Acyen Multien (VII Corps).

The 45th Division was drawn along in the second line through Dammartin. Hence the army had made but little progress. It was very far from its objective, Chateau-Thierry.

Aviators reported that German columns from the south seemed to be falling back across the Marne. Gallieni recognized the importance of these movements; here also he took action and addressed in the evening the following message to French:

> The Sixth Army this morning began its offensive toward the east as planned. At 9o'clock its front was coming abreast of Meaux on the line: Chambry – Barcy – Forfry – Oissery. General Maunoury is meeting with serious resistance and believes himself confronted with the entire IV Reserve Corps. Furthermore, he reports that two enemy columns, each of one division, are coming up from the south and at 9 o'clock reached the Marne at Varreddes and Lizy. Operation is therefore well under way. To increase the strength of, our offensive I am putting all my forces at the disposal of General Maunoury. But it is absolutely necessary that the action of the Sixth Army shall not remain isolated and that the Germans shall not be able to bring up against it any units facing the English army. I therefore earnestly request Marshal French to be good enough, on his part, to push his army forward in accordance with the instructions of General Joffre, so that the general offensive contemplated for today may be really general and in order that there may exist between the different armies such harmony as alone can assure a decisive success.

It is clear that no great confidence existed in the vigor of Marshal French. The events were destined to justify that doubt.

Though the British army had had some rest and had also supplemented its armament and materiel, Marshal French believed that the situation demanded prudence. In his opinion, practically the whole of the German First Army had already arrived south of the Grand Morin and had left only one to two divisions north of the Marne. He therefore believed that he could not reach the Grand Morin on the 6th. The I Corps advanced through Rozoy in the direction of Vaudoy – Orneaux, the TI Corps farther north, the III Corps followed as a reserve behind the left wing. The realization gradually dawned that the enemy was retreating under the protection of rear guards. French will have it that at this moment he ordered a vigorous pursuit. The march was continued in the direction of Choisy – Coulommiers – Crecy. The Grand Morin was not reached, however, until the next day, as French himself admits. In the evening he received from Gallieni the letter quoted above. Joffre, also, asked him during the night to take a more northerly direction.

The French are highly displeased with the manner in which the English army advanced in the course of that day. They say that while French moved forward only with hesitation, the Germans had fallen back behind a thick curtain of cavalry."The consequences of that hesitation were serious," says General Canonge.[9] The German independent cavalry had done its duty well that day.

On September 3 General Franchet d'Esperey had assumed the command of the French Fifth Army. He was assigned the task of attacking in the general direction of Montmirail by advancing beyond the line: Sezanne – Courtacon. His right flank was to be covered by the Ninth Army. But in the course of the battle events were such, according to the French versions, that instead, General Franchet d'Esperey was obliged to support the Ninth Army with a corps on September 7and also to cover its flank with another corps, so that finally he had only two corps in addition to his reserve divisions with which to attack Montmirail.

On September 6 the II Cavalry Corps (Conneau), on the left wing, advanced to Courtacon then, from left to right, the XVIII Corps to Sancy, the III Corps to Courgivaux, the I Corps to Esternay, the X Corps to Moeurs. The 4th group of reserve divisions (General Valabregue) followed as a reserve. Thus the Fifth Army collided essentially with the left wing of the German First Army (III and IX Corps), the right wing of the Second Army being farther in rear. The French were not in a position to derive advantage from the very much exposed situation of the two corps.

According to the French report, the Fifth Army arrived in the afternoon, after violent fighting, as far as the line: La Villeneuve – Esternay – Courtacon.

The French Ninth Army, under General Foch, had been drawn up between Sommesous and Sezanne. On the left wing, to the north

---

[9] *La bataille de la Marne*, Paris 1918

of Sezanne, were the 42nd and Moroccan Divisions farther east the army was protected by the swamps of St. Gond. The IX Corps was facing Fère Champenoise, the XI Corps Sommesous. The reserve divisions were in rear. Between the right wing of the Ninth Army and the left wing of the Fourth at Sommepuis there was a gap of 20 kilometers which could not be filled by the 9th Cavalry Division at Mailly. By a curious coincidence, as we have already stated, a gap had also been formed, on September 5 precisely in front of this spot as a result of the change of front to right and left by the German Third Army.

Foch was assigned the task of supporting the offensive of the Fifth Army with his left wing and furthermore to remain on the defensive until the advance of the Fourth Army would permit'him to join in the attack. But his army was attacked on the left wing by the German Second Army wheeling around Montmirail and thrown back slowly in the course of heavy fighting. "The day was not favorable to the Ninth Army," says General Canonge.[10]

General Langle de Cary, commander of the Fourth Army, was to adapt his movements to those of the Third Army which was to advance in the westerly direction north of Revigny. The Fourth Army stood south of the Ornain from Sermaize to Sompuis, separated by a gap from the Ninth Army, as already stated. Here also heavy fighting occurred, which made it necessary to reenforce the Fourth Army by the XXI Corps. This latter, coming from the First Army, arrived at Joinville and Vassy in the period of September 4-6.

The Third Army set out from the line: Souilly (southwest of Verdun) – Beauzee – Vaubecourt – Revigny and advanced in a northwesterly direction, the right wing resting onVerdun.

The First and Second Armies, in the vicinity of Pont à Mousson, covered the rears, protected Nancy and held out on the general line: Luneville – St. Die.

---

[10] Loc. cit.

September 7

On September 7 the French Sixth Army received reenforcements, which were brought to the decisive left wing.[11] Sordet's cavalry corps (1st, 3rd and 5th Cavalry Divisions) reached the vicinity of Betz, in a high state of exhaustion. Cornulier-Lucinière's cavalry division received orders, in the night of September 6-7, to move from the valley of the Marne to the left wing and rejoin the cavalry corps. On the Marne, it had been in a bad position from the start. The 61st Reserve Division of the Ebener group was transported by rail from Paris to Le Plessis Belleville, that is, to the immediate rear of the field of battle and then pushed from this point to the left wing by way of Sennevières.

September 7 was a hard day for Maunoury. The attack of the Sixth Army was to begin at 4 o'clock in the morning, the Lamaze group (55th and 56th Reserve Divisions, Ditte's Moroccan brigade and 45th Division) attacking by way of Chambry – Barcy – Marcilly, the VII Corps by way of Puisieux – Acy en Multien, the 61st Reserve Division by way of Bois de Montrolles – Etavigny farther north, was the independent cavalry. Thus a powerful envelopment of the German right wing was under way when, on the 7th, the German reenforcements arrived in time precisely at that place. They collided at Etavigny with the 61st Reserve Division which had just arrived, and hurled it back beyond Villers St. Genest. According to the French account, this division reassembled in the evening 2 kilometers west of Nanteuil le Haudouin! A crisis occurred in the battle. The left wing (VII Corps), also, began to give way it was held up, however, thanks, it appears, to the bold pushing forward of the artillery under Col. Nivelle. As a result of this reverse, Sordet's cavalry corps, which had been advancing upon Cuvergnon, began to fall back upon Nanteuil le Haudouin by way of Betz. The envelopment sought by Joffre and Maunoury had failed.

On the French right wing the fighting wavered backand forth, without decisive results. The effects of the German heavy artillery,

---

[11] See Sketch 15.

established between Varreddes and May en Multien, was keenly felt by the French. On the other hand, our infantry emphasized repeatedly the powerful effects of the Frenchartillery. It was said that siege artillery must have arrived from Paris. The powerful burst of the French explosive projectiles was manifestly the cause ofthatsupposition.

At the end of the day the Sixth Army stood, according to the French data, on the line: Penchard – Chambry – Barcy – Marcilly – Puisieux – west of Etavigny. Hence it had not made a single step forward and had suffered a defeat on its left wing.

In the course of the afternoon Maunoury had been informed that German troops in front of the English and the Fifth Army were falling back beyond the Marne. General Franchet d'Esperey asked him to attack the retreating Germans in the flank. But, as Hanotaux remarks, Maunoury was by no means confronted with Germans in retreat, but with a powerful enemy force provided with plenty of artillery and which was attacking him: "He had nothing left to do but stand his ground or, if required, to attack."

Meanwhile the IV Corps at last arrived. The 8th Division was stopped and detrained, September 6, at the Lagny station for the purpose of establishing liaison with the English and supporting their left wing. In a letter dated September 8 to the Minister of War, Gallieni relates that he did everything in his power to induce Marshal French to advance and that the latter finally consented on the express condition that his flank should be covered: "I was consequently obliged to send to the south of the Marne the 8th Division, whose place would have been on Maunoury's left wing, in order to operate against the German line of retreat." The division was to push forward south of the Marne through the Grand Morin, but it appears that on the 7th it remained for a time east of Lagny. At any rate, it was absent from the decisive point and, due to the hesitant advance of the English, failed to come into action on the right wing. On the other hand, thanks to the vigorous action of Gallieni, the 7th Division was brought up in due time to the left wing. It had been detrained at Pantin in the course of the afternoon of the 7th. Gallieni, having recognized the danger which menaced his left wing, requisitioned 1300 Parisian taxicabs with which, in the night of the 7-8th and up to 8 o'clock in the morning, he transported five battalions into the region of Nanteuil le Haudouin. The rest of the infantry was transported by rail, and the artillery went on foot.[12]

On September 7 the British army crossed the Grand Morin on the line: La Ferté Gaucher – Coulommiers – Crecy, but went little farther. French himself gives as the line on which the English stood on the morning of the 8th Jouy sur Morin (I Corps) – Aulnoye (II Corps) – La Haute Maison (III Corps). On the right wing was Conneau's cavalry corps.

In the French accounts, the extremely slow advance of the English is much deplored. It is said to have had a very important influence on the issue of the battle. What a success could have been obtained if they had pushed forward through La Ferté-sous-Jouarre and Meaux!

According to the order of General Franchet d'Esperey, the Fifth Army was to digin on the evening of September 6 on the line attained, namely: La Villeneuve – Esternay – Courgivaux – Montceaux – south of Augers, in such manner as to "resist any attack at whatever cost." That doesn't look very enterprising. The resistance of the German III and IX Corps, in conjunction with the advance of the Second Army, had had such a powerful effect that the Fifth Army had evidently been continued on the defensive. There is nothing surprising about that when we consider the state of the Fifth Army at the beginning of the French offensive.[13]

On the morning of the 7th, however, numerous German columns were reported retreating from the region north of Courtacon – Esternay toward the north. These were the III and IX Corps, which, as a result of the defensive attitude of the Fifth Army, had been able to execute in broad daylight, without being disturbed, the retiring movement according to previous orders. Conneau's cavalry corps was proceeding toward La Ferté Gaucher in the course of the day it observed that the adversary had everywhere disappeared and that La Ferté Gaucher was clear of

---

[12] Illustration of September 4, 1920.

[13] See page 213.

enemy troops.

The Fifth Army was able in these conditions to continue its forward movement, but at the end of the day had only reached the locality: La Recoude – Morsains (I and X Corps), La Ferté Gaucher (III and XVIII Corps and in rear the Valabregue group of reserve divisions). Hence the right wing had made no progress whatever.

As regards the Ninth Army (Foch), the situation was less favorable; it was attacked by the left wing of the Second Army and by the right wing of the Third. The line wavered in the, region Fère Champenoise – Sommesous giving rise to some concern. At the center, the army held the passes south of the marshes of St. Gond. On the west, General Franchet d'Esperey had to support its left wing by putting his right-wing corps (X) at the disposition of Foch. General d'Esperey then found himself in a difficult situation as regards the continuance of the operations. If he marched farther toward the. north, he would lose connection with the Ninth Army. If he turned toward the right to support the Ninth Army, he would abandon, Maunoury to his fate on the Ourcq. If he split up his forces, it would be still worse.[14]

The fighting in which the Third and Fourth Armies were engaged brought no decision whatever.

On the whole, very little had been attained on September 7. For the Sixth and Ninth Armies the day had been unfavorable. The English were far in the rear. The Fifth Army, which had already been constrained to the -defensive, had finally advanced only when the III and IX Corps had been recalled by the First Army. Joffre jumped to the conclusion that this retirement was a general retreat of the German right wing.

On September 7 the French commander-in-chief issued the following order:

> 1. The German First Army seems to be falling back toward the northeast before the combined efforts of the allied armies on the left wing. The latter will follow the enemy with the whole of their forces, in such a way as still to preserve the possibility of surrounding the

---

[14] Hanotaux, loc. cit.

German right wing.

2. The march will therefore be executed, in general, in the northeasterly direction, in an arrangement which will permit engaging battle in case the enemy makes a halt and without leaving him time in which to organize substantially.

3. To this end, the Sixth Army will make successive gains of ground toward the north on the right bank of the Ourcq. The British forces will attempt to gain a foothold successively beyond the Petit Morin, the Grand Morin and the Marne.

4. The Fifth Army will speed up the movement of its left wing and will employ its forces on the right to support the Ninth Army.

5. This latter will strive to hold out on the front it now occupies until the arrival of the reserved forces of the Fourth Army on its right will enable it to participate in the forward movement.

Limit of the zones of action between the Fifth Army and the British Army: Dagny [Dragny on general map] – St. Remy – Sablonnières – Hondevilliers – Nogent l'Artaud – Chateau-Thierry (this route to the British Army).

On the morning of September 7 the staff of the German First Army moved from Charly to Vendrest (immediately in rear of the combat front on the Ourcq), where it arrived at 7 o'clock. Quarters and supplies were here of the most limited. The staff was unable to find sufficient space for its offices. We installed ourselves for work in the open air. There could be no thought, moreover, of sleeping. Communications were poor, the telephone failed to function regularly. The connection with the different corps had to be effected mainly by the officers of the staff.

In the forenoon we received from the High Command the following communication: "According to an order of Joffre's, picked up today, decisive battle for all French armies prescribed for today."

During the night of the 6-7th, while the IV Corps was marching toward the Ourcq in the general direction of La Ferté-sous-Jouarre – Crouy, its commander, General Sixt von Armin, betook himself to the staff of the II Corps, where he arrived at 3:30 in the morning. It was agreed to push the 7th Division to the right wing for the purposes of envelopment, but to intercalate the 8th Division via Lizy into the sector held by the IV Reserve Corps, which was exhausted and very much weakened. Such a measure was not desirable, but could not be avoided. General von Gronau pushed the 15th Brigade and the artillery of the 8th Division into the position of the 7th Reserve Division and kept the 16th Brigade in rear as a reserve. But this latter was sent later to the right wing to take part in the flanking attack. The 3d Division, which stood on the left wing in the vicinity of Varreddes, also called for support. It was, in fact, in a difficult situation and suffered from the fire of the enemy artillery which, from the vicinity of Meaux, was firing into its left flank and almost against its rear. The emplacement at Varreddes, with the Marne and the canal at its back, had been poorly selected in the first place. No support could be furnished, however, by the army command. The idea which governed the conduct of the fighting was to hold firm on the left wing and to surround the enemy with the right wing by spreading out to the north. That was where the decision lay, that was where the enemy also wished to envelop. Crises arising on the front had to be taken as part of the game; they existed, moreover, on the enemy side as well as on ours. Frontally, no progress could be made by either.

Toward noon the introduction of reenforcements into the fighting front was so far advanced that General von Linsingen, who on that day still retained command of the II and IV Corps and IV Reserve Corps was able to pass to the attack. The IV Corps had just accomplished an extraordinary march. It had set out from the vicinity of Choisy on the 6th and had marched throughout the night except for one brief rest. The 7th Division on the outside wing had covered more than 60 kilometers. Because of the mixture of units, it had been necessary to distribute the available troops in three groups. The north group (7th and 4th Divisions, 16th Brigade of the 8th Division), under General Sixt von Armin, was to attack by way of Antilly – Acy en Multien; on the center, in the region Vincy Manoeuvre – north of Trocy, the 8th Division (less the 16th Brigade)and the 7th Reserve Division, under General von Gronau, were to join in the attack of the north group in as far as their advance would permit; the left wing (22nd Reserve Division and 3rd Division) was to maintain a temporizing strategy in the region: Trocy – Varreddes. The 4th Cavalry Division stood southwest of La Ferté Milon on the right wing.

Captain Bücrmann of the army staff, who had seen the 7th

Division during its march to the fight, and who accompanied it during its attack, reports on the matter: “It was wonderful the way the battalions, which I had seen a few hours previously dragging along painfully, now advanced to the attack with sprightly step and in perfect order as on the drill field, well supported by the field artillery set up in along line.”

The attack of our right wing collided, as already pointed out, with the French 61st Reserve Division, itself on the way to the field of battle, and completely repulsed it. From all indications, the importance of this success was not fully recognized by us. It even appears that our right wing was a bit drawn back in the evening. In the center, no great attack occurred. Our center and left wing held firm.

The reports received up to noon by the staff of the first Army at Vendrest showed that the British Army was advancing only with hesitation. Aviators announced that at 10 o’clock columns were marching from Pezarchesupon Coulommiers, that at the same hour rather important bivouacks were installed in the woods northeast of Tournan, and finally, that south of the Marne there was no enemy force west of La Ferté-sous-Jouarre. At 6 o’clock in the morning the 2nd Cavalry Corps, also, had reported “no enemy force whatever at Coulommiers”; and three hours later it had seen only a few English troops south of Coulommiers, and at 12:30 p.m., only small forces of cavalry and artillery at and facing Coulommiers to the west.

On the other hand, it appeared from reports received with, regard to enemy forces facing us on the Ourcq, that railway movements and detrainments were in progress at Le Plessis-Belleville. Assemblies of troops at Crépy en Valois as well as between Dammartin and Nanteuil le Haudouin, which were announced by our airmen, permitted the conclusion that the enemy was considerably reenforcing his north wing. It could be assumed with certainty that Joffre, in the decisive battle which he was seeking, was devoting his main effort to the envelopment of our right wing.

If the First Army were to be thrown back upon the eastern bank of the Ourcq, toward which at the time its columns and trains were still crowding together, there would inevitably result the greatest danger not only to the First Armybut to all the German armies. The fate of the whole battle of the Marne was at stake.

The army command considered once more whether the task of the army could be accomplished defensively. A defensive position behind the Ourcq could only make our situation worse; compressed in the angle between the Ourcq and the Marne, the army would have fallen into an unfavorable tactical situation without escaping envelopment. To draw the army back in the midst of combat, say with the left wing upon Chateau-Thierry, was extremely risky. After a little while, the army would have found itself confronted again with the samesituation. With the cooperation of the English army henceforth assured, the enemy was able to initiate his enveloping movement more effectively.

Nothing but the offensive offered a possible solution. The enemy had to be thrown back. It was the best way of protecting the flank. But to that end it was necessary to call up the III and IX Corps. This was the sense of the decision reached by General von Kluck.

To be sure, the gap which already existed between the First and Second Armies was thus increased and the flank of the Second Army, which the First Army was charged with protecting endangered. We were going on the assumption, however, that the English, after their repeated defeats, their heavy losses and their continued retreat since the battle of Mons, would hardly be in a position to pass at once to a vigorous offensive. It appeared to us to be possible to hold them, at the latest, on the Marne until the decision could be obtained on the Ourcq. If the Second Army continued, as we expected, to wheel to the right and to make progress between the Seine and the Marne in the westerly direction, the gap was sure to become narrower. The course of the fighting up to the evening of September 6, both as regards the Second Army and the III and IX Corps had given no cause for concern.

On September 6 the Second Army had ordered that the fighting be resumed at daybreak of the 7th. This order had been transmitted to the III and IX Corps with the following supplement: "By agreement with the, First Army, the III and IX Corps come provisionally under my command. I prescribe: the IX Corps will resume the attack at daybreak; the III Corps will assure protection of the right flank of the Second Army." But meanwhile, during the night of September 6-7, the III and IX Corps had received orders from the First Army to fall back behind the Petit Morin to the right wing of the Second Army. The two corps began this movement on September 7 at dawn without the least interference from the enemy. The orders which had been issued to them by the Second Army with a view to the attack where thus countermanded. They continued, however, by reason of their arrangement in echelon, to assure protection of the right flank of the Second Army.

But at 11 a.m., the First Army had been obliged to send the following radiogram to the Second Army: "Intervention of III and IX Corps on Ourcq urgently needed. Enemy being greatly reenforced. Request that corps be sent in direction of La Ferté Milon and Crouy."

This was another considerable disarrangement in the plans of the Second Army. The command acceded, however, to our request, although its army was engaged in hard fighting and its flank menaced. The III Corps was started off in the direction of Charly, and the IX Corps was drawn back on September 7as far as the vicinity of Chezy (south of Chateau-Thierry).

At 1:15 p.m., orders were despatched from Vendrest to the two corps to push as far as possible in the course of the day in the direction of La Ferté Milon – Crouy so as to be able to come into action not later than the 8th with the right wing of the army. The IX Corps remained in position at Chezy; the III Corps reached the vicinity of Charly – La Ferté-sous-Jouarre. The last troops arrived after midnight; a large part of them had covered up to 60kilometers during the day.

In the afternoon Captain von Schtitz of the staff of the First Army, who had been sent to the left wing of the fighting front, attached to a communication regarding the tactical situation an air report which caused us great concern. According to this report, a column marching toward the southwest had passed through Villers-Cotterets without firing on our aviators flying at a height of 2500 feet. "The aviator is convinced that they were German troops." Now we were expecting the Lepel brigade of the IV Reserve Corps, which was coming up from Brussels by way of Péronne.

The communications inspectorate informed us from Chauny that this brigade had arrived to the south of Péronne with five battalions and that one-battalion was already probably at Noyon. It could not, then, have passed through Villers-Cotterets during the day. On the other hand, the communications inspectorate, at the request of the army, had assembled in its zone a number of available troops and had started them off, under the command of Colonel von der Schulenburg, from Chauny bound for Villers-Cotterets. The reports of the communications inspectorate regarding this matter arrived at Vendrest at 4:45 p.m. So it might have been these troops which the aviators had seen.

In the course of September 7 the II Cavalry Corps also effectually retarded the English advance. At 12:15 p.m. it received a radiogram sent from Vendrest by the First Army: "Our left wing at Varreddes, north of Meaux, is seriously menaced by the enemy artillery from direction of Meaux. Flanking attack by artillery from direction of Trilport urgently needed as soon as possible." According to the report of Captain von Schütz, sent into this region by the army command, the 3rd Division was engaged in heavy fighting at Varreddes and still suffered under artillery fire from the direction of Meaux. We erroneously believed that the English had entered into line in that region and we considered it urgent to send reenforcements. The army command now had at its disposal only the units charged with assuring its own protection at Vendrest: one battalion and one section of machine gunners, one section of artillery. These, with the exception of one company, were pushed forward upon Lizy. Unfortunately, as a result of the radiogram despatched at 12:15, the whole 9th Cavalry Division also advanced upon Trilport. According to its war journal, it was unable to pass over to the north bank because of the enemy's heavy artillery. And the width of the valley did not permit it to come into action with its artillery from the left bank. It appears that it still made an effort to come into action at Germigny, and then remained to the southeast of Lizy. As the 4th Cavalry Division occupied a position on the right wing of the army, the 2nd Cavalry Division finally found itself alone before the English. In the evening it passed over to the north bank of the Marne at La Ferté-sous-Jouarre.

After the departure of the III and IX Corps, the I Cavalry Corps fell back behind the lower Petit Morin.

On the evening of September 7 the situation of the First Army was regarded at Vendrest as more unfavorable than it was in reality. The accounts we had received of 'the conditions of the struggle in the vicinity of Varreddes caused us great uneasiness. I remember distinctly that we were expecting at any moment to see the English arrive in the elbow of the Marne, at Trilport, in the back of the 3rd Division. The success of Sixt von Armin's group is not mentioned in the army order of the evening, which merely states that the army held firm on the line: Antilly – Puisieux – Varreddes. I recall the strong impression produced by the report of the chief of staff of the IV Corps when he arrived at Army Headquarters at Vendrest during the night of 7-8th. The war journal of the IV Corps states that doubts were expressed at headquarters as to whether it would be possible to hold out. The losses were heavy, the enemy artillery seemed to be superior. The troops were exhausted. The picture presented by the chief of staff was far from encouraging. But the commanding general of the corps had issued orders to stand firm, regardless of cost, and await the arrival of the III and IX Corps. The army command could only approve that decision. In the evening large bivouacs were reported in the vicinity of Nanteuil-le-Haudouin, Silly le Long, St. Soupplets and westward. He awaited the morrow anxiously. When would the English appear on the Marne?

Today we know that, as frequently happens in war, the anxiety was still greater on the side of the enemy.

The army order which was issued from Vendrest at 9:15 p.m. prescribed that the left wing at Varreddes be drawn back during the night in case of need into a more favorable position. Furthermore, considering our view of the situation, the task of the army during the day of the 8th was, because of the enemy reenforcements which had arrived, to hold out on its positions until the attack could be released on the right wing after the arrival of the III and IX Corps. The grouping under General von Linsingen was to be adhered to until that time. Striking camp at 2 o'clock in the morning, the IX Corps was to advance by way of Chateau-Thierry upon La Ferté Milon, the III Corps from Montreuil aux Lions and La Ferté-sous-Jouarre upon Mareuil and Crouy. So that on both sides during the night new troops advanced in all haste toward the vicinity of Betz, some by rail and in automobiles, the others by forced marches, for the purpose of surrounding the enemy wing.

At 5 p.m. the following report was addressed to the High Command: "As result of intervention of IV Corps on right wing, fighting of II Corps and IV Reserve Corps has progressed toward line: east of Nanteuil – Meaux. III and IX Corps coming up. Attack will be continued tomorrow with prospects of success. II Cavalry Corps covering toward Meaux – Coulommiers, where no important enemy force has moved forward. Enemy has employed much heavy artillery, apparently from Paris. Opponent: English forces and apparently French V and VII Corps."

On September 7, after the departure of the III and IX Corps, the Second Army inserted the 13th Division on its right wing on a vast front extending from Fontenelle to Montmirail. The division was not attacked on the 7th. Farther left, the right wing of the Second Army was unable to continue its progress in the course of the day, and thc same is true of the center on the marshes of St. Gond. Following a French counterattack, General von Bülow drew his reserve, the 14th Division, stationed north of Montmirial, from his highly menaced right wing, and pushed it forward upon Champaubert, where it was inserted in a gap existing in the center of his front. The command of the VII Corps also remained in that neighborhood up to the 8th. On the left wing, the enemy was thrown back at Fère Champenoise – Sommesous, in conjunction with the right wing of the Third Army. The I Cavalry Corps was charged with holding the enemy on the Petit Morin.

On September 7 the commander of the Third Army recognized that the French offensive was directed essentially against his right wing on Lenharree and against his left wing on Sompuis – Vitry le Francois, while in front of his center, facing Sommesous, the principal force was only one division of cavalry. General von Hausen considered that there was no longer any reason for fearing a breakthrough at the rather thin center of the Third Army. On its left wing, this army held firm against powerful French attacks, while on its right wing the course of the fighting was favorable, as already stated. On receipt of the communication stating that the German right wing (First and Second Armies) was heavily attacked and that it was menaced in its flank by troops coming up from Paris, General von Hausen reached the absolutely correct decision to attack all the more vigorously on the 8th, starting from the German center, and regulated his attack for that day in conjunction with the two armies on his flanks. It might have been considered whether the Third Army, on its part, should not have attempted to break through in the direction of Mailly by penetrating the gap which was known to exist in the French front, instead of spreading outto the right and left. Unfortunately, the Third Army was quite weak. It is possible that such was the reason which led to the adoption of a more wary attitude.

The fighting of the Fourth Army on the Marne-Rhine canal continued during the following days of the Battle of the Marne without decisive results.

The Fifth Army was unsuccessful in making any considerable progress on the days of September 7 and 8.

September 8

The intentions of the command of the German First Army for the conduct of the battle are clear from written instructions remitted to Captain von Schütz, the army's liaison officer with General von Linsingen. It would have been highly desirable to attain a decision as quickly as possible on the Ourcq before the English appeared on the Marne and menaced our communications with the Second Army. On the other hand, it had to be seen to that the reenforcement arriving should not be hurled into the battle by handfuls but should produce a combined effect. The envelopment of the enemy wing was therefore to be delayed if possible until September 9 and then carried out with the maximum of forces, with the aid of the III and IX Corps, after they had completed their concentration. The preliminary condition for that was that the center and left wing should stand firm throughout the day.

The envelopment sought was not an easy matter. It could not be effected, as required by theory, with the aid of army units coming up from a distance in a favorable direction. The troops charged with the envelopment were to be brought from the left wing to the right wing by filing past in rear of the entire front, at the cost of the most strenuous marching efforts, and it was only then that they could wheel for the purpose of executing the envelopment. That was a. very difficult movement, which was also very much hampered by regard for the columns of ammunition and the trains behind the front. The two corps to which this task was confided were obliged first to getaway from the enemy. It was to be feared that in the course of their march behind the front a part of their elements would be turned aside by calls for aid.

The III and IX Corps were to strike camp at 2 o'clock in the morning. But the army order failed to reach them early enough. The IX Corps aroused its divisions at 2:10 after the arrival of the order, in spite of their highly exhausted condition, and, starting from the vicinity of Chezy, continued its movement. The III Corps also had been unable to set out from Charly and westward until an early hour of the morning.

At 6:45 a.m. there was received from the Ourcq front a report of Captain von Schütz stating that a powerful French attempt to break through in the center, in the vicinity of Trocy, appeared imminent and that the IV Corps was not yet strongly attacked for the moment: "Aid by way of Lizy urgently needed."[15] In such a case Napoleon would let the troops of his front line be completely spent before bringing his reserves into action. Here the situation was different: "Since noon of September 5 the infantry and field artillery of the IV Reserve Corps had fought almost uninterruptedly against an enemy considerably superior in numbers, almost the whole of those forces being deployed in the first line, without reserves, throughout the day under the burning sun, without water and without food, waiting in vain to be relieved and reenforced."[16] If the enemy broke through our front, the whole movement of the III and IX Corps which was being effected in the rear would be upset and the envelopment of the enemy front would become impossible. At 7 o'clock in the morning, the army command

---

[15] See Sketch 16.

[16] Communication by General von Gronau.

ordered the commander of the III Corps to have his left column (5th Division) oblique at once in several columns, with the artillery in front, upon Trocy. General von Linsingen provisionally brought up the 9th Cavalry Division behind the menaced part of the front, toward the locality east of Le Plessis Placy.

The enemy break-through at Trocy failed to come off. The 22nd Reserve Division whose fighting strength was very much weakened, was attacked. The village of Trocy, taken under the powerful and concentrated fire of the enemy artillery, became the prey of flames. From the rear the situation appeared more dangerous than it really was. The troops evacuated the locality, but the lines of sharpshooters in front of the village held out.[17] The 5th Division was able to concentrate in rear and remain for the most part available. The army command regretted having turned it aside from its march objective, but on the following day had it on. hand when the advance of the English on the Marne made it necessary to reenforce the troops in that region.

After the 5th Division had been excluded from the troops assigned to the projected envelopment, the IX Corps received orders at 9:15 a.m. to march upon La Ferté Milon and Mareuil, the 6th Division upon Crouy. The reports received in the course of September 7 regarding the advance of the English beyond the Grand Morin led the First Army. Command on the 8th to create a reserve to support theindependent cavalry charged with the defense of the Marne. It therefore ordered the IX Corps to leave at its disposition at Montreuil aux Lions (northeast of La Ferté-sous-Jouarre) an infantry regiment and an artillery group belonging to its left column. But the commanding general of the corps was further advised not to let himself be diverted on any account from his advance upon La Ferté Milon by the enemy marching upon Coulommiers, for the decision was to be obtained on the right wing.

A little later, contrary instructions had to be issued to the IX Corps. At 10:10 a.m. , aviators announced that enemy columns were marching from Crecy upon La Haute Maison, from Boissyle

[17] Communication by General von Gronau.

Chatel upon Doue, and from La Ferté Gaucher upon Rebais. The report was accurate and timely. The English army appeared now to be acting in earnest and speeding up its movement. The enemy had evidently noticed the retirement of the III and IX Corps. It appeared doubtful that the cavalry alone would suffice to defend the Marne until the decision had come on the Ourcq. At 11:20 a.m., Generalvon Kluck reluctantly decided to order the IX Corps to leave two brigades of infantry and two regiments of field artillery for the defense of the Marne line between La Ferté-sous-Jouarre and Nogent l'Artaud. To this end, the army reserve (one infantry regiment and one artillery group), established at Montreuil aux Lions was put back at the disposal of the corps. The II Cavalry Corps was assigned the task of defending the Marne at La Ferté-sous-Jouarre and westward. The Marne line was to be held at all cost and the bridges destroyed.

This order reached the commander of the corps at 1 p.m., during the march. Contrary to the army order, he decided, due to the depletion of his effectives, to leave in the rear only one infantry regiment and one regiment of field artillery, which were to join hands at Montreuil aux Lions with the army reserve, with which they formed the Kraewel brigade. He thought that otherwise he would not be in a condition to obtain the decision on the right wing so insistently urged upon him. The result of this decision arrived at independently by General von Quast, was that, on September 9, he was able to lead his splendid corps to victory, while the army commander was in a position to fill the deficit on the Marne by means of the 5th Division.

In the course of the day the Kraewel brigade was placed under the command of General von der Marwitz, commander of the II Cavalry Corps, under whom now devolved the whole defense of the Marne. He was also, if possible, to take command of the adjoining 5th Cavalry Division, which belonged to the I Cavalry Corps. In addition to his four battalions of chasseurs, he also had at his disposal a detachment of the 3rd Division at Mary.

It is extremely regrettable that a single command was not established on the Marne in the gap which existed between the First and Second Armies. All the efforts of the two cavalry corps to keep in liaison could not make up for that lack. On the morning of September 8 General von der Marwitz had established the 2nd Cavalry Division at Ussy (west of La Ferté-sous-Jouarre), while General von Thumb with one brigade of cavalry and four battalions of chasseurs was to cover south of the Marne, facing the enemy forces reported at Coulommiers and Pierre Levee. General von Thumb fell back later before the enemy advance to the heights north of La Ferté-sous-Jouarre. Toward 2 p.m. this division received orders to set out at once by way ofLizy.

In the course of the forenoon an enemy cavalry division was beaten back on the Marne. The II Cavalry Corps in conjunction with the battalions of chasseurs then defended this river at La Ferté-sous-Jouarre.

The I Cavalry Corps had attempted to stop the enemy on the Petit Morin in the locality of St. Cyr – Verdelot in order to cover the right wing of the Second Army which had been drawn back on September 7th from Montmirail upon Fontennelle. This corps repulsed a strong cavalry force at St. Cyr, but the latter broke through later at Verdelot – Sablonnieres. The I Cavalry Corps fell back with the Guard Cavalry Division upon Condé-en-Brie, while the 5th Cavalry Division withdrew by way of Chateau-Thierry to the north bank of the Marne.

In the course of the day the enemy forces at Coulommiers advanced upon La Ferté-sous-Jouarre and by way of Rebais upon Orly. At 8:20 p.m. the II Cavalry Corpstransmitted the following report: "Marne still being held in spite of powerful enemy force and violent artillery fire. Schmettow (9th Cavalry Division) is just coming in." The II Cavalry Corps assumed command of the Kraewel brigade.

This latter arrived at Montreuil aux Lions at nightfall of the 8th. Its commander had been assigned the task of holding at any cost the line of the Marne between La Ferté-sous-Jouaree and Nogent l'Artaud.[18] He hesitated to disperse his forces atnightby sending detachments to the different crossing points. The pioneer company which had been promised him failed to arrive. So he kept his troops concentrated during the night at Montreuil aux Lions.

---

[18] See page 248.

The first Army held firm on the 8th all along its front extending from Antilly up to a point in front of Trocy, Passing through Acy en Multien, the eastern edge of Vincy Manoeuvre and the region west of Le Plessis Placy. The 3rd Division on the left wing was drawn back upon Gue a Tresmes – Congis. The bridge at Germigny was destroyed. The left wing now found itself relieved of the danger which constantly menaced its flank, and was protected against envelopment. As for the 5th Division, which byarmy order had been turned aside upon Lizy by way of Cocherel, only a few of its units had to be used; the larger part of its forces were established east of Le Plessis Placy. The army command forbade its employment in executing a partial attack.

From the aviation reports received, it appeared that during the forenoon enemy troops had advanced from the west upon Macquelines, from Boissy and Fresnoy[19] toward the northeast, and that others had passed through Nanteuil le Haudouin. At 10:45 they seemed to be assembling, with a strength of approximately one division, at Levignen. The menace of an envelopment existed in that vicinity. It would have been desirable that the IX Corps, to which the 6th Division had been subordinated, had still been able to come into action during the day on the right wing. But it was not until evening that the 6th Division, which had set out at 6 a.m. from Charly, arrived very much fatigued at Thuryen Valois – Cuvergnon, too late to enter into action. As for the IX Corps, its 18th Division advanced during the night as far as Ivors, and its 17th Division, marching in the direction of Vaumoisse, as far as the region northwest of LaFerté Milon.

One has to marvel atthis marching performance of the III and IX Corps. Both corps had been engaged in hard fighting throughout the day of September 6. On the 7th, the IX Corps had struck camp at daybreak and, marching until midnight, had attained the vicinity of Chezy, covering approximately 37 miles. On the 8th it had been aroused at 2:10 in the morning and had marched throughout the day with only one brief pause, up to an advanced hour of the night, again covering 37 miles. On the morning of the 9th, the IX Corps

[19] Separate towns, shown on map as one.

and the 6th Division attacked. Such an unheard-of performance was possible only by reason of detailed marching instructions, the arrangement of timely halts, the creation of depots of food and water along the route, the transportation of the bags on all the available vehicles including the cannons, and finally of the utilization of the automobile columns temporarily available. The morale of the troops remained excellent throughout the march, and eventheir humorheld up well. The marchingobjective was attained without any considerable loss from straggling.[20] Colonel Auer von Herrenkirchen, at that time senior staff officer of the IX Corps, says on this point: "The sight of our proud troops will remain in my memory always. It was a gripping experience to see those thinned ranks dragging painfully along and yet displaying the greatest willingness." On the following morning those troops were going to swing into action and throw the enemy left wing far back upon Nanteuil le Haudouin!

In the course of the afternoon the staff of the First Armymoved from Vendrestto La Ferté Milon, on the decisive wing. The IX Corps had not yetarrived, the 4th Cavalry Division was in the vicinity of Thury en Valois. When wearrived in the afternoon in the neighborhood of La Ferté Milon, we collided with French cavalry. It was the 5th Cavalry Division of the Sordet corps which was executing a raid upon the rear of the First Army. The staff was obliged to prepare for a fight on foot, and it was only by the narrowest margin that it escaped capture. We were unable to get back to our headquarters until late in the evening, after the arrival of the head of thecolumn of the 17th Division. In the darkness, the men, exhausted and covered with dust, dragged along painfully through the village. The following morning at 3 o'clock they were again advancing to battle.

According to the army order issued in the evening at La Ferté Milon for the day of the 9th, the decision was to be obtained that day, starting from the region north of Cuvergnon, by the enveloping attack of the IX Corps, the 6th Division, and the 4th Cavalry Division, which were placed under the command of

[20] Communication by General von Kluge.

General von Quast. The Lepel brigade of the IV Reserve Corps which had come by way of Compiegne as far as Verberie, was ordered to advance upon the rear of the enemy by way of Rully – Baron. The 10th landwehr brigade, made available by the communications inspectorate and which had advanced as far as Ribecourt (southwest of Noyon), was to push its landwehr squadron and its battery forward upon the Lepel brigade and rapidly follow this brigade with the remainder of its units. Two battalions which the communications inspectorate had also started off under command of Colonel von der Schulenburg had already arrived on the right wing of the 6th Division. The last available man had thus been brought up for the decision, and the right wing had been assigned a direction which assured a complete envelopment. Although at Chauny the communications inspectorate was in a very uncertain situation, menaced on its flank and rear and very much impeded in its relations with the army by the French cavalry in the forest of Villers-Cotterets,[21] General von Bertrab, inspector of communications, and his chief of staff, Lt. Col. von Müller, did not hesitate to send to the front all the troops which they had at hand.

The Sixt von Armin group (16th Brigade, 7th and 4th Divisions) was to join in the attack of the Quast group in so far as circumstances would permit. The left wing, under General von Linsingen – namely, the von Lochow group (section of the 7th Reserve Division with the other attacked units), the von Gronau group (section of the 22nd Reserve Division), the von Trossel group (section of the 3rd Division) – was to hold its positions.

At La Ferté Milon, still in the course of the evening, we listened in on a radiogram from the Third Army to the Second: "Fighting here going on well. Heights south of Sommesous carried." We also learned that Maubeuge had capitulated. For our part, we were convinced of having acquired on the Ourcq superiority over the enemy. , The victory seemed to us assured for September 9. The enormous tension we had experienced was beginning to relax in the expectation of the imminent decision.

---

[21] See page 227.

On the right wing of the Second Army, the 13th Division held firm in its extended position against all attacks. When the enemy succeeded, under cover of darkness, in penetrating its front at one point, it fell back, at an advanced hour of the evening and in perfect order, upon Montmirail – Artonges. As the 26th Brigade had remained, with an artillery group before Maubeuge, this division comprised but six battalions and three groups. For this reason General von Bülow, in the night of the 8th-9th, drew his right wing back upon the line: Margny – Le Thoult. The First Army having recalled its III and IX Corps, the Second Army having brought up its reserve (14th Division) from its right wing toward its center, and the I Cavalry Corps having fallen back toward Condé-en-Brie, a menacing gap of 20 miles (air line) was opened between the First and Second Armies.

Whether the drawing back of the right wing Upon Margny was the proper procedure must remain an open question. The local irruption of the enemy which was announce4 as having occured at the 13th Division proved insignificant. The division had put up a valiant defense on the 8th, was by no means beaten, but in perfect order and in the best of spirits.

The center was unable to make any marked progress on the marshes of St. Gond. On the other hand, a great success was obtained to the east of this region. Here the left wing of the Second Army and the right wing of the Third threw the enemy back beyond Fère Champenoise – Sommesous on the Maurienne sector between Corroy and Semoine. The right wing of Foch's army was thoroughly beaten; at Mailly the gap seemed open for a breakthrough in the enemy front. A great victory was in prospect.

The left wing of the 3rd Army came up against powerful forces and made no marked progress southwest of Vitry le Francois. The 24th Reserve Division arrived September 8behind its right flank. The army commander believed therefore that he could look forward with full confidence to the continuation of the offensive of the 9th for the purpose of supporting the Second Army, which was engaged in heavy fighting, by a vigorous action of his right flank in the southwesterly direction upon Sezanne.

Lt. Col. Hentsch, of the General Headquarters, who had been sent by General von Moltke to the different armies and who was at the headquarters of the Third Army that evening, was able to send from that point the following report to the High Command: "Situation and view of the Third Army entirely favorable."

In so far as can be determined from the available French accounts, (Hanotaux and Palat have not yet reached that point), on September 8, Maunoury wished to attack his adversary by surrounding him from the north. To that end he had at his disposal on the left wing, in addition to the VII Corps and the 61st Reserve Division, the 7th Division just arrived. Confronted with the German right wing, which was reenforced by the IV Corps, Maunoury could obtain no success whatever. Nor was an attack of the 45th Division on the right wing in the direction of Etrepilly attended by any result. Sordet's cavalry corps on the extreme left clung to the side of the infantry, which was now put under the command of General Bridoux.

"When, toward 8 o'clock in the evening, firing ceased on both sides, General Maunoury realized that it was going to be difficult to throw his powerful adversary back beyond the Ourcq and to follow him there. He consequently gave orders to organize a supporting position on the line: Monthyon – St. Soupplets – Le Plessis Belleville, to which end the 62nd Reserve Division was to be employed."[22] Gallieni wished to send him this division, from the vicinity of Dammartin, by automobiles. General Mangin also confirms the statement that a supporting position was to be organized the 8th.[23] Gallieni proceeded in the course of the day to Maunoury's headquarters at St. Soupplets: "When the latter expressed to him his well-founded fear of being surrounded himself, Gallieni endeavored to calm him and asked him, in case he was forced to retreat, to maneuver in such a way as to keep the enemy facing west so as to facilitate the advance of the English."[24] To leave nothing possible undone, Gallieni that night sent a detachment of zouaves in automobiles to Creil and Senlis to harass

---

[22] Canonge, loc. cit.

[23] Loc. cit.

[24] Canonge, loc. cit.

the German communications. But he could not ward off the inevitable.

"In the night of the 8-9th Maunoury reported to the commander-in-chief regarding the terrible situation in which he found himself. He declared that his troops, exhausted and very much depleted, would hardly be in a condition to continue the fighting. Though recognizing the truth of these statements, Joffre gave orders to hold on to till the last man."[25]

On the English side also, it is confirmed that Maunoury's situation was critical on September 8. It is stated that he was hard pressed all along his front and menaced with envelopment on his left wing, that the Germans had taken Betz and pushed forward upon Nanteuil le Haudouin, and finally that a part of the troops of the Sixth Army, in particular the VII Corps, was exhausted. Joffre wrote to Maunoury the following day, the 9th, a letter which is characteristic of the situation on the 8th: "I have been kept informed hour by hour of the stubborn combats waged the last three days by the army under your command and of the superhuman efforts imposed upon your troops. By keeping a large part of the German forces engaged on the Ourcq front you have obtained an immense advantage which permits the operations of the allied armies to unfold in the manner which I desire."

As regards the English army, its I Corps, on the morning of the 8th, occupied a position at Chailly and Jouy sur Morin, its II Corps one at Aulnoy, its III Corps one at Haute Maison. According to his own statements, the English commander in chief believed, as regards the situation, that. almost the whole German First Army had turned against Maunoury. The French Fifth Army, moreover, had met with violent resistance. Marshal French considered that he could most effectually relieve the Sixth Army by advancing rapidly beyond the Petit Morin and the Marne, in the rear of the First Army, and at the same time maintaining connection with the French Fifth Army. He assumed that in this direction he would probably find in front of him nothing but German cavalry supported by a strong artillery force and detachments of infantry.

---

[25] Fabreguettes, *Les batailles de la Marne*, page 61.

As usual, however, he displayed his hesitancy, for, as he says himself, he had known the German cavalry from the time of his trip to Germany in 1911 and respected it accordingly. He declares that it was highly experienced in rear-guard fighting, that it was equipped with numerous machine guns and a great number of chasseur battalions, and that accordingly the passage of the Marne between Changis and La Ferté-sous-Jouarre was destined to be difficult and that a strong detachment of heavy artillery was reported at Varreddes. Fortunately for us, the English commander-in-chief was not a Blücher.

The English army advanced toward the Petit Morin, the I Corps upon La Trétoire, the II Corps upon Doue, the III Corps upon La Ferté-sous-Jouarre – Changis. According to the French account, aviators announced at 1p.m. the general retirement of the Germans toward the north and northwest, under the protection of rear guards established on the Petit Morin, and from that time on the advance was more rapid. On the Petit Morin, at Orly and St. Cyr, the I and II Corps met with violent resistance from the German independent cavalry, but still arrived before night as far as Hondevillers – Boitron – Bussieres. The III Corps did not succeed in crossing the Marne at La Ferté-sous-Jouarre. The bridge over the Marne at that point was destroyed, while, according to the English accounts, the others were intact. The French 8th Division pushed forward by way of Pierre Levee – Villemareuil, but was called back to the Ourcq by Maunoury on the 9th. Its despatch to the south of the Marne had been quite useless.

The French Fifth Army (I, III, and XVIII Corps and Valabregue's reserve divisions) advanced that day, according to the French account, as far as the region: Vauchamps – Marchais, hence to the other side of Montmirail. On the right wing the X Corps supported the Ninth Army by moving forward in the direction of Le Thoult.

On September 8 the Ninth Army unquestionably suffered a defeat on its right wing. Foch had, to be sure, pronounced the situation "excellent" and had wished to take the offensive. But his right wing (XI Corps) at Fère Champenoise was thrown back behind the Maurienne. The army headquarters at Pleurs was endangered and had to be moved in haste to Plancy. The right wing was completely battered in. The IX Corps behind the marshes of St. Gond, was menaced in its rear.

"It can reasonably be maintained that rarely has an army found itself in such a critical situation. What would have happened if the Germans had pushed resolutely in the direction of St. Loup?"[26]

Civrieux also declares that the situation on the right wing was extremely serious in the afternoon.[27] The danger existed that on the 9th the Germans would drive the whole Ninth Army toward the west and break through.

At the end of the day the Moroccan division stood at Mondement – Allemant, the IX Corps from this point to Connantre, the XI Corps and the 18th Division to the south of the Maurienne sector from Gourgancon to Semoine. The 42nd Division on the left wing was drawn back from the front during the night.

As regards the Fourth Army, no important change occurred in the situation on September 8.

The Third Army, strongly attacked on its front, found itself menaced in the rear when the pressure of the German V Corps, which had remained on the right bank of the Meuse, increased against the Hauts de Meuse and the bombardment of the fort of Troyon began. Sarrail nevertheless held fast to his connection with Verdun and accepted his share of the enormous danger incurred by his army if the battle of the Marne was lost.

September 9

The German First Army, which had been subjected to a flank attack on September 5, was ready on the morning of the 9th to attack the enemy in flank and rear. As for the English, we hoped to hold them. It was only the situation of the right wing of the Second Army which caused us any concern. Everything hinged on whether

---

[26] Canonge, loc. cit. , page 41.

[27] *Revue militaire generale*, February, 1920.

we could hold the enemy there until the expected victory of the First Army, on the one hand, and the great successes of the left wing of the Second Army and of the Third Army, on the other, had definitely changed in our favor the situation of the whole German right wing.

The staff of the First Army was moved to Mareuil at 8:30 in the morning, but most of the staff officers were on the way toward the most important points of the field of battle so as to keep the army command in constant touch with the situation.

The first reports soon arrived. The 5th Division was still at the disposition of the General von Linsingen southeast of Le Plessis Placy. At 8:15 the Lepel brigade had reached the heights between Rully and Baron without encountering the enemy. It was followed by the 10th landwehr brigade. The attack on the rear of the enemy was beginning.[28]

From the right wing, the staff officer of the First Army, who had been sent to General von Quast, at 10:15 reported that the order for the attack of the north group (IX Corps and 6th Division) had been issued and that General Sixt von Armin had been invited to take part. The right wing of the IX Corps (17th Division) pushed forward past Gondreville to the south of Rouville; the left wing (18th Division) through Ivors upon Boissy – Fresnoy; the 6th Division was later to join in the attack by setting out from the line: Villers Les Potees[29] – Antilly and advancing upon Betz – Villers St. Genest. The officer also stated that enemycavalry had advanced from Levignen upon Crépy en Valois, that the edge of the forest on both sides of Levignen was occupied, that a division was marching presumably from Villers St. Genest toward the north, and finally that the 4th Cavalry Division was marching upon Freigneux (north of Crépy en Valois).

So the battle was hastening toward the decision. After enormous efforts the troops of the right wing were moving forward to execute the enveloping attack. General von Voss, staff officer of

---

[28] See Sketch 17.

[29] Not on map; 4 km. E. of Betz.

the 17th Division at the time, says with reference to the march of this division, which we had seen just a few hours before entering La Ferté Milon at night in a state of complete exhaustion: "I shall never forget the effect produced on our gallant division by the news that we were marching again to meet the enemy. The weary-faced braced up, all fatigue was forgotten; the attack took place as if it had been on the drill ground. The advance of General von Lepel by way of Baron was known and communicated to the troops. We could distinctly see the artillery battle in which the divisions on our left were engaged. The conviction arose that a great success was under way."

From the Marne we received numerous reports. As early as 7:35 in the morning we had been advised by the Second Army that it had drawn its right wing back upon Margny – Le Thoult. Thus the English had a clear path and were no longer troubled by the Second Army in their march toward the Marne. We learned also that the Guard Cavalry Division had fallen back upon Condé-En-Brie and that the 5th Cavalry Division had been thrown back toward the region north of the Marne and had retired as far as Marigny en Orxois. It thus came into the radius of action of the II Cavalry Corps. At 9:15 the latter had reported that all was still quiet before its front. At 10:28 we listened in on a radiogram from the Guard Cavalry Division to the Second Army, stating that strong infantry and artillery elements had crossed the Marne bridge at Charly. A report of the II Cavalry Corps, despatched at 10:50 a.m. and arrived at 11:10, said that a strong infantry force was marching by way of Charly – Nanteuil. But the continuation of the report was interrupted by the radio station with the explanation: "I must get away quick."

The situation on the Marne appeared, then, to be growing menacing. The right wing of the Second Army having fallen back and the English having crossed the Marne, the situation of our left wing on the Ourcq to the north of Congis was becoming untenable. Behind this whole wing there were only two substantial bridges over the Ourcq at Lizy and Crouy. A retreat behind the deeply-indented Ourcq could become fatal if it was not undertaken until the last moment and under pressure of the enemy. Accordingly the left wing had to be drawn back at the opportune moment. But the attack of the right wing was to be continued only the more vigorously. Against the English too, relief was to be afforded by an attack.[30]

At 11:30 General von Kluck ordered General von Linsingen to draw the left wing back behind the Ourcq and to direct the 5th Division upon Dhuisy for the purpose of attacking the English. Sixt von Armin's group was to cover the movement by attacking in the direction of Villers St. Genest – Acy en Multien the Quast group was to "cooperate by a thrust in the direction of Nanteuil." This latter expression was not definite. The sense of the order was that the attack of the center and right wing was to be continued. That was the best way of covering the movement of von Linsingen's group.

From the war files there can be no doubt that this order was first transmitted provisionally to the II Corps in a different form, by telephone. According to the first form, Sixt von Armin's group also should have fallen back be hind the sector: Antilly – Mareuil, "the left wing in direction of Crouy with flank cover via Coulombs in direction La Ferté Milon – Neuilly St. Frond." This form is not clear in itself. The communication plainly rests on a misunderstanding either on the part of the army officer charged with transmitting the order or on the part of the officer of the II Corps who received it. It is now impossible to get any further light on the question. The command of the corps forthwith presented objections by telephone. There was still time for the misunderstanding to be cleared up.

General von Linsingen ordered the left wing of the army under his command to fall back onto the line: May en Multien – Coulombs: Lochow group ("7th Reserve Division, remains of the 8th Division together with any foreign elements attached to it") upon May en Multien, left wing on the Ourcq; Gronau group ("22d Reserve Division and elements attached to it") upon Fussy; von Trossel group (3rd Division elements attached to it and detachment

---

[30] See Sketch 18.

at Mary) upon Certigny[31] – Coulombs. This order also gives an idea of the mixture of the units.

The order reached the different groups about 1 o'clock in the afternoon, and between 2 and 3 o'clock the movement began in perfect order and without the slightest molestation from the enemy. The last elements of the left wing passed the crossroads of Beauvoir au Beauval [Beauvoir] at 3:40. Captain von Schütz of the headquarters staff remained at that point a long while: "During all this time the French percussion shell and shrapnel continued to burst at the same spot as before. No enemy force was visible. When no one was left at Beauvoir, I set out by automobile for May en Multien and went up into the very high steeple of that village. To the southwest in the clear evening sky, rose the Eiffel Tower. The fire of the French artillery had almost entirely ceased. In spite of the excellent view obtained over the whole surrounding country, nothing was seen of the enemy, not even a cavalry patrol." Also farther south, no infantryman, no trooper followed the Gronau group.

The enemy force in front of our left wing was thoroughly worn out. It appears not to have had the slightest suspicion of our retirement. I have not found it mentioned in any French report.

It was not without reason that at 2 p.m., the commander of the II Corps, General von Linsingen, was able, as noted by the war journal of this corps, "to acquire the conviction that in drawing back the left wing of the army full account had been taken of the menace arising from the English and that the offensive of the right wing, which was well under way, was bound to result in a victory for the first Army."

At 12:34 p.m., Capt. Bürhmann transmitted from the right wing a report to the effect that the attack was crossing the line: southern edge of the forest west of Grondeville – Ormoy – Antilly, in the direction of Levignen – Betz, that apparently no important enemy forces were being met with, that Betz was clear of enemy troops and that there was enemy cavalry at Crépy en Valois. At 1:55 he added that the Bois du Roi seemed to have been evacuated by the

---

[31] Shown in error on General Map No. 2 as Crotigny.

enemy, that to the east of Nanteuil a rallying position appeared to be contemplated, and that according to an air report of 12:30 p.m., the Lepel brigade was engaged at Baron.

Hence the circle seemed to be closing around the enemy wing at Nanteuil le Haudouin when an unexpected intervention occurred.

Toward noon Lt. Col. Hentsch,, coming from the Second Army and acting in the name of the High Command, appeared at Mareuil. I informed him regarding the situation and told him that in order to assure the safety of the left flank we had just ordered our left wing to be moved at once to the rear because the right wing of the Second Army had fallen back upon Margny. There then took place, in the presence of Col. von Bergmann, quartermaster general of the First Army, a discussion which was decisive for the issue of the Battle of the Ourcq. Both Col. Bergmann and myself were perfectly aware of the enormous importance of that hour. After the discussion of September 9 there was not a minute to lose for issuing, on the basis of the decision arrived at, the most urgent orders. It was not until the next day that we had time to set down on paper the details of the discussion. Each word had remained deeply impressed upon our memory and was put in writing after careful reflection. I first reproduced the text of this document:

La Ferté Milon, 9/10/1914.

> Yesterday noon Lt. Col. Hentsch of the High Command appeared at the army headquarters at Mareuil and made the following communication: The situation is not favorable. The Fifth Army is blocked in front of Verdun, the Sixth and Seventh Armies in front of Nancy – Epinal. The second Army is now only "residue." Its retreat behind the Marne is irrevocable; its right wing (VII Corps) has been thrown back, not drawn back. It is therefore necessary to displace all armies at the same time: the Third Army to the north of Chalons, Fourth and Fifth Armies on its flanks upon Verdun by way, of Clermont en Argonne. The First Army must therefore also fall back, direction: Soissons – Fere-en-Tardenois, and even in the most extreme case upon Laon – La Fère. With a charcoal pencil he sketched on my map the approximate fronts to be attained by the armies. He added that a new army was to be concentrated at St.

Quentin and that a new operation might thus begin.

I observed that we were in the midst of an attack, that a retreat would be a very delicate matter, that the army was all mixed up and at a point of extreme exhaustion.

He declared that nevertheless there was now nothing else to do. He conceded that a retreat in the prescribed direction from the scene of the present fighting was not practicable, but that we could fall back straight to the rear of us, at the most upon Soissons with the left wing behind the Aisne. He emphasized that these instructions were determining and were to remain so regardless of any communications which might be made to us later, for he has full powers.

VON KUHL,
Brigadier-General and
chief of staff of the First Army.

I hereby confirm the above statements, which were made in my presence.

VON BERGMANN,
Colonel and Quartermaster-
General of the First Army.

The interview lasted a long while. I opposed in the most vigorous manner the proposition to retreat and insisted over and over again on the favorable situation of our right wing. All the possibilities of continuing the fighting up to the final victory were examined. But when it, had been made clear that the decision of the Second Army had been reached that morning, that its troops were already in full retreat in the afternoon and that that decision could no longer be recalled, the army command had to submit. Even a victory over Maunoury could not have prevented us from being encircled by superior force on our left wing and from being cutoff from the rest of the German Armies. The First Army would have been isolated.

I appeared before the commander in chief to make my report. With a heavy heart, General von Kluck was obliged to accept the order. Upon my return, Lt. Col. Hentsch departed, after being informed of the decision arrived at. Colonel von Bergmann gives the following account of the proceedings as he remembers them:

I was present from beginning to end of the discussion which took place on September 9 with Lt. Col. Hentsch in the office of General von Kuhl. Lt. Col. Hentsch recounted what he regarded as the rather unfavorable turn which events had taken on the western theater and insisted particularly on the situation of the neighboring Second Army. I recall distinctly that he depicted this situation in very gloomy colors and that his description of the very low morale of the staff of the Second Army impressed me particularly. It was evident to us that the lieutenant-colonel had formed, from the information given him at the Second Army, a completely erroneous picture of the situation of the First Army and that the much more favorable appraisal made to him by General von Kuhl surprised him exceedingly. To the serious objections presented by General von Kuhl against the retreat required of the First Army, whose right wing was engaged at the time in executing an attack which was progressing favorably – objections in which I joined, also insisting on the technical difficulties and the condition of the troops – Lt. Col. Hentsch always replied by saying that the retreat of the Second Army behind the Marne, already begun, was an irrevocable necessity. In view of this communication and the further declaration of Lt. Col. Hentsch to the effect that he had full powers to order a retreat of the army in the name of the High Command, nothing remained for General von Kuhl but to propose to the commander in chief to retreat, the more so as at that time there was no connection permitting a direct exchange of ideas with the High Command. To this end he appeared before General von Kluck to make his report, while I remained alone in the room with Lt. Col. Hentsch until General von Kuhl returned with the approval of the commander in chief.

All the officers of the staff of the first army who were charged with the operations felt the historical importance of the instructions given us by Lt. Col. Hentsch, and as early, as the afternoon of the 9th Captain von Alien suggested to me the necessity of having the two witnesses – General von. Kuhl and myself – state in writing the tenor of the negotiations which took place with the envoy of the High Command. But the great number of questions which on that day still demanded the attention of the staff up to alate hour of the night did not allow of putting this plan in execution until the following morning at 10o'clock at LaFerté Milon. The well known document reproduces textually the essential points of the statements of Lt. Col. Hentsch, statements which had made on us a profound impression and which accordingly were still quite fresh in our memory. I vouch for the accuracy of said document.

Though seeing the goal within reach of his hand, the commander-in-chief was obliged to renounce attaining it. The measures to be taken for the retreat were difficult. The army's energy, which in the rush of the offensive was still sufficient, was in danger of failing in a retreat. The units were all mixed up; the baggage, columns and trains were not prepared for a retreat and did not have the necessary start. Their movements had to be regulated solely by the staff of the army in order to avoid congestion of the roads and bridges. Behind the army was the Aisne with its wooded heights and steep slopes. It was necessary to prepare and cover its passage and to take account of the fact that the powerful enemy cavalry in our right flank might beat us to it. Everything had to be arranged in the greatest haste in order to begin the retreat the very next night. On September 5 the army stood beyond the Marne facing south; during the Battle of the Ourcq it had been facing west, then southwest; now, on September 9, it was obliged to fall back very nearly toward the north. Any specialist will realize the enormous difficulties which resulted from these changes for the movement of the troops, the baggage trains, the ammunition columns and the convoys as well as for resupplying with food and ammunition and for the sanitary measures.

During the interview with Col. Hentsch the following radiogram, the transmission of which had been delayed by motor trouble, was received from the Second Army at 1:04 p.m.: "Aviator reports advance of four long columns toward the Marne. At 9 a.m. heads of columns at Nanteuil sur Marne, Citry, Pavant, Nogent l'Artaud. Second Army initiating retreat, right wing Damery." This last point was recognized on the following day to be erroneous, following an inquiry of the First army, which had listened in on other radiograms from the Second Army. It was not Damery near Epernay that was meant, but Dormans.

At 2 p.m., the army first got in touch with the 4th Cavalry Division, which at that time stood in the vicinity of Vaumoise (east of Crépy en Valois); it was informed that the Second Army was going to fall back in the direction of Epernay, and the First Army with its left wing on Soissons. The division was ordered to start off at once in advance on the Aisne and occupy the bridges from Soissons to Attichy.

Once the army command had become clear regarding the general manner in which the retreat was to be executed, the II Cavalry Corps was informed at 3:15 p.m. that the First Army would fall back during the day upon the line: Antilly – Brumetz, then farther on in the course of the night. The corps was ordered to cover this movement, the 5th Division being placed under its command to this end.

Meanwhile the army order had been completed. General von Kluck in the afternoon directed General von Linsingen to move the left wing of the army under his command behind the sector: Montigny l'Allier – Brumetz, while the Sixt von Armin group would move behind the line: Atilly – Mareuil. The Quast group was not to push its attack farther than necessary to get away from the enemy and was then to join in the movement of the other groups.

Prior to the despatch of the army order, the various corps were given provisional information at once by telephone and through liaison officers charged with explaining to them the decision arrived at. This decision met everywhere with violent opposition, particularly at the IX Corps. Captain Bührmann of the staff of the First Army, who was then at the IX Corps, announced that the troops had absolute confidence in victory and that the morale was excellent in spite of the unexampled fatigue of the last few week sand especially of the last few days. The enemy was everywhere on the point of yielding. When the army command instructed Captain Bührmann by telephone to transmit the retreat order to the commander of the IX Corps he resolutely refused and had me called to the phone myself. I explained to him the reasons for the decision arrived at. Captain Bührmann reports as follows on what took place later at the staff of the IX Corps: "Meanwhile the army order prescribing retreat had arrived. General von Quast raised a violent protest and urged me to have the order countermanded. I again called General von Kuhl, who once more explained to me in detail the whole situation and the necessity for the retreat. During this time, the order had come to the knowledge of the divisions. As for of staff of the IX Corps told me that General von Kluge, commander of the 18th Division, refused to execute the order, which was quite incomprehensible to him, saying that the enemy was in full retreat upon Paris and that his own troops wished to exploit their victory to the limit and were in a situation to do so. He suggested calling the army command once more. His Royal Highness the grand duke of Mecklenbourg-Schwerin, who was accompanying the IX Corps, joined in this demand. The army command replied that the decision was irrevocable."

The situation on our right wing was excellent in the afternoon.

At noon the 18th Division had taken Bargny and the edge of the forest south of Levignen, then carried the heights east of Boissy Fresnoy and Villers St. Genest. Our superiority was quite evident. The fire of the enemy artillery was rather light, our losses small. Then in the afternoon arrived the order of the corps directing that no further advance be made. General von Kluge protested by telephone and stated that if the attack continued, his success was certain. At the same time he gave orders to his division to carry Boissy Fresnoy and Villers St. Genest and urged the adjoining division to cooperate with him. These localities were taken by storm without great losses, when a new order of the corps arrived forbidding further advance. Again the general protested against the order, in the conviction that if we continued to advance on September 9 we would certainly win a decisive victory over Maunoury, whose left wing was beaten and surrounded. But the order had to be executed.[32]

Meanwhile, farther to the right, the 17th Division had advanced by way of Levignen through the northern part of the Bois du Roi and was encircling the enemy. The 4th Cavalry Division was advancing by way of Crepyen Valois. Lepel's brigade, followed by the 10th Landwehr Brigade, had moved forward from Verberie through Baron – Droiselles and was arriving upon the rear of the enemy. The 6th Division was marching upon Villers St. Genest by way of Betzand wassupporting the 18th Division.

Sixt von Armin's group, also, had advanced to the attack at an early hour. Its original plan had been not to join in the attack of the Quast group until the latter had crossed the line: Levignen – Betz. But when the enemy seemed to be withdrawing forces from Villers

[32] Communication of General von Kluge.

St. Genest and pushing them toward the north, General Sixt von Armin decided to attack. His right wing was making progress through the Boris de Montrolles.

Such was the situation when the retreat had to begin. It was executed with the utmost calm.

The army order by which it was regulated reached General von Linsingen at 4 p.m., when the rearward evolution of the left wing upon the line: May en Multien – Coulombs, ordered at noon, was in course of execution. At 5:10 p.m., at Crouy, he ordered the movement continued provisionally as far as Montigny l'Allier – Brumetz.

The Sixt von Armin group was released from the enemy without any difficulty. No one followed; the enemy lost all contact.

Quast's group remained on the terrain won and did not start its retreat until the following morning.

At 8:15 p.m., the army sent from Mareuil the order to continue the movement and to push that same day with the main body up to the linc: Gondreville (southeast of Crépy en Valois) – La Ferté Milon – the Ourcq line above this point and northward. The Lcpel bridge fell back by way of Verberie. General von Kluck expressed to the troops of the First Army his profound gratitude for the devotion and the extraordinary performances accomplished by them up to that timein the course of the offensive.

The staff then moved, late in the evening, to La Ferté Milon, where it had difficulty in finding lodgings. In the course of the night it was necessary to decide on the measures which remained to be taken for regulating the communications in rear of the various corps, the movement of the columns and trains, supply of rations and ammunition and numerous other matters. Enemy cavalry detachments were seen in the afternoon in the forest of Villers Cotterets; they prevented the communications inspectorate from sending rations and ammunition to the army columns.

At the end of the day the following report was addressed to the High Command: "Right wing of the army was throwing the enemy back in the direction of Nanteuil. Center and left wing were holding their positions. II Cavalry Corps, reenforced, was holding the enemy on the Marne at and above La Ferté. Conformably to the order of the High Command, the First Army then fell back, without being pressed by the enemy, upon the line: Crépy en Valois – La Ferté Milon – Neuilly. English crossing the Marne in the section La Ferté-sous-Jouarre – Chateau-Thierry. Plan for September 10: continue the movement beyond the Aisne."

On September 9, on the Marne, the II Cavalry Corps succeeded in holding firm through the day at and below La Ferté-sous-Jouarre, where the bridge had been destroyed. East of this city, the bridges. fell intact into the hands of the enemy. There was no serious local resistance in this region. Kraewel's brigade had established itself on the 9th at Montreuil aux Lions. The I Cavalry Corps having fallen back, the passage was open to the enemy. At Montreuil aux Lions Kraewel's brigade engaged in combat in the course of the day with the enemy forces which had crossed the Marne at Saacy – Nogent l'Artaud. In the afternoon, the 5th Division, marching from Vendrest upon Dhuisy, arrived. General von der Marwitz then decided to attack with these troops and with the cavalry corps stationed near Cocherel. According to information furnished by the cavalry corps and the 5th Division the enemy was thrown back again in the afternoon. General von der Marwitz then initiated his retreat, which was not disturbed by the enemy. General von Kraewel is of the opinion that his brigade completely fulfilled its task of stopping the English.[33] He also believes that in view of the good condition of his troops and the unskillful tactical conduct of the English, his brigade would also have been able to hold them on the 10th, in conjunction with the 5th Division and our numerous cavalry.

Several air reports on the advance of the English beyond the Marne reached the First Army up until evening. At 3:30 p.m. the vicinity of Chateau-Thierry was clear of enemy troops. At La Ferté-sous-Jouarre no crossing had taken place; at Nanteuil a column crossed the Marne. North of Charly small detachments had been seen in process of formation. The bridge at Chezy was not destroyed.

On September 9, according to the orders of the headquarters staff, the Second Army was to stand on the defensive with its right

---

[33] *Militär-Wochenblatt*, 1919, no. 74

wing, drawn back upon Margny, continue to attack with its left wing, and join in this attack with its center. On the morning of the 9th, however, General von Bülow reached the decision to retreat behind the Marne, though a number of his staff officers opposed the plan. He justifies the decision in his report with the statement that it was necessary to reckon with a breakthrough of strong enemy forces between the First and Second Armies: "If the enemy advanced beyond the Marne in the rear of the First Army, the latter would run the risk of being completely surrounded and thrown back in the westerly direction. When, therefore, on the morning of September 9, the enemy crossed the Marne in numerous columns between La Ferté-sous-Jouarre and Chateau-Thierry, it was no longer doubtful here that the tactical and strategic situation made the retreat of the First Army inevitable and that the Second Army, also, had to fall back to avoid complete envelopment of its right flank."[34]

General von Bülow had become convinced that the First Army had to fall back behind the Aisne and seek to reestablish contact with the Second Army in the direction of Fismes. A new front was thus to be constituted on the Aisne. The orders for the retreat were given in the course of the forenoon and the retreat began in the afternoon.

At 2:30 p.m., the following report was sent by the Second Army to the High Command: "First Army falling back, left wing Coulombs – Gandelu. In accord with Hentsch, Second Army suspends its offensive, which was progressing slowly, and advances toward north bank of the Marne, right wing at Dormans." The statement in this report regarding the retreat of the First Army rests on a radiogram of the first army which did not reach the Second or was not heard by it until 12:30 p.m.; that is, at a time when the retreat of the Second Army was already ordered and when Lt. Col. Hentsch had already arrived at the First Army. Furthermore, in this radiogram apparently addressed to the Second Army, the reference was not to a retreat of the First Army, but only to the drawing back of its left wing, a matter which had been

---

[34] Loc. cit. , page 60.

discussed on various occasions.

On September 10, General von Bülow transmitted another report of the same tenor: "In accord with Hentsch, situation appraised here as follows: Retreat of First Army. behind Aisne necessitated by strategic and tactical situation. Second Army must support First Army north of Marne if right wing of German forces is not to be pressed in and taken progressively in flank."

Thus it appears that on the morning of the 9th General von Bülow was not accurately informed regarding the situation of the First Army. As is clear from the foregoing narrative of the events of September 9 and confirmed by the situation of the enemy, still to be examined, that the decision of the Second Army to retreat can not be justified essentially by the situation of the First Army. The English did not cross the Marne on the morning of the 9th in numerous columns between La Ferté-sous-Jouarre and Chateau-Thierry. Sketch 3 attached to the report of General von Bülow (situation at 10 a.m. of the 9th)[35] does not represent the situation accurately. On the evening of the 9th the English had by no means advanced so far forward. Besides, we were not defending the Marne with cavalry alone. And particularly, on sketch 3 [General von Bülow's report] the French and Germans stand facing each other frontally in the Battle of the Ourcq, while in reality the French left wing was completely encircled and attacked in the rear.

There can be no doubt that the situation of the First army on September 8 and 9 was considered extremely unfavorable at the staff of the Second Army. This fact is also confirmed by Capt. Bührmann, who had been sent by the First Army to the Second. It was said there that the first Army was beaten and could scarcely be used any more.

The High Command, also, had regarded the situation of the First Army as a cause for much concern. This is the explanation of the task assigned to Lt. Col. Hentsch and the manner in which he accomplished it. To be sure, the First army had fallen into a great danger, but the danger was averted. And for a time thereafter, it was thought that the First Army had suffered a defeat on the

[35] Not Sketch 3 in back of this book

Ourcq. On September 14, 1914, General von Stein, the quartermaster general, had appeared at the headquarters of the First army at Vauxaillon and, in my absence, left a letter from which it appeared that at that time the High Command was still of the opinion that the IV Reserve Corps had been beaten in front of Paris, and that the Battle of the Ourcq had taken, at least on the right wing, a rather unfavorable turn. As late as October, 1914, the High Command asked us if we had lost 120 cannon. Now in reality, during the retreat toward the Aisne, nine pieces were abandoned by a corps, and in another corps eleven batteries were formed from twelve as a result of loss of materiel. Futhermore, we lost a dozen baggage wagons, caissons, and forges.

There has been much dispute regarding the mission assigned to Lt. Col. Hentsch. Unfortunately, it was not expressed in writing, as the importance of the case certainly required. Lt. Col. Hentsch accepted it only with reluctance, and was perfectly conscious of the great responsibility incurred. He was not at all inclined from ambition to act independently or to exceed his authority. From working with him for years, I knew him as a very intelligent, very prudent, and very reserved staff officer in whom one could have absolute confidence. General Tappen states that his mission was to inform himself regarding the situation at the various armies.[36] In case retiring movements had already been ordered by the army commands, he was to act in such a way that the cohesion of the armies among each other would be reestablished; for the First Army, the direction Soissons would then be considered. General Tappen declares, moreover, that the despatch of the envoy was preceded by a detailed examination of the situation, in the course of which it was emphasized that the question was henceforth one of holding firm and preventing any backward movement. This is confirmed by others. General Tappen affirms that Lt. Col. Hentsch was not authorized to order retiring movements in the name of the High Command. General von Moltke expresses himself on the subject as follows: "The only commission entrusted Lt. Col. Hentsch was to say to the First Army that if a retreat became

---

[36] Loc. cit. page 24.

necessary, it was to fall back upon the line: Soissons – Fismes in order thus to resume contact with the Second Army. He was by no means authorized to say that the retreat was inevitable." Lt. Col. Hentsch himself represents his mission as follows: "I was authorized to order, in case of need, the retreat of the whole army onto the line: St. Menehould – Reims – Soissons – Fismes. I was formally vested with full powers to issue orders in the name of the High Command."

By way of summary, from the foregoing the following may be established: The plan of the High Command was to act upon the right wing in such manner as to lead it to maintain its positions. It took account, however, of the fact that retreat might become necessary, and for the eventuality mentioned Soissons at that time as the direction to betaken by the First Army. In case retiring movements had already been ordered by one army, Lt. Col. Hentsch was to concern himself with reestablishing the cohesion between the armies and with giving orders to that end; which is the case that actually occurred. He was not authorized to order, of his own accord, a retreat by any army unless these preliminary conditions were fulfilled. Neither did he do so, nor did he pretend to possess such a right.

Upon arriving at the Third Army on September 8, he found the situation favorable and reported accordingly to the High Command.[37]

It was otherwise at the Second Army. When he arrived on the evening of September 8 at Montmort, he found the baggage of the army staff ready for leaving. Retreat had already manifestly been contemplated but was not yet decided upon. At 10:30 p.m. he transmitted the following report to the High Command: "Situation serious, but not desperate on the right wing of the Second Army." On the morning of the 9th, General von Bülow decided to beat a retreat. The determining factors in this decision were: the situation of the First Army, regarded at the staff of the second Army as extremely menaced; the excessively unfavorable idea which he entertained with regard to his own right wing, and the gap existing

---

[37] See page 254.

between the First and second Army. No one suggests that Lt. Col. Hentsch, acting in the spirit of his mission, exerted his influence in the contrary direction and demanded that any army remain in place. He saw the situation as it had been depicted to him at Montmort and accepted the point of view of General von Bülow without being able to verify the bases of his decision.

When, on the morning of September 9, he left Montmort for Mareuil, it was determined that the Second Army would begin its retreat in the afternoon. In accord with General von Bülow, Lt. Col. Hentsch was convinced of the necessity of the retreat of the First Army upon Soissons – Fismes.

It was not until about 12:30 p.m. that he arrived at the headquarters of the First Army, after having been obliged, as a result of the congestion of the roads, to stop along the way and to make a long detour. The discussion at Mareuil lasted until 2 p.m. Here he suddenly found himself confronted with a very different conception of the situation. The First Army Command was conscious of the seriousness of the situation and did not at all underestimate the danger of the gap which existed between the First and Second Armies. But it was precisely in the forenoon of the 9th that the complete reversal had begun to arise in our favor, in the Battle of the Ourcq. We hoped to be able to hold the English sufficiently by the measures already adopted. Everything might be made to come out well if the Second Army held firm a little longer. In these conditions I resolutely refused to accept the order to retreat and did not issue such an order until after long negotiations and for the reasons already stated.[38] To convince me of the necessity of the retreat, Lt. Col. Hentsch painted the situation of the Second Army in the darkest colors. His statements on this point were not in accord with the facts.

It follows from the foregoing that Lt. Col. Hentsch did not go beyond the task assigned him. Once the retreat of the Second Army had been decided upon and got under way, he was obliged to restore the cohesion of the different armies among each other. It was impossible to attain that otherwise than by the retreat of the

---

[38] See page 263.

First Army. Now the High Command had prescribed that the First Army should take the direction: Fismes – Soissons. Lt. Col. Hentsch therefore had the right to order the First Army to retreat in that direction. He was guiltless of any unjustified intervention in the decisions of the First Army Command and is not responsible for the retreat which followed the battle of the Marne. The one who bears the responsibility for what happened is the one who assigned him that mission, the one who at the gravest hour of the campaign turned over to him the burden of adopting the decision.

According to General Tappen, Lt. Col. Hentsch declared later that he gave no order to retreat to any army and that when he arrived at the headquarters of the First Army the retreat orders were already issued by the command of that army. That is certainly an error on the part of General Tappen. Lt. Col. Hentsch made no such assertion in his report, but on the contrary states "I referred at the first army to the order I had received, and I ordered the retreat in the name of the High Command."

Whether, from the point of view of the High Command, Lt. Col. Hentsch was obliged to approve the decision arrived at quite independently by General von Bülow, or whether it was his duty to seek to prevent it conformably to the instructions he had received, is another question. When he arrived at the staff of the Second Army, he was unaware of the real situation of the First Army. He saw that situation as it was assumed to be at that staff. Moreover, he was inclined, by his very nature, to see things from the dark side. It was a matter of regret that he did not begin his tour with a visit to the First and Second Army, whose fate was at stake, instead of traveling about a whole day by auto from the left wing to the right wing and taking in all the armies. More regrettable still is the fact that there was no intermediate superior organ for harmonizing the divergent ideas of the commands of the First and Second Armies. An army-group command would, as happened constantly later in similar cases, have quickly clarified the situation by speaking personally with the two army commands. General von Bülow would then have had an accurate idea of the point at which the fighting of the First Army had arrived.

The situation of the Second Army on September 9 was not such as to make its retreat necessary. Its right wing, which was drawn back, was not attacked at all on the 9th before the beginning of the retreat. The 13th Division had been able to occupy and fortify its new position in all tranquility. It was then able to recover the hours of sleep which it had lost. Two battalions and two batteries of heavy howitzers arrived to reenforce it. It is evident that the French had not realized their local success of the evening of the 8th. On the morning of the 9th they had lost contact with the 13th Division. The flank of this division was not menaced. "The order to retreat burst like a bomb in the midst of the leaders and the troops. It was no easy matter to make the order acceptable to the troops by referring to the repulses undergone at another point. It could not be explained from our own situation." The division commander, General von dem Borne, believes that he could have held his position on the 10th against any enemy attack. At the time of the retirement, he had almost the whole of his infantry file past him; it was in perfect order.[39] These troops were not "merely residue"; they proved it in the course of the following days.

Colonel von Caprivi, who was then the senior staff officer of the staff of the VII Corps, and Major von Platen, then staff officer at the 13th Division, confirm the foregoingdescription. The commander of the VII Corps General von Einem, went on horseback on the morning of the 9th to the 13th Division, at a time when it was preparing its defensive organizations in broad daylight. It bore not the slightest resemblance to a beaten body of troops but, on the contrary, made a fresh impression. "It would certainly have conducted itself as well on the 9th and the following days in the face of an enemy attack as it had done on the 8th throughout the day. But no enemy showed up, at no point did they come into contact with him. At 1:30 p.m. we received the army order to fall back behind the Marne. It was the greatest surprise to us, for we had heard of the successes won by the left wing of the army. During the retreat we were subjected to nothing but artillery fire. The enemy followed in the evening only as far as the

[39] Communication of General von dem Borne.

Verdonnelle sector."[40]

On the 10th the Marne was crossed on either side of Epernay.

The left wing of the Second Army and the right wing of the Third won a brilliant victory on September 9. The third Army took Mailly and threw the enemy back beyond the Maurienne and the sector: Corroy – Semoine, while its left wing held firm at Sompuis and eastward. During this time the left wing of the Second Army had progressed as far as Connantre and La Colombiere. The Mont d'Aout was stormed, Allemant attained, Mondement taken.

A combatant of the Second Army, Lt. Col. Dietrich, describes as follows the splendid situation of the army at noon. "The enemy came down in a hasty retreat from the Mont d'Aout toward the west and southwest; French batteries were getting away at a rapid pace and were subjected to shrapnel from three sides. The victory of the left wing of the Second army, obtained in conjunction with the right wing of the third, and the thrust through the army of Marshal Foch, were clearly discernible and perhaps already effected. Then arrived the orderly officer of the regiment, his face pale and grave, with the message: 'At 4p.m. the retreat will begin.' We did not want to believe him, we wanted to laugh him off, we pointed out to him the imminent victory which lay before us. But we soon felt, wonderingly and with bitter pain, that his message was serious."[41]

General von Hausen is convinced that he was on the point of breaking through the enemy front when he suddenly received the announcement of the Second Army that it was retreating. This communication was followed at 5:30 p.m. by a radiogram from the Second Army, despatched at 2:45 p.m. : "First Army falling back. Second Army starting retreat upon Dormans – Tours. Order to retreat has been transmitted to Kirchbach." The retreat of the First Army is given as the determining motive. General von Kirchbach, who commanded the right wing of the Third Army fighting in contact with the Second, had received directly from the Second

---

[40] Major von Platen.

[41] *Militär-Wochenblatt*, 1920, No. 10.

Army the order to retreat. With a heavy heart, General von Hausen decided to fall back.

The Fourth and Fifth Armies made no marked progress whatever on September 9. In front of the former, however, the enemy seemed to be growing paralyzed.

As regards the French Sixth Army, the French reports for September 9 are incomplete. But all of them recognize that the situation of this army was seriously menaced. Its left wing was beaten and thrown far back beyond Villers St. Genest and Nanteuil le Haudouin upon Silly le Long; the advance of a German column through Baron upon the rear of the French was hastening its retreat. Its right wing, suffered heavily from the powerful fire of the German artillery. Thus the French accounts themselves admit that Maunoury suffered a heavy defeat. It was plain that his right wing was still scarcely in a condition to fight, and his left wing was thoroughly beaten. It is clear that only a final thrust was required to drive Maunoury from the field. "At last night came, a night full of anxiety. What will happen tomorrow? Human strength has its limits."[42]

At the end of the day the Sixth Army stood on the line: Chambry – Etrepilly – Puisieui – Silly le Long. Its right wing had thus remained in place after the retreat of the German left wing. Manifestly, this retreat had not been at all noticed. The 8th Division, which on September 8 had still pushed forward to the English left wing southwest of La Ferté-sous-Jouarre, had to be brought back on the 9th to the left wing of Maunoury's army. To that end it would have had to march for two days, and even by rail it could no longer arrive in time. Hence it failed to come into action either north or south of the Marne. No other reenforcements for Maunoury were available. Nothing remained but to "hold on to the ground" and if necessary "to be killed on the spot." The troops had suffered heavy losses, and were exhausted; they had "reached the limit of their strength." Their situation would have become extremely serious if they had been attacked once more on the morning of the 10th. Maunoury was looking forward to this day

---

[42] Fabreguettes, loc. cit.

with the greatest anxiety; "he breathed again when, in the morning, he acquired the certainty that the Germans had fallen back during the night."

An expressive description of Maunoury's situation is furnished by the *Journal des Débats* of November 28, 1914. It relates that a number of war correspondents, with an official pass had visited the battlefield of the Ourcq, and that the battle was explained to them by a military personage. The events of September 5 and 6 are then briefly described. It is stated that during those days the German IV Reserve Corps offered a vigorous frontal resistance, while other German corps coming back across the Marne were returning toward the Ourcq without resistance on the part of the English who were advancing but slowly. "On the 7th, the French VII Corps was beaten at Acy en Multien; the left wing was also strongly attacked at Etavigny and thrown back upon Bouillancy and Villers St. Genest. General Maunoury concentrated all his reserves at that point. But on the evening of the 8th it was clear that the movement toward the east had failed. The left wing had to front to the north. General Maunoury was further reenforced with the IV Corps, but was obliged to yield one division to the English, who thought they were faced by highly superior forces. Instead of encircling the German right wing, Maunoury had to see to it that he was not enveloped himself. All the still available troops of the IV Corps were brought up upon Nanteuil le Haudouin, by rail, by automobiles requisitioned in part at Paris, and on foot. Meanwhile the enemy was reported in a direction which occasioned still greater concern: a German column; was reported at Baron on the road from Nanteuil to Senlis. It was learned from German prisoners that these were landwehr troops which-had been charged with covering the communications farther north but which at that critical moment had been called to the front. On the afternoon of the 9th the IV Corps had to fall back upon Nanteuil. Speculation was rife concerning the situation on the following day. Meanwhile the commander in chief recommended holding firm at any price so as not to jeopardize the success of the whole Marne battle. General Boelle, commander of the IV Corps, ordered that the troops let themselves be killed on the spot rather than yield ground. The emplacement of the left wing was, however, unfavorable; it was situated in a plain where the troops had neither cover nor point of support. But on the morning of the 10th only rear guards were still encountered."

The situation of the French is represented as still more unfavorable from the English side. General Maurice says that General von Kluck endeavored on the 9th to encircle Maunoury "in order to consummate the defeat of the French before the English could come into action."[43] Advancing by way of Betz, the Germans took Nanteuil. "It was now only a matter of hours to see whether the German plan from this point of view would or would not be crowned with success." Reenforcements, landwehr troops from the occupied territories, arrived."Maunoury's troops were quite as exhausted as those of Kluck. The latter was surrounding the French left wing. A few hours more of strenuous efforts might procure him such a victory that all the dangers into which he had fallen by reason of his rapid march beyond the Marne would disappear." General Maurice asserts that the retreat of the Sixth Army was already regarded as inevitable and that the latest troops despatched in all haste by Gallieni were only to serve to cover the retreat. At the moment when we were crossing the Marne, the French army had reached the limit of its force of resistance. Gallieni had already started to take the measures required for preparing the retreat. And he adds that "the English advance determined the German retreat" and that "Maunoury was saved at the moment when his danger was serious."

It was not in reality the English who saved Maunoury.

According to the French accounts, on the evening of the 8th the French Fifth Army had reached Vauchamps (I Corps), Montmirail (III Corps) and Marchais (XVIII Corps). The X Corps had faced toward the east to support the Ninth Army.

On the evening of the 9th, after the German Second Army had fallen back, the XVIII Corps is said to have got as far as the locality: Viffort – Essises, the III Corps up to Montigny – Le Breuil, while the I Corps made no progress, it appears, but was stopped at Fromentièes to support the X Corps. This latter corps

---

[43] Loc. cit.

was employed by General Foch to relieve the 42nd Division on his left wing.

On September 9 the left wing of the German Second Army and the right wing of the Third Army continued to progress without interruption. On the right wing of the French Ninth Army the XI Corps was thrown farther back beyond Semoine, Gourgancon, Corroy and Connantre. On the center, the IX Corps was menaced in its flank by this retirement and fell back in the afternoon upon Lin thes by way of Mont d'Aout. Mondement, the point of support of the French center, was lost. Poincaré, in his discourse to the French Academy at the time of the reception of Marshal Foch, described the situation of the Ninth Army as follows: The right wing (XI Corps) evacuates Fère Champenoise; the IX Corps menaced in the center and rear, falls back. Then Marshal Foch is said to have addressed to the commander in chief the following report: "My right wing is hard pressed; my center is falling back; it is impossible for me to take a new position. The situation is excellent; I attack." But the Guard throws back the Moroccan Division and takes Mondement: "One final pressure on the part of the enemy and the gap is opened." At this moment there arrives on the right wing of the Ninth Army the 42nd Division, which the general brought up from his left wing.

A legend has become attached to this appearance of the 42nd Division. It is regarded as one of the boldest and most skillful maneuvers which has ever changed the situation at the decisive moment. The situation has been the subject of a brilliant military picture: under a rain of artillery projectiles, the 42nd Division moves from the left wing to the right wing by filing past in rear of the whole front. At a charging pace; it falls on the flank of the astonished enemy masses. General Mauricc, also, describes the intervention of the 42nd Division in a similar manner: the division throws the enemy back; the whole line of the Ninth Army proceeds to the attack and wins the victory. Foch seized the weak point of the enemy at the favorable moment and transformed the critical situation into a thorough victory.

This legend has been destroyed by the French military

historians themselves.[44] The real facts do not correspond in the least to the beautiful picture made from them. Thanks to the support of the Fifth Army, General Foch was able, in the night of September 8-9, to withdraw the 42nd Division from the front of his left wing. Its relief by the X Corps was prolonged into the forenoon of the 9th. Filing behind the front, the division then advanced from Soizy aux Bois through Broyes and St. Loup upon Lin thelles, where it arrived completely exhausted in the evening, after the Germans had already left. It was no longer capable of attacking; it bivouacked at Linthes and Pleurs. It could no longer have changed the fate of the Ninth Army."On the morning of the 10th, there was no longer any doubt that the enemy had fallen back. Happily surprised, the troops took up the march."

We have seen that as early as the afternoon of the 9th, at the same time that he formed the decision to draw back his own army, the commander of the Second Army had also ordered General von Kirchback, commander of the right wing of the Third Army, to retreat.

So we lost in that region the opportunity to win a certain and great success which could not have failed to have its effect on the advance of the French Fifth Army and of the English Army.

The situation in the locality of Fère Champenoise also exercised an influence upon the French Fourth Army, which drew back its left wing.

The attempt made by the French Third Army to attack the German left flank had completely failed; but Sarrail still held on the 9th.

"On the evening of the 9th," says the French military writer de Civrieux in *L'Illustration* of September 4, 1920, "the situation at the two focal points of the fighting was as follows: Maunoury, exhausted and very much worried about his left flank, wonders if it is not his duty to prescribe a retreat upon Paris. It is only at the urgent request of the commander in chief that he defers his decision. Foch has lost Fère Champenoise and moved the 42n4d Division from his left to his right wing to support the XI Corps

---

[44] De Civrieux, be. cit.

which is partly annihilated. He does not know what is in store for him on the following day. But when that day dawned, the enemy had disappeared from the field of battle where a few hours earlier it had attacked stubbornly and with success." And de Civrieux adds that that retreat was "unexpected by all."

The headquarters of the English Army on the 9th was at Coulommiers. The I Corps was moved that day upon Nogent l'Artaud – Charly by way of Sablonnières and La Trétoire, its II Corps upon Nanteuil sur Marne and Mery by way of Orly and St. Ouen, and its III Corps to the west of these points, upon La Ferté-sous-Jouarre. The English reports describe as follows the events of September 9:

Allenby's cavalry, going on ahead of the army, seized the bridges at Charly and covered the passage of the I Corps.

The center succeeded in crossing the Marne in the course of the afternoon. The 3rd Division crossed it at Nanteuil, the 5th Division at Méry. But its advance was arrested by the German artillery established northwest of Montreuilaux Lions. As the two flank corps were still in retreat and had not yet crossed the Marne, French was reluctant to let the II Corps advance alone. Smith-Dorrien received orders to halt. At the end of the day, units of the II Corps that were the farthest forward had reached Bezu le Gúery.

The I Corps advanced only with hesitation. French will have it that he had received information indicating great masses of troops between Chateau-Therry and Margny; adding, however, that they were regarded merely as strong rear guards, for columns were reported as marching toward the north. At any rate, following the receipt of this information, French became uneasy about his flank. General Maurice confirms the statement that the I Corps was held back until the afternoon, because an attack was feared from the direction of Chateau-Thierry. It was not known that the enemy troops reported in that region comprised only Richthofen's cavalry corps, and as long as any danger appeared to exist on the flank the enemy did not dare to attempt the crossing. At the end of the day the advanced elements of the I Corps are said to have reached Domptin. On the 9th, on the left flank, the III Corps was unable to cross the Marne. French betook himself-to that wing and observed that all the attempts which were made to pass the river failed under the enemy artillery fire. It was not until the morning of the 10th, long after we had already fallen back, that the corps was able to cross.

The attempt which was made to open the passage of La Ferté-sous-Jouarre by sending ahead a division of the II Corps upon Dhuisy into the rear of the defenders failed. "The 5th Division, which was assigned to this task, was unable to triumph over the enemy resistance." The reference here is manifestly to the struggles with the Kraewel brigade, the 5th Division which was coming up, and with the II Cavalry Corps. General Maurice, also, confirms that General von Kluck had time to organize the defense of the Marne between Chateau-Thierry and Lizy and to bring up reenforcements. He acids that in the afternoon violent fighting took place with these reenforcements and that Richthofen's cavalry corps also came into action. He criticizes the fact that the bridge at Chateau-Thierry had remained undamaged and was not defended at all, although the ground was entirely favorable to such defense.

French denies having asked for the support of Maunoury and having thus brought it about that the French 8th Division took no part in, the struggle. He declares that on the contrary Maunoury twice urgently asked him, in the course of September 9 to release him from the pressure to which the Germans were subjecting him. But Gallieni has proved that without the despatch of the 8th Division he could not have induced French to move forward.[45]

There is no doubt that on September 9, just as in the course of the preceding days, the English advanced only with extreme caution. General Maurice considers it a bit of bad luck that a greater number of troops did not cross the Marne on the 9th. "Those are accidents of warfare." It was not an accident, but serious negligence on the part of our enemies. The French consider that it was due to the hesitant advance of the English that General von Kluck was, able to bring up his whole army against Maunoury.

---

[45] See page 234.

Retrospect

The great Franco-English offensive had struck the German right wing in an unfavorable situation. The flank was not sufficiently covered. This covering task was confided by the High Command to the First Army, which to this end had been ordered to follow in echelon. But the First Army thought that the enemy was being held by our attack all along the front, including the front on the Moselle, and believed it could cover the flank sufficiently by remaining in echelon upon itself.

The French, who according to the reports of the second Army had been beaten in a decisive manner and were in flight, could not be encircled and driven back except by the First Army. This goal, upon which rested the whole plan of campaign, the First Army sought still to attain at the last moment.

The High Command changed its design when the Sixth and Seventh Armies had failed to break through on the Moselle. It recognized the danger in the vicinity of Paris when it obtained knowledge of the French transportations toward the west.

The encirclement was abandoned; the First and Second Armies were ordered to front toward Paris, astride the Marne. What would have been the situation on September 6 if the First Army had remained in rear as an echelon since the 3rd? To obtain that echelon formation it would have had to stop on the 3rd and 4th, and on the 5th it would probably have advanced to the Marne. The encounter of the IV Reserve Corps with Maunoury on the 5th would no more have taken place than the general offensive of the French on the 6th. This latter was due principally to the pressure of Gallieni, who realized on September 3 and 4. that the First Army was filing past Paris toward the southeast. Joffre would therefore probably have ordered the retreat continued to a position behind the Seine. The orders of the High Command could have been executed. The First and Second Armies could have fronted Paris. There is no doubt that we would have been in a better position if, later, an attack had proceeded from the capital. Our flank would have been sufficiently covered. But it is hard to say how our maneuver should have been continued in order to obtain at once a great decision.[46] The campaign had failed.

As the events actually unfolded up to September 5, a serious crisis arose on the German right wing. In order to judge the decisions of the First Army from that time forward, we can not set out from what we know at the present time but from the situation as it was known at that time and from its progressive development. On September 6 the First Army was on the point of beginning, on orders of the High Command, to fall back upon the north bank of the Marne in order to oppose offensively any enemy enterprises proceeding from Paris. Such a case arose as early as the night of September 5-6; the IV Reserve Corps had come up against the enemy. Was it then the duty of the First Army to take at once a defensive attitude? At that moment the High Command and the First and Second Armies were quite unaware of the fact that a general French offensive was imminent all along the front. At noon of September 6 the Second Army still assumed that the French were in full retreat behind the Seine. The Second Army was beginning to face toward Paris. The situation called for an offensive by the First Army.

A defensive attitude would by no means have enabled it to fulfill its task. There was no question of a position on the Ourcq. Such a position was too far forward and could easily be surrounded. There was no time for organizing it. If combat was accepted on the Ourcq, it could only be done offensively.

Still less could there be any thought of bringing the First Army to the right flank of the Second, say onto the line: Montmirail – Chateau-Thierry and northward, that is, of forming a defensive flank. From the front: Coulommiers – Esternay up to that line, would have involved two strenuous days of marching. The columns and trains would have had to be pushed forward and the movements covered on the Ourcq up to the 8th. The weak IV Reserve Corps was not capable of such afeat. It would have had to be reenforced by at least one corps, and even then the matter would have been doubtful. If the covering troops posted on the Ourcq had been thrown back while the First Army was executing its flank

---

[46] See page 168.

movement in the narrow space behind them and a part of its units was crossing the Marne, it might have suffered the most disastrous defeat. The situation on the Ourcq would probably have obliged the command to gradually reenforce the troops in that region, contrary to its original designs.

But even if the movement had succeeded, the security of the German flank would not have been assured. The French Sixth Army was advancing north of the Marne and might have outflanked us; the English, in such a case, would have followed south of the river. The German right wing would have been encircled.

In the face of such a situation the offensive was the most certain means of assuring the protection of our flank. The best defense is to strike. A firm will, the desire to attain a definite goal, rapid movements directed with unity of view, could guarantee success.

The First Army Command was confronted anew with the question when on September 7 the necessity arose for bringing up to the Ourcq the III and IX Corps as well. This measure, which was of decisive importance to the course of the battle of the Marne and seriously endangered the right wing of the Second Army, has been repeatedly subjected to criticism.

Field-Marshal von Bülow does not approve the decision of the First Army Command to advance beyond the Ourcq with the II Corps, IV Corps, and IV Reserve Corps, on the ground that the gap between the First and Second Army was thereby increased.[47] Still less, he thinks, should the III and IX Corps have been brought into that region. If, he says, the First Army was confronted on September 7, to the west of the Ourcq, with such large forces that the II Corps, IV Corps and IV Reserve Corps were unable to handle the situation without the intervention of the III and IX Corps, it would still have been preferable on September 7 to break off the fighting west of the Ourcq with the three corps on the right and regain contact with the Second Army, say toward Chateau-Thierry. The III and IX Corps could then have been brought up

[47] Loc. cit. page 56.

behind the Dollau. The First Army, he thinks, would thus have renounced the possibility of winning a tactical success which could not have been exploited anyhow by reason of the proximity to Paris, but it would have fulfilled its main task, that of assuring the safety of the German right flank. The enemy would have found himself faced with a single front which he could neither have broken through nor outflanked.

Whether this plan was tactically feasible is a question which must remain unanswered. The III and IX Corps could easily have been brought upon September 7 behind the Dollausector. But to draw back the three other corps beyond the deeply indented Ourcq in order to push them, during the night of the 7-8th and day of the 8th, toward the locality north of Chateau-Thierry would have a very audacious measure exposing us to the greatest danger. At the least, it would have strengthened the enemy's will to conquer and exercised a depressing influence upon our troops.

If, however, the three corps were no match for the enemy west of the Ourcq, in an attack and with the prospect of being reenforced, they would have been still less so after their retreat by keeping on the defensive north of Chateau-Thierry. Maunoury's pursuing army, animated by its success, would have encircled them by the north while the English would have attacked their left wing south of Chateau-Thierry. In any case, the situation of the German right wing would have been dangerous. It is hard to say how the operations would have had to be continued.

Setting out from a different conception of the situation, the anonymous author of the *Critique de la Guerre Mondiale* is of the opinion that the First Army had no need at all of the III and IX Corps for the struggle against Maunoury. He declares that from the eve of the very first day of the battle, that is, from September 6, the crisis was averted: "Maunoury's army was hopelessly blocked in a costly struggle...The balance leaned already in favor of Kluck." And he adds that the bringing up of the III and IX Corps formed on the north wing of our defensive west flank an excess of forces which was no longer in relation with its purely defensive mission and that on September 7 the First Army turned from a successful defensive to a superfluous strategical offensive. The critic of the World War places the center of gravity of the German maneuver on the break-through at Mailly which, in his opinion, promised success. Abandoned, however, on its right wing by the First Army, attacked at Montmirail by the superior forces of the French Fifth Army, the Second Army no longer had the strength to advance to a decisive attack on its left wing. This attack took the form of a disengaging thrust at Fère Champenoise; the Third Army, instead of breaking into the gap of Mailly, was turned aside in a westerly direction to support the Second Army; and on the 9th the Second Army, now nothing but"residue," was not in a condition to fulfill its task, namely, to repulse a powerful attack on the right, and to attack on the left itself. The Mailly break-through, which would have succeeded if the Second and Third Armies had been sufficiently massed, remained a mere "possibility."

The author concedes, it is true, that the First Army acted quite correctly within the limits of its commission; it had no means of knowing that the Second Army had meanwhile been strongly blocked by the French attack, that the order of the High Command of September 5 had been left in the air and that the III and IX Corps could not be brought up toward the north. He says that the task which now fell to the First Army was that of flank protection both north and south of the Marne. Only the High Command could judge of all that. It seems to me, however, that the author fails to realize exactly the situation at Mailly and on the Ourcq and the condition of the Second Army, which was by no means "residue." The thrust at Fère Champenoise would not have remained a mere possibility; it would have become a reality if we had not discontinued the fighting. To be sure, it would have come about earlier and in a much more effective direction if the Third Army had not weakened at an inopportune time. It would then have been able not only to rout the right wing of Foch's army but also to enter at once into the gap at Mailly. At any rate, the victory would have been obtained on September 8 and 9 at Fère Champenoise and would have been of the greatest importance when the battle was continued.

In view of all that, we have no right to minimize the significance of the Battle of the Ourcq. To say that Maunoury's army was hopelessly deadlocked on September 6 and that the fighting had already turned in favor of Kluck is not in accord with the facts. On the evening of the 6th, the First Army Command was very uneasy and awaited impatiently the arrival of the IV Corps. We have shown how unfavorably the situation of the right wing was viewed on the evening of the 7th both at army headquarters and at the IV Corps. At the center and on the left wing the weak IV Re-serve Corps and the hard-pressed 3rd Division held with difficulty. To support them, the army command was obliged to deprive itself of the small detachments which assured the guard of its headquarters. I shall never forget the anxious night of September 7-8 at Vendrest. It was manifest that General Joffre wished to envelope our right wing and that he was daily reenforcing the Sixth Army. The enormous danger which menaced all the German armies if the First Army was repulsed was perfectly plain to us. There was no thought of "superfluous forces on the Ourcq." Without the III and IX Corps we would have been no match for the enemy. That is still my conviction today, and every commander who during those difficult days was obliged to hold on at Varreddes, Trocy, and Acy en Multien while anxiously awaiting reenforcements will confirm my opinion. On the morning of September 9 the forces confronting each other on the Ourcq were increased on the French side to eight and one-half divisions of infantry and four divisions of cavalry, on the German side to eight divisions of infantry and one division of cavalry. In the matter of reenforcements, Maunoury had on the march to the field of battle the 8th Division, while the German First Army had Lepel's reserve brigade and the 10th Landwehr Brigade. One division of German infantry and two, divisions of cavalry were employed on the Marne to face the English. If we brought up the III and IX Corps, it was better to employ them offensively than defensively. A rapid blow was calculated to give us breathing space. The offensive was not "strategically superfluous."

I still believe that the best means of meeting the danger in the flank was to swing the First Army around westward to the attack. The crisis thus arising on the right wing of the Second Army could have been endured up to the 10th. On that day, in so far as the human understanding was capable of judging, victory would have been obtained in the forenoon at Fère Champenoise and on the Ourcq, while the English would have been held until that time.

With Maunoury thrown back upon Paris, the communications of the English would have been menaced in the highest degree. In all probability, they would have fallen back.

The decisive point was at Montmirail. It was there that the issue of the Battle of the Maine was to be decided. Who was in the more dangerous situation: the German Second Army whose right wing was menaced but whose left wing was progressing victoriously, or General Franchet d'Esperey who found the road open on his left while on his right the Germans, closely pursuing the defeated Ninth Army, were menacing his rear? Once the English had fallen back and the advance of a part of the units of the First Army toward the Marne had become noticeable, the French Fifth Army would have been menaced anew with a Cannae defeat as at Namur and St. Quentin, and the more menaced as it moved farther forward. Would it then have been equal to the situation? That is highly doubtful, now that we know the condition in which it found itself at the beginning of the French offensive.[48]

As a matter of fact, it was only in the course of September 10, after the retirement of the Second Army, that Franchet d'Esperey arrived at the Marne. It would have been necessary, of course, that the German First Army, after its victory, should still have had the strength to move forward with its left wing toward the Marne into the uncovered flank of the Fifth Army, while the left wing of the Second Army and the right wing of the Third would have continued their victorious offensive. Now the First Army started its retreat during the night of the 9-10th, directly on coming out of a five-days' battle, and continued it uninterruptedly in strenuous marches up to behind the Aisne, where it stood on September 12, highly fatigued but ready for fighting. After a victory, it would still have certainly found in the offensive the impetus for the march upon Chateau-Thierry. It might be stated that once the left wing of the army, under Linsingen, had been drawn back toward the line: May en Multien – Coulombs, in accordance with the order of noon of the 9th, the Gronau and Trossei groups (22nd Reserve Division and 3rd Division) would have been ready on the left bank of the

---

[48] See page 213.

Ourcq at Fussy – Certigny – Coulombs, after a victorious issue of the battle, to attack either the English or the flank and rear of the French Fifth Army in conjunction with the II Cavalry Corps, the 5th Division and the Kraewel brigade.[49]

So, on September 9, a crisis existed on both sides. The situation hung by a thread. Whoever was to resolve the crisis to his own advantage had to possess the stronger nerves. To be sure, it was taking a great risk to carry the battle through to a decision. But the prize was worth it. We should have had the audacity. It could not have turned out worse for us than it did after four hard years of war.

As regards the High Command, it absolutely did not direct the Battle of the Marne. On the German right wing, it took no action whatever. It could not do so from Luxembourg. The communications were not sufficient and we had no liaison officer of the General Headquarters at the First Army. There can be no doubt that we would have been victorious in the Battle of the Marne if the XI Corps and the Guard Reserve Corps had not been sent to the eastern front. The Third Army would certainly have broken through at Mailly with the aid of the XI Corps, while the Guard Reserve Corps would have been able, on the right wing of the Second Army, to fill, at least up to the Marne, the gap which existed between the First Army and the Second. Yes, a single division on the Dollau sector would probably have sufficed. Unfortunately, the 13th Division lacked the reenforced 26th Brigade, which had been left in front of Maubeuge. The First Army alone could have handled the French Sixth Army and the English.

If there had been even one army-group command for overcoming the divergences in the views and measures of the right-wing armies, for organizing a unified defense of the Marne between the two armies, and diminishing the dangers of the gap, all could have come out well. Negotiations between the commands of the First and second Armies could not make up for that need.

In an excellent article in *Wissen und Wehr* regret is expressed for the absence of a constant exchange of ideas and of a sign of

---

[49] See Sketch 18.

understanding between the two commanders placed in position of such high responsibility.[50] Now it was impossible for the two commanders in chief to have personal interviews. Furthermore, their chiefs of staff were unable to leave their posts a single moment, either by day or by night. At headquarters, the reports, communications, orders, and decisions followed each other ceaselessly. Communication by telephone with the corps was insufficient. Most of the staff officers of the First Army were detached and assigned to units. Between the staffs of the First and Second Armies there was no communication except by radio. Anyone who witnessed the life at headquarters during those days can have an idea of the overexertion of the staff. The exhaustion was so great that a number of persons saw their strength desert them or fell asleep while working. During those critical days the two army commands sent staff officers back and forth without interruption in order to keep each other informed regarding their situation and their plans. But it frequently happened that they were unable to reach an agreement.

From the tactical point of view, the conduct of the Battle of the Ourcq by the First Army Command may be subject to criticism. Considering the origin and development of the battle, the leadership could not be exemplary. The mixture of units was thoroughly undesirable, but could not be avoided, since the troops could be entered only gradually at the points most menaced at the moment. The corps commanders were very much provoked at having under their orders all sorts of units in the place of their corps as originally constituted. The headquarters staff continued to hold firmly to the governing idea of the encirclement and sought to bring the main body of its forces to the decisive right wing. The preliminary condition for that was that the center and left wing should be able to hold until the encirclement had taken effect. Now this was the first time that our troops found themselves uncovered under the heavy fire of the enemy artillery. It was accordingly necessary to lend direct support to the weak IV Reserve Corps; otherwise the whole of the IV Corps could have been employed

---

[50] No. 4 of 1920, page 377.

from the beginning on the right wing. One division of the III Corps was also shoved to the left wing because of the critical situation at that point.

The distribution into groups was a necessary evil. The first reenforcements which arrived, as well as the IV Reserve-Corps, were placed under General von Linsingen, commander of the II Corps, who gradually assumed command of the IV Reserve Corps and of the II and IV Corps. This question also could not at first be regulated in any other way. At the beginning the army command was so absorbed with the situation as a whole, the orders to be issued to the troops on the south bank of the Marne, the negotiations with the Second Army, then with the measures to be taken for defending the Marne in the gap which had opened, that if. was unable to regulate the details of the Battle of the Ourcq. Furthermore, all the movements of the columns and trains had to be directed by the army command if hopeless disorder was to be avoided. General von Linsingen established his quarters very far forward, at Beauvoir au Beauval [Beauvai]. It is possible that he was here too much under the direct influence of the heavy fighting on the front and was thus too much inclined to reenforce that front. The responsibility, however, falls upon the army command, which confided to him the direction of the battle up to September 8. After the coming into line of the III Corps, General von Linsingen retained the direction of the left wing of the army (groups of von Lochow, von Gronau and von Trossel). It was impossible for the army command itself to keep control of the confused situation in that region. It laid the main emphasis of its leadership upon bringing into action the adjoining groups of the right, those of Generals Sixt von Armin and von Quast, with a view to the encircling attack.

The importance of the encirclement in the Battle of the Ourcq has already been referred to. On the other hand, a break-through would have had a chance of success for the enemy on the Marne and for us at Mailly. In both cases the possibility of breaking through rested upon the existence of a gap in the enemy front. It was the menace of a break-through by the English and by the French Fifth Army which brought about the decision in the Battle of the Marne.

Our independent cavalry was at the proper point. Still it would have been well to have on the right wing, in the vicinity of Crépy en Valois, a stronger cavalry force than the 4th Cavalry Division. The enemy cavalry at that point was considerably superior in numbers, but used up. For us, it was more important to have a strong cavalry force on the Marne. Here the First and Second Cavalry Corps were concentrated together. The First Army was operating on the inner line between the English and the French Sixth Army. The space for such a maneuver was very limited, the two adversaries too close together. Everything depended on holding the English army long enough on the Marne.

In the defense of the Marne the results were not such as might have been expected. The army command had counted upon a more vigorous resistance. The Marne is an important obstacle; its banks are enclosed by wooded heights which permit the defender to use to advantage his artillery and infantry. The forces available for the defense of the river comprised at first the II Cavalry Corps and Four agar battalions, then on the evening of the 8th the Kraewel brigade, and on the afternoon of the 9th the 5th Division. The thing lacking was a unified command. On the 7th at the latest, once the decision to bring up the III and IX Corps was arrived at, the army command should have given orders to take the necessary steps for destroying the Marne bridges. The defense of the river at La Ferté-sous-Jouarre was confided to the II Cavalry Corps, and between La Ferté and Chezy to Kraewel's brigade. Both were advised on September 8of the importance of the defense of the Marne and charged with destroying the bridges. It was not until later that the Kraewel brigade and the 5th Division were subordinated to the II Cavalry Corps. That should have been done at the very beginning. And the necessary forces and technical means should have been placed in due time at the disposal of the II Cavalry Corps. The defense could then have been organized in such manner as to place at the most important points – La Ferté-sous-Jouarre, Nanteuil sur Marne, facing Nogent l'Artaud and Chezy – detachments charged both with blowing up the bridges and with assuring the local defense. In rear, one or two reserves should have been held in readiness to provide for the possibility that the enemy would break through at any point. The main task was a local defense, stopping the enemy and gaining time, and not assuring permanently the defense of the river and defeating the enemy. The matter of keeping the forces concentrated and carrying out an offensive defensive by advancing to meet the enemy crossing the river was a minor concern. If we succeeded in preventing the enemy from passing on the 9th and 10th, the goal was attained. After it had crossed the Marne, the cavalry corps was obliged to operate mainly as infantry and make use of its artillery.

The course of events did not conform to the foregoing. The only bridge blown up was that of La Ferté-sous-Jouarre this had been destroyed by the English in the course of their retreat and was restored by our IV Corps with any means at hand. We have seen how the destruction of this bridge retarded the enemy. It was not until the 10th that he succeeded in crossing the river at this point, although, contrary to the English account, the crossing was not opposed by large forces but only by a few detachments of cavalry and chasseurs. All the other bridges fell intact into the hands of the enemy. Otherwise not an Englishman would have crossed the Marne before the 10th.

Kraewel's brigade was too weak to hold the Marneline by advancing offensively from a central position to meet the enemy crossing the river. It remained in place on the 9th. The 5th Division did not arrive until the afternoon of the 9th, at a time when the only course still possible was to attack the enemy who had passed the Marne.

The sending of the 9th Cavalry Division into the region of Lizy was a mistake.

The news received on the morning of September 9 regarding the insufficiency of the Marne defense and the great retirement executed by the right wing of the Second Army, determined the First Army at noon to draw back its left wing. From the point of view of the moment, this measure appeared advisable. It would have been foolhardy to leave the left wing at Congis when the English were crossing the Marne in the rear of the German forces along a broad front and the French Fifth Army was advancing sensibly upon Chateau-Thierry. The measure had no influence on the course of the events of the 9th, for the movements were not got under way until the afternoon when the retreat of the. whole First

Army was already decided upon. But it might have had great importance if the battle had been waged to a decision. The success of our encircling movement would have been increased if the enemy had also been attacked frontally by our left wing. General von Gronau has described the anticipation which followed, on the morning of the 9th, the arrival of the army order prescribing the general attack. All preparatory measures were taken at once. The activity of the enemy artillery facing us was now but weak: "I was more and more convinced that the prescribed attack was destined to lead to a complete victory." Then came the order to withdraw. Besides, if a general attack had taken place all along the front, only von Gronau's and von Trossel's groups would have been lacking. VonLochow's group, which stood on the right bank of the Ourcq at May en Multien, would have been in a position to join in the attack. With my present knowledge of the events on the Marne in the course of September 9, I regret the drawing back of that wing. And yet, the bold idea of the First Army, to compel the English to retreat by winning a complete victory over Maunoury and then turning against the French Fifth Army, might have led at the last to staking everything like a reckless gambler, on that one card in order to win atone grand stroke or else collapse.

Could the same idea, at noon of September 9, have induced the commander in chief of the First Army to refuse to obey the order brought by Lt. Col. Hentsch and resolutely to continue the attack to a decision? Such a proposition has often been maintained. General von Francois says: "The troops of the First Army had accomplished extraordinary feats in the matter of marches and combats, and General von Kluck could think with justified pride of the exemplary manner in which he had directed the Battle of the Ourcq, which will remain in military history as a classic example of the transformation of an encirclement by the enemy into a flanking attack upon that enemy. He would have been the hero of the Battle of the Marne if he had refused to accept the order to retreat delivered by Lt. Col. Hentsch and if, on the contrary, he had induced this latter to stop the retreat of the Second Army until our supreme commander himself had reached a decision. Thus the necessary time would have been gained for realizing the hopes of victory which the First, Second, Fourth, and Fifth Armies had correctly placed in their attacks already launched or in course of preparation."[51]

General von Kluck would not have hesitated to act contrary to the order if there had been any possibility of doing so. But the retreat of the Second Army could no longer be stopped. This fact was established in the course of the discussion with Hentsch. The latter had been very late in arriving at Montmirail, as we have already stated. Meanwhile, noon had struck; the Second Army was in retreat. There was no communication with it except by radio, which required hours and permitted no exchange of ideas. We know today that General von Bülow had also issued retreat orders directly to the right wing of the Third Army, and this in turn led General von Hausen to join in this retreat with the other units of his army. How could all these measures have been annulled, and how could the orders have been transmitted in time to the troops already on the march? The first Army could not remain in place if the Second and Third Armies fell back. To ask for a decision from the High Command was out of the question in view of the defective communications.[52]

Lieutenant-Colonel Müller-Loebnitz, in his book on the Battle of the Marne, which is by far the best which has been written on the subject, says that on September 9 between 11 o'clock and noon it was still quite possible for the First Army Command to induce the Second Army to withdraw its order to retreat by addressing to it a vigorous radiogram.[53] But at that moment the command of the First Army was still unaware that its neighbor had adopted that decision. We learned of it only through Lt. Col. Hentsch. The facts as previously set forth show that it was no longer possible to have the order of the Second Army countermanded by acting contrary to the advice and instructions of Lt. Col. Hentsch.[54]

---

[51] *Marneschlacht und Tannenberg*, 1920, page 109 ff.

[52] See page 41.

[53] *Der Wendepunkt des Weltkrieges*, page 58.

[54] See page 262.

The dispute which has been waged with regard to whether it was the High Command or Lt. Col. Hentsch who must bear the responsibility for the retreat of the First Army is trivial. There is no doubt that the latter gave the order to retreat in the name of the High Command. The command of the First Army executed that order because there was nothing else to do. The decision was reached at Montmort and not at Mareuil.

This retrospective glance over the events on the German side during the Battle of the Marne can not be closed without homage to the remarkable performances of our troops in all the armies. If the marching performances were greater for the armies on the marching right wing, the left wing too was obliged to make its way past strongly defended sectors, in difficult terrain, and with almost uninterrupted fighting. No one army deserves less credit than another.

The First Army entered the Battle of the Ourcq after uninterrupted and unparalleled marches. Its corps usually reached the field of battle by night marches of enormous length. All the corps deserve mention in the same manner: the gallant IV Reserve Corps which with its small force clung to the ground for five days and lost 163 officers and 4000 men; the II Corps which in the night of September 5-6 hastened up to the battle and held out on the left wing in the most difficult situation; the IV and III Corps which had to cover an enormous distance by marching day and night without halt. Astonishing is the performance of the IX Corps which, setting out from Esternay, marched without stopping on the 7th and. 8th by way of Chateau-Thierry and La Ferté-Milon, and on the 9th victoriously threw the enemy back beyond Nanteuil le Haudouin. It is hard to determine which would be admired the more: the energy of the commanders or the spirit of sacrifice of our gallant troops giving their last strength without reserve.

On the French side, the course of the battle did not meet the expectations of Joffre. The Battle of the Marne was not a Cannae. Maunoury's flank attack lacked determination. Cooperation with the English was nonexistent. The Sixth Army was too weak to accomplish the decisive task confided to it. It was not yet assembled when the attack was launched earlier than anticipated. The reenforcements arrived only gradually. The premature encounter of September 5 prevented surprise. Gallieni declared later that the plan of encircling the German right wing had failed because the Sixth Army had not been supported sufficiently. But neither was that army skillfully led. From the very beginning it was massed upon its right, although in that locality the Marne prevented extending the wing and encircling the enemy. The left wing, charged with the encirclement, was too weak and was reenforced but gradually. General von Kluck, on the contrary, held resolutely from September 6 to 9 to his idea: remain on the defensive with small forces on his left wing resting on the Marne, and bring up, regardless of all the difficulties, the main body of his forces to his right wing in order to execute an outflanking attack. Though on September 9 Maunoury's forces were, on the whole, superior to those of the First Army, he was still the weaker at the decisive point.[55]

The English were plainly a disappointment. The French Third Army was not in a condition to attack the German left flank. It was itself menaced in its rear. The Ninth (Foch) Army was beaten.

Such was the situation when a gap unexpectedly opened to Joffre in the German battlefront west of Montmirail. Instead of the planned encirclement, it was the breakthrough, now beginning, which led to the goal and which, contrary to expectations, reversed the situation which was otherwise entirely unfavorable. That was the "Miracle of the Marne."

The result was a great French success. To determine whether the French are entitled to call it a victory would lead to a vain discussion. We evacuated the field of battle. The essential disadvantage to us in the Battle of the Marne was the blow to our military prestige. France breathed again at the moment when she was on the point of being conquered. From that time began the strengthening of her power of resistance and her faith in the final victory.

---

[55] See page 290.

Chapter IX – The German Retreat After the Battle of the Marne

September 10-13

On September 9 the High Command still held to the intention of continuing the offensive with the center, and that same evening ordered that the Third Army should remain south of Chalons, ready to resume the attack. The Fifth Army in the night of the 9-10th and the Fourth Army when there was prospect of success should also attack and to this end establish connection with the Third Army. On September 10, however, when Lt. Col. Hentsch had returned to General Headquarters and made his report on the retreat of the First and Second Armies, the High Command decided to draw back the other armies also. The First Army was placed under the command of General von Bülow, the Second Army was ordered to fall back behind the Vesle, with the left wing at Thuizy, the Third Army behind the Marneon the line: Mourmelon le Petit – Francheville; the Fourth Army, on the flank of the Third, was to take up a position north of the Marne-Rhine canal as far as the vicinity of Revigny; the Fifth Army was to remain in the positions already attained. The various armies were to fortify and hold their positions.

On the 10th, the Second Army crossed the Marne on either side of Epernay. Rear guards were left south of the river. The Second Army Command ordered the First Army to fall back behind the Aisne and there draw up to the right wing of the second Army. The first army that day reached the vicinity of Villers Cotterets with its rear guards, without being pressed by the enemy. At the news of the retreat of the Second Army, the Third Army had originally desired to fall back on the 10th behind the Marne to the north of Chalons, but on the evening of the 9th it received the order of the High Command to remain south of Chalons and resume the offensive on the 10th as soon as possible. It consequently adapted its movement to that of the Second Army so as to stand on the 10th between Vertus and Vitry le Francois. It got away from the enemy without any special difficulty. Only its left wing, which had remained in place west of Vitryle Francois, was attacked in the afternoon.

On September 11 it occurred to the Second Army that the enemy marching toward the east was seeking to break through in the zone of the Third Army. A rather long enemy column had been seen the evening of the 10th marching along the road: Champaubert – Bergères. On September 11, the Second Army addressed to the High Command a radiogram in which it was stated that an enemy breakthrough on the front of the Third Army appeared imminent. General Tappen declares that by such a breakthrough the Fourth Army and especially the right wing of the Fifth could have been pressed against the fortress of Verdun and exposed to annihilation, which would have meant the loss of the war. He adds that the High Command then decided to draw back the Third, Fourth and Fifth Armies onto a single position, and that the necessity for this measure was confirmed in the course of a conversation with General von Inflow at Reims, to which place General von Moltke had journeyed.

Consequently, on the evening of the 11th, the High Command despatched a new order, according to which the Third Army was to attain the line: Thuizy – Suippes, the Fourth Army the line: Suippes – St. Menehould, the Fifth Army the vicinity of St. Menehould. The positions were to be organized and held.

Whether it was advisable, on receipt of the foregoing reports, to order such a retreat and consent to such an abandonment of the ground already won, must remain an open question. From the account of General von Hausen it appears simply that the advance of powerful enemy forces in the direction of Vitry le Francois and the march of the enemy upon a large front beyond the line: Fere-en-Tardenois – Damery – Mareuil in the northeasterly direction against the Second and Third Armies indicated only that an enemy attempt to break through was possible and not that that break-through was already imminent.

The First Army crossed the Aisne September 11, mainly between Soissons and Attichy, and left strong rear guards south of the river. It was not until late in the afternoon that enemy advance guards warily appeared beforeourfront.

To put our thoroughly mixed-up army back into order was a measure no less urgent than difficult. The most divergent proposals were made. The difficulty was finally overcome in the following manner: on the 11th, some comparatively unmixed units were left as rear guards south of the Aisne by the different groups, while the remaining elements were displaced north of the river in such manner as to reconstitute in a fashion the different corps. The rear guards then crossed the Aisne on the 12th and rejoined their corps. At all the passages and crossroads, sketches bearing mention of the points of assembly were held in readiness to be distributed to the small isolated units. We thus succeeded in establishing the army on the Aisne very rapidly and in an order sufficient for a new combat. It was not possible, however, to resume contact with the Second Army by a leftward displacement; a considerable gap still remained. No later than the afternoon of the 12th, the army was attacked on the position Attichy – Soissons.

On the 12th the Second Army occupied the reconnoitered position on the Vesle on either side ofReims.

On September 13 the First Army held firm on its positions and extended its left wing as far as Vailly. The first elements arriving from the Seventh Army, VII Reserve Corps and XV Corps, could be inserted in the gap between the First and Second Armies. It was owing to the VII Reserve Corps in particular that the First Army was rescued from a great danger; it arrived on the left wing just at the proper time, September 13, after a very strenuous march.

In conformity with the new instructions of the High command, the Third Army crossed the Marne on either side of Chalons on September 11, destroyed the passages behind it and continued its movement to the north of the river without being molested. On the 13th, it attained the position Prosnes – Souain, henceforth assigned to it, and was joined by the Fourth Army on the left.

The armies now stood ready for the defense. When, later, the struggles over the western flank and the "race to the sea" had led the two adversaries to extend the front all the way to the channel, the whole front in the west settled down to position warfare.

Chapter X – The Engagements of the Sixth and Seventh Armies on the Moselle

The operations which unfolded on our left wing In Alsace and Lorraine, during the events which we have just described, were of great importance to the course of the Marne campaign. The objections to which the strength, the grouping, and the task of the Sixth and Seventh Armies gave rise have already been considered.[1] Whether by executing the prescribed offensive in the direction of the Moselle below Frouard and in the direction of the Meurthe, those armies would succeed in holding the forces supposed to exist in that region or in inflicting a decisive defeat upon the French in case the latter advanced in their turn between Metz and the Vosges, remained to be seen. The future was also to show whether the troops employed in Alsace-Lorraine would not be needed on the right wing at the decisive moment or whether, once their task had been accomplished, it would be possible to transport them to that point at the opportune moment.

The course of events on our right wing has already enabled us

---

[1] See page 20.

to realize that the hopes which had been placed in the operations of the Sixth and Seventh Armies were not fulfilled.

When the French advanced with their VII Corps and8th Cavalry Division from Belfort upon Mulhausen and took possession of this city on August 8, General von Heeringen counter-attacked from Colmar with the XV Corps and from Neubreisach and Neuenburg with the XIV Corps throwing them back upon Belfort on the 9th and 10th. This success, though gratifying in itself, drew the Seventh Army far toward the south and retarded the operation which it was to execute in conjunction with the Sixth Army. It was not until August 19 that it was entirely brought back to the side of the Sixth Army. Meanwhile, on August 9, it had been placed under the command of his royal highness the Crown Prince of Bavaria, commander of the Sixth Army.

The engagement at Lagarde on August 11, together with other information received, showed that the French Second Army had begun to penetrate into Lorraine. The design of the Crown Prince of Bavaria was to accomplish his task offensively, if possible, but he wished for the present to await the arrival of the Seventh Army, which was to concentrate in the region Saverne [Zabern]-Molsheim. To this end he would stand on a line somewhat as follows: southeast of Metz – Delme – Chateau Salins – Blamont – Cirey.

However, up to August 13 it appeared that very important enemy forces, perhaps the main ones, were assembling on the line: Raon l'Etape – Pont-à-Mousson. A great French offensive was to be expected between Metz and the Vosges. It was quite possible that the war would be decided in that locality. A premature attack on an enemy very superior in point of numbers had to be avoided. The great part of the German forces (First to Fifth Armies) could not be assembled and ready to cooperate before August 18. Consequently, on August 13, the High Command informed the commander in chief of the Sixth and Seventh Armies that it had no intention of having these two armies advance between Metz and Frouard and over the Meurthe; that such an advance could not be contemplated until a large part of the enemy forces had been transported to another point or had marched off; and finally, that if confronted with a highly superior enemy force, the Sixth Army should retire.

It was evidently the design of General von Moltke, in case the main body of the enemy forces in Lorraine took the offensive, to shift the center of gravity to that region and seek the decision there. The Fourth Army was informed that its cooperation would probably be required if the view entertained with respect to the enemy's designs should be confirmed. In such a case, the Fifth Army was to come into action by debouching from Metz and from the Nied position. Even the ersatz divisions were brought up behind the Sixth Army. The strategical views of Moltke thus already departed from those of Count Schlieffen. The latter believed that a French counter-offensive in Lorraine was desirable. He was opposed to leaving more than four and one-half corps in Lorraine, in addition to the cavalry, the fortress garrisons, and the landwehr. The sweeping movement through Belgium was to be executed even though in Lorraine the French should advance to the attack. Count Schlieffen assumed that they would turn back. General von Moltke, on the other hand, wished in such a case to strike. In the course of a journey of the General Staff, at the close of the campaign, he had declared that the aim of the great movement through Belgium was to attack the enemy in the open field, outside his fortresses, and that if the French accommodated us by an attack in Lorraine that aim would already be attained. He criticized the German leader for having continued the movement into Belgium in such a case, and said that he should have executed a change of front and advanced to the decision. Such a situation seemed to occur in August 1914.

In the middle of August the Sixth Army began to turn back in the direction of Saarbrücken – Sarrguemines [Sarrgemund] – Sarrburg but stopped on the line: Sanry – Han a.d. Nied – Fenestrange [Finstingen] – Sarrburg, when the information received showed that the main body of the enemy forces was not assembled in Lorraine. The High Command no longer expected the decision in Lorraine but by going around through Belgium. The Sixth Army was then assigned the task of covering the German flank. Crown Prince Rupprecht was left entirely at liberty to decide whether he would accomplish this task offensively or defensively. The High Command gave him orders to this effect on August 17.

But enemy forces in Lorraine were still to be reckoned with. It appeared inadvisable to fall back before them in case they took the offensive. For if a trap were set for them between Metz and the Nied position, on the one side, and the Seventh Army concentrated north of the Vosges, on the other, it was doubtful that they would follow. The Crown Prince of Bavaria decided to carry out his mission offensively and to advance to meet the enemy. The success obtained showed that he wasright.

On August 20 the Sixth Army debouched from the front: Wallersberg – Lauterfingen, and the Seventh Army from the locality of Pfalzburg and southward, as well as from Schirmeck, upon Baccarat – Raon l'Etape. They collided with the French First and Second Armies, which at the middle of August had also taken the offensive.[2] On August 20-22 the enemy was beaten in the Battle of Lorraine and pursued by the Sixth Army up to the frontier in the direction of Luneville.

Crown Prince Rupprecht had accomplished his mission: the German left flank was covered. The last moment had arrived at which it was still possible to bring up forces toward the right wing as provided for in the original plan. General Tappen objects that the destruction of the Belgian railway system rendered the thing impossible. But it was to be expected that those railways would be destroyed. If, then, the Lorraine forces could not be transported at that date and were lacking on that wing, then the initial concentration had been at fault. But it was still quite possible at that time to displace large forces by rail as far as Aix-la-Chapelle and to have them follow in echelon.[3]

The High Command adopted the grave decision to continue the pursuit in Lorraine in full force in order, by following upon the heels of the enemy, to break through the upper Moselle. It was believed, from the experience with the fortresses of Liege, that the French fortresses could quickly be disposed of. If the break-through succeeded, it would be possible, in conjunction with the

---

[2] See page 76.

[3] See pages 124-125.

detour through Belgium, to effect an encirclement of both enemy wings, a complete encirclement, a new Cannae. There would then be the prospect of a rapid termination of the war. General Tappen believes that that decision was entirely in accord with the original plan. I personally believe that the plan was completely abandoned.

It was less the existence of the barrier forts than the natural strength of the Toul – Epinal sector and the fact that both wings were supported on the great fortified zones of Toul – Nancy, on the one side, and Epinal on the other, which rendered the success of the breakthrough highly improbable. This is not a mere *a posteriori* affirmation. That it was impossible to cross the Moselle between Toul and Epinal, that is to say, in the trouée de Charmes, was known in time of peace. The French knew what they were doing when they left this sector unfortified. Several years before the war the, General Staff had an appraisal on the subject, based on personal investigations, of the following tenor:

This sector is an enormously strong one. The river is very important, forming with the deep canal along its banks a double and difficult obstacle. The valley of the Moselle is 1000 yards to one and one-half miles broad, in part quite flat and withoutcover. The terrain on the left bank is more favorable to the defender than that of the right bank to the assailant. The defender's two wings are supported on great fortresses. "The Russo-Japanese war has shown that a purely frontal attack on such a position would at least require much time. The war would assume the character of position warfare." As regards the Moselle front of Belfort – Epinal – Toul as a whole, the appraisal stated: "To attack in that direction would be to fall in with the desire of the French. The country's system of defense would be put to full use. The fortified organizations cooperate with the natural strength of the sector to compel the assailant to turn from movement to position warfare. The French then hope that behind this sector and under cover of their fortresses they will be able to regroup their forces in such manner as to take the offensive at some point in superior numbers."

On August 24, by order of the High Command, the Sixth Army, covering toward Nancy, took up the pursuit in the direction of Luneville, and the Seventh Army with its left wing in the direction of St. Die. On the same day the chief of staff of the Sixth

Army, General Kraft von Dellmensingen, reported that he had no thought, as the High Command appeared to believe, of a pursuit such as took place after Jena or Waterloo. He declared that the advance was but slow, that the independent cavalry could not do much in that region, that the different corps were highly fatigued. On the right, the attack scarcely proceeded farther than the Mortagne [river], and on the left the locality of St. Die. The enemy offered vigorous resistance; he made a counter-thrust from Nancy and also attacked the German left wing from the south.

The attack had not turned out so successfully as was expected. At the end of the month there arose the question as to what further should be done. On August 31 the Sixth Army reported that it had not yet been able to ascertain that the enemy was withdrawing before its front or displacing forces by rail; that consequently it was not yet necessary to march toward the Moselle to hold the enemy; that. the troops had suffered heavy losses but that the same was certainly true of the enemy and that it was hardly possible that the latter had any fresh forces. "And so the army command would by no means regard the attack over the Moselle between Nancy and Epinal as having no chance of success." Also on September 1 the Sixth Army reported that it was inclined to believe itself still confronted with strong enemy forces, and that further preparations for the continuance of the offensive were being made.

After discussing the question in detail with the command of the Sixth Army, the High Command, as General von Tappen says, pronounced in favor of continuing the attack, in the hope that the break-through would still succeed or that it would be possible at least to hold large elements of the French forces. While the right wing of the Sixth Army, reenforced by heavy artillery brought up from the interior, was to attack the advanced positions of Nancy, its left wing was to try to break through in the direction of Bayon. The Seventh Army was to take part in this operation and cover the left flank facing Epinal. The attack began on September 4.

Once the retreat of the French armies was under way, the First and Second Armies had been assigned, by order of the High

Command of August 25, a purely defensive task.[4] They were to hold the forces opposed to them, while the other armies would first get away from the enemy and a powerful offensive group would be formed on the extreme left. The first and Second Armies had completely accomplished their task up to that time, although their operations had lacked unity. Almost at the same time that the Germans were deciding to continue the attack against the Moselle, the French General Headquarters believed itself in a position to withdraw forces from the region of the Moselle and move them toward the other points of its front. These withdrawals began on September 1.

This was not noted at once by the Germans. In the evening of September 3 the Sixth Army sent the following report: "No retiring movement, no withdrawal of forces by rail, has yet been noted on the army front. On the other hand, powerful forces and much artillery are still found in and behind the enemy position."

The attack on Nancy was launched September 4, at a time when the High Command was perfectly aware that the French had begun to transport forces from the east toward the west. The fortified position established on the heights which form a vast arc of a circle around Nancy are called by the French the "Grand Couronne de Nancy." Work had been going on therefor years. The German attack on these positions made but slow progress. The Seventh Army, also, was only approaching the locality of Rambervillers on September 5.

On the same day the High Command decided to withdraw from the front the headquarters of the Seventh Army, the 7th Cavalry Division, the XV Corps and a corps of the Sixth Army and transport them to the right wing. It was the eve of the Battle of the Marne. The Belgian railways had meanwhile been sufficiently restored. The transportation of the 7th Cavalry Division began September 7, and of the XV Corps September 8, by way of Liege – Brussels – Mons.

The attack on Nancy was at first continued, but it could no longer have any other purpose than that of holding the enemy. Only

---

[4] See pages 173-174.

the Fourth and Fifth Armies, by advancing toward the south, could henceforth open the passage of the Moselle to the Sixth Army. On September 8 arose the necessity of withdrawing further forces from the Sixth and Seventh Armies for reenforcing the German right wing. An advance of the Fourth and Fifth Armies to the left bank of the Meuse could no longer be counted on. On September 8 the High Command conferred on this matter with the commander in chief of the Sixth Army. The latter would have still preferred to continue the attack: the losses up to that time had been considerable; to renounce the offensive after such sacrifices was the equivalent of a defeat. The High Command decided, however, in view of the general situation, to stop the offensive. It gave orders on September 8 to hold the I Bavarian Corps ready for entrainment on the 9th. It also announced that further considerable withdrawals would be made. On the 9th the following order was sent to the Sixth Army: "The attack on the advanced position of Nancy will not be pushed farther. The design is to render available as quickly as possible all the elements of the Sixth Army which are not indispensable, with a view to a different employment. Preparations will therefore be made at once for the occupation of a defensive position in the rear." Position warfare then began here also.

It is interesting to note that according to Palat's account the situation at Nancy from September 5 onward was regarded as very critical by the French. He says that after the withdrawals which had been effected the Second Army had at its disposal only two regular corps in addition to its reserve divisions; that Joffre and the commander of the Second Army, General Castelnau, had considered the question of abandoning Nancy and falling back on the fortified positions of the forest of Haye in front of Toul, but that it was decided to hold Nancy for the present. This is confirmed by Mangin. He says that after violent fighting the Germans made progress on September 6 and 7, although at the cost of heavy losses, and that the French had resigned themselves to the idea of falling back behind the Meurthe and the Mortagne.[5]

The troops which the French right wing had been obliged to

---

[5] Loc. cit.

yield were distributed as follows between the different armies:

In the first place, the Army of Alsace was disbanded on August 28.[6] The VII Corps (14th Division and 63rd Reserve Division) was assigned to the newly formed Sixth Army.[7] On August 30 the 8th Cavalry Division was pushed upon Chalons-sur-Marne, where it was assigned to the II (Conneau) Cavalry Corps.

The First Army, comprising originally the VIII, XIII, XIV, and XXI Corps and the 6th Cavalry Division was obliged on September 2to yield a corps (the XXI), which was entrained in the locality of Bruyeres and Epinal and transported to the Fourth Army. On September 7 it yielded the 6th Cavalry Division and the XI and XIII Corps, and later the VIII Corps.

The Second Army comprised originally the XVIII, XX, XV, and XVI Corps. Of these forces, the XVIII Corps had already passed at the middle of August to the Fifth Army; half of the IX Corps had been pushed into the gap between the Fourth and Fifth Armies. On September 1 the withdrawal of the 10th Cavalry Division was ordered: it was assigned to Conneau's cavalry corps. On September 2 orders were issued for withdrawing the XV Corps and the rest of the IX Corps. The XV Corps struck camp on the 3rd, mostly by night in order to conceal its departure, pushed through Bayon – Haroue and executed fatiguing forced marches in order to pass to the Third Army. The elements of the IX Corps fell back during the night of September 2-3 upon Nancy and were transported to Arcis sur Aube in order to pass to the Ninth Army, where the other fractions of this corps were stationed.

The Army of Lorraine yielded to the Sixth Army the 55th and 56th Reserve Division which on August 29-30 were disembarked south of Montdidier.

The IV Corps which arrived at the Sixth Army beginning September 6, came from the Third Army.

Thus we see that on the French side an important displacement of forces from the right wing to the left took place early. As for us,

---

[6] See page 176.

[7] See page 82.

the displacement of our forces began too late, and the transport lines at our disposal were by no means so good as those of the French. But that was a matter which we were in a position to foresee; we should have been grouped accordingly from the beginning, at the time of the concentration.

Conclusion

The retrospective glance over the German operations from the beginning of the campaign up to the Battle of the Marne might be headed by Moltke's saying, that an error committed in the concentration can scarcely be compensated in the course of the whole campaign. The German right wing remained too weak, the left wing too strong.

The strength of our left wing led to the attempt to break through the French fortified front of the northeast, an enterprise which we had wished to avoid by the detour through Belgium.

On the right wing our forces were not sufficient for encircling the enemy wherever he appeared, as Schlieffen desired. The more deeply the offensive led us into the enemy country, the more numerous were the withdrawals made from that wing in order to cover the communications and besiege the enemy fortresses, while no other troops were brought up in the second line. Speed had to take the place of what we lacked in the matter of forces. Many things were done precipitately under constraint of necessity. The operations oscillated between the farthest extremes. The right wing had first to be extended toward the southwest as far as the lower

Seine, then it had to change front toward the southeast by filing past in front of Paris, until finally, on September 5, the whole campaign plan collapsed. We stood before Paris and could do nothing with it.

There is in general no great use in wondering, after a war, what would have been the result if such or such thing had happened. But in the present case it is a question of proving that in 1914 the German army undertook nothing which was beyond its powers.

If our concentration had been effected logically, according to the Schlieffen plan, the success, in so far as the human understanding can judge, could not have failed to be ours. Our advance to the north of the Marne completely surprised the French and upset their campaign plan. The great August battles might already have brought the decision; the battle of the Marne or of the Seine could certainly have brought it in September when Joffre's measures presented us with the brilliant opportunity of throwing the French back toward the southeast.

The plan of Count Schlieffen was not outmoded; it was instinct with life, not "the recipe of the deceased Schlieffen." But we did not follow it.

The campaign would still have been won, however, if we had not, in addition, adopted defective measures.

Instead of bringing up behind the right wing everything available in the way of troops, two corps were withdrawn. The ersatz divisions were brought up behind the left wing; the landsturm troops were raised too late. On August 23 or even on August 30 there would still have been time to effect a regrouping of our forces from the left wing to the right.

Leadership at the top was lacking. From Koblenz or Luxemburg it was impossible to manage the reins. Communications were wholly insufficient, exchange of ideas totally impossible. By the time long written orders reached the armies they were outstripped by the events. the army commanders were often thrown upon their own resources and advised that they should come to an understanding between themselves. With what result, the events have demonstrated. They did as well as they could from their own point of view, but not always in accord with their neighbors and within the framework of the great strategic situation. The High Command let itself be pushed; it often failed to take action when the armies adopted other courses than those which it had prescribed, but approved their conduct later.

Thus, August 23 on the Sambre and Meuse, August 29-30 on the Oise, the opportunity was lost for striking the enemy a heavy blow. On the Marne, the First and Second Armies separated.

We would not have lost the Battle of the Marne if we had only hung on. The victory on the Ourcq, the break-through at Fere-Champenoise, more than counterbalanced the difficulties of our situation at Montmirail and on the Marne.

After the August battles, a second German victory on the Marne would have had, as the French concede, the most widespread effect and would have been a crushing blow to the morale in France. Paris and Verdun, the two pillars of the French military structure, would probably have fallen.

Would we then have been in a condition for continuing the operations? We would certainly not have done so at once and within the term established up to that time. We would have had to regroup our forces, regulate our communications and provide for the rationing of our army. The offensive could then have been carried farther.

As regards munitions, the situation of the First Army during its rapid advance was sometimes difficult, in certain isolated instances disquieting, but never so critical as to seriously menace the operations. The fact that there was no lack of ammunition was due to the excellent cooperation of the staff officers of the First Army, who had charge of supplies, with the perfectly functioning depot service and to the splendid performances of the columns and parks. During the battle of the Ourcq in particular, we had plenty of ammunition.

Because of the swiftness of our advance, the railways of Belgium and Northern France had not been destroyed so completely as might have been expected. The chief of the railway service had had the foresight to engage numerous railway construction companies behind the First and Second Armies. None the less, the railway situation was unfavorable at the beginning of September. The supply line: Aix-la-Chapelle – Liege was not sufficient to meet all the demands of the armies and of the depot service, and it was obliged moreover to serve for transporting the landwehr, the IX Reserve Corps and the artillery designed to be used against Antwerp.

But the needs of the combatant troops were fortunately not very great apart from ammunition. The harvest was ripe; oats and other cereals stood in ricks or sheaves in the fields. Meats of all sorts were abundant. The troops lacked nothing but time and experience for making a rational use of the provisions. Still, the great mass of the cavalry suffered seriously on several occasions from the lack of oats. But in Courland, Volhynia, and Macedonia, much greater difficulties arose in the course of the war and were still surmounted.

Even though it had not been possible to exploit our victory to the full extent, even though we might have settled down to position warfare, our situation would have been incomparably better than it actually turned out later. The occupation of the Channel ports particularly would have been of the greatest importance.

The judgments which our operations have called forth in the French and English accounts of the campaign are worthy of mention.

General Maurice says: "The German campaign plan was bold and simple in its conception and based on the most painstaking study of the war. If it had been executed on the field of battle with the same skill with which it had been established in the offices of the staff, it would have led to the complete annihilation of our first five divisions, the fall of Paris and the loss of the north of France." General Maurice believes, however, that even such a success would not have resulted in final victory to the Germans. He objects to the German plan that the crossing of Belgium determined the whole world to turn against us. As if England was not already decided to enter the struggle anyhow.

Marshal Foch's opinion of the German command in the battle of the Marne was expressed in the course of an interview with the correspondent of a Parisian newspaper.[1] He thinks that the German plan of operations was rigid and made no allowance whatever for

---

[1] *Petit Parisien*, September 7, 1920.

the unforeseen. But the marshal here confuses the plan with its execution. He then says that the German High Command allowed each one of its generals to go his own way and that none of them concerned himself with his neighbors. The strategists of Berlin had assumed as a matter of course that everything would come off as set down on paper. General von Kluck, who had been assigned the task of encircling the enemy left wing, pushed up before Paris in astonishing marches and with an unheard-of rapidity without paying any attention to Gallieni, who then turned up suddenly in his flank in the midst of the most beautiful of maneuvers. At that moment there was only one natural thing for the German High Command to do; to take back the reins which had dropped from its hands and to give firm guidance to the hesitant armies. Instead of that, the High Command remained at Luxembourg and lost all view of the situation as a whole; the uncertainty infected the leaders, until the confusion became complete.

As for the fact that his own army was beaten on September 8-9, the marshal skips over this point with the remarkthat there were difficult hours, that on the evening of the 9th he had issued orders to attack, but that the attack had to be delayed until the following day, when suddenly the completely unexpected news of the German retreat reached him.

He unreservedly recognizes the value of the German troops: "That German Army of 1914! It was a magnificent tool! Never thereafter did Germany find an army of that stamp!"

De Thomasson condemns our ideas of trying to breakthrough beyond the Moselle with the Sixth and Seventh Armies. In doing this, did we not attack the fortified front which we wished to go around? It would have been better, he thinks, if we had done as old Moltke desired, that is, encircled the French right wing at the very beginning in order to drive the French back on Belgium instead of driving them back onto the interior of their country. If necessary, he says, we could have had recourse to crossing Switzerland. We had good reasons for avoiding that.

The judgments expressed by Hanotaux on the operations of the First Army can for the most part scarcely betaken seriously. It is only occasionally that one finds a practicable idea among the numerous fairy tales with which he regales the reader. As an example of these fairy tales, we may state that according to Hanotaux General von Kluck wanted to seize Paris. A flag 20 meters wide, he says, had been prepared for planting upon the Eiffel Tower. The entry into Paris was set for September 2. Palat, who is otherwise so moderate in his statements, himself relates that event before the Battle of the Marne ten wagon loads of medals representing the entry into Paris were held in readiness.

On September 1 the staff of the First Army stopped for several hours at Lassigny. General von Kluck's host, M. Albert Fabre, counselor at the Paris court of appeal, made certain declarations before an investigating committee with reference to our sojourn there which Hanotaux reproduces. A superior officer, he says, entered first and announced that in three days the Germans would be at Paris and that the city would be completely destroyed. Then an officer left the automobile, in an impressive attitude, "tall, majestic, with hard features and a terrible glance. I had before me the image of Attila. It was Kluck!" General von Kluck, says Hanotaux, then hesitated between taking Paris and seeking connection with Bülow; the fact that he abandoned Paris proves his lack ofenergy.

Le Gros expresses a different opinion on the matter. He declares it unjust to reproach Kluck with not having continued the march on Paris and with having sought to encircle the French left wing. It was impossible to do both at the same time. "He acted entirely in accordance with correct strategic principles in seeking first of all to come to terms with the combatant armies before turning against the fortress of Paris. A French defeat in the open field would quickly have resulted in the fall of the fortress. His misfortune consisted in not having known of the presence of Maunoury's army."

As for the motive behind the First Army's crossing the Marne in advance of the Second, Hanotaux, by dint of his gifts of imagination, finds it in the personal ambition of General von Kluck. He wished to annihilate the enemy, and now he had to stop all at once, pass into the background and let Bülow go on ahead and gather the laurels!

The First Army's rapid change of front toward its flank in order to face Maunoury in the Battle of the Ourcq is thoroughly appreciated by the French. "Our staff renders full justice to the skilful measures of Kluck...That evolution to the rear will be reckoned, when it is better known, among the most interesting maneuvers executed in the course of the war. Von Kluck saved the Germans from defeat by his decision and swiftness of execution."[2] When von Kluck was attacked in the flank,"he showed himself an eminent tactician. His energy and audacity never failed him in those difficult days of September 8 and 9 when he turned about and indented Maunoury's left flank."[3] Hanotaux, also, believes that on September 5 Kluck recognized his error: "He again becomes what he is in reality – an experienced leader, calm and collected and decided. He was warned, and he turned about before we could strike a decisive blow." And he adds that by operating on the inner line, he regained the initiative. General Canonge sums up his estimate with the statement that Kluck has often been blamed unjustly. "His renown as an instructed and vigorous general was not unmerited."[4]

As regards the measures adopted by General von Bülow, Hanotaux reproaches him with having added to the difficulties of the encirclement by drawing directly to himself the neighboring armies to lend him support. In addition to this action upon the progress of the operations, Hanotaux imputes to him a direct influence, increasing in the course of the campaign, upon the High Command. This was particularly true, he says, as regards the order of September 4 by which the encirclement was definitely abandoned. Hanotaux is naturally unable to furnish any proofs of these statements.

On September 9, 1914, the Marne campaign was lost to us, but not the war itself. We were, to be sure, obliged to abandon all hope of a rapid decision, but the spirit of the army was intact and would have remained so to the end if the country had remained behind it.

---

[2] Fabreguettes, loc. cit. , pp. 45 ff.

[3] General Malleterre, *Un peu de lumiere sur les batailles d'aout et de septembre*, 1914, page 57.

[4] *La Battaille de la Marne, Paris*, 1918

It is said that our "system" was to blame for the loss of the war. In so far as concerns the army, the "system,"of instructing our troops, of forming our corps of officers and the activity of our staff were excellent. Apart from the unfavorable political conditions of our entrance into the war, it was mainly due to the leadership that we lost the campaign of 1914. It was not the system which failed us, but the directing personages.

But it is said to have been the fault of the system that we did not have the proper men at the proper places. Under the same system King Wilhelm I found a Bismarck, a Moltke and a Roon. Does a democracy guarantee that the men at the head are at the same time the best of the nation? One must wait to answer that question. At the present time the proof of that, as concerns us, has not been furnished.

We must confess to many errors committed in the course of the campaign just described. Only our troops were impeccable. Never did they fall short, they made the impossible possible. In them lived the German fidelity, which we hope to see reappear. The deeds of our troops inspire hopes of a better future.

Maps and Sketches

Map No. 1

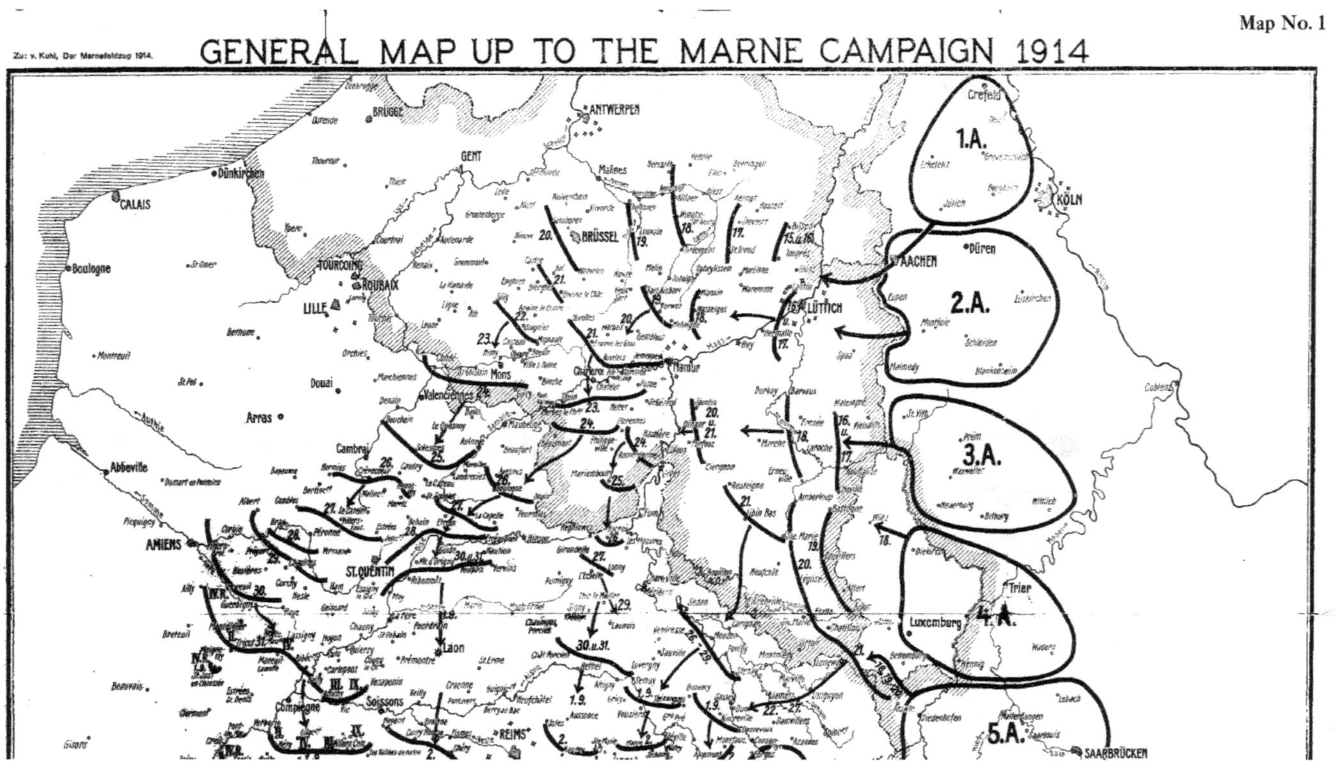
Zu: v. Kuhl, Der Marnefeldzug 1914.
GENERAL MAP UP TO THE MARNE CAMPAIGN 1914
1.A.
2.A.
3.A.
4.A.
5.A.
KÖLN
Crefeld
Düren
AACHEN
LÜTTICH
Namur
ANTWERPEN
BRÜSSEL
BRUGGE
GENT
Dünkirchen
CALAIS
Boulogne
TOURCOING
ROUBAIX
LILLE
Douai
Arras
Cambrai
Mons
Valenciennes
Charleroi
Abbeville
AMIENS
ST. QUENTIN
Laon
Soissons
Compiègne
REIMS
Luxemburg
Trier
SAARBRÜCKEN
Malines
Montreuil
Beauvais
Coblenz

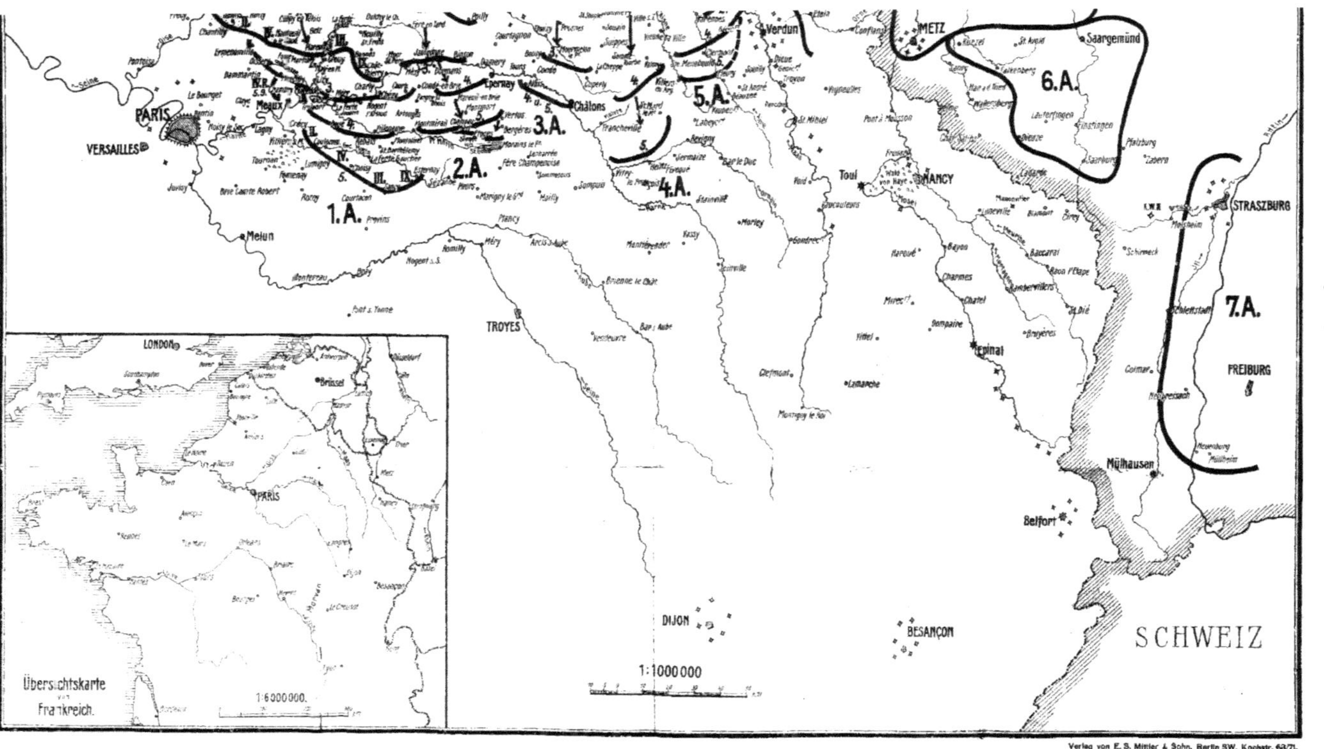
1.A.
2.A.
3.A.
4.A.
5.A.
6.A.
7.A.
PARIS
VERSAILLES
Meaux
Melun
Epernay
Châlons
Verdun
METZ
Saargemünd
Toul
NANCY
STRASZBURG
FREIBURG
Mülhausen
Belfort
Epinal
TROYES
DIJON
BESANÇON
SCHWEIZ
1:1000000
LONDON
Brüssel
PARIS
Übersichtskarte von Frankreich
1:6000000
Verlag von E. S. Mittler & Sohn, Berlin SW, Kochstr. 68/71.

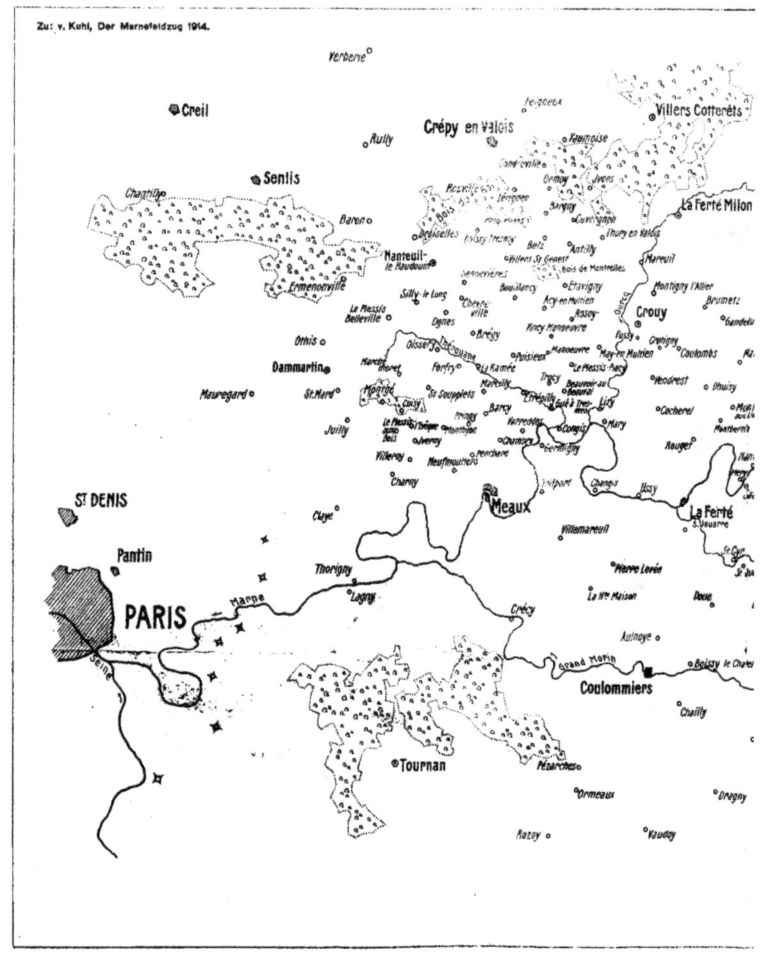
Zu: v. Kuhl, Der Marnefeldzug 1914.
Verberie
Creil
Crépy en Valois
Villers Cotterêts
Rully
Senlis
Chantilly
Baron
Nanteuil-le Haudouin
Ermenonville
Betz
Antilly
Etavigny
Bois de Montrolles
La Ferté Milon
Thury en Valois
Mareuil
Montigny l'Allier
Brumetz
Crouy
Le Plessis Belleville
Silly-le Long
Ognes
Brégy
Othis
Oissery
Forfry
Puisieux
La Ramée
Marcilly
Trocy
Étrépilly
Lizy
Vendrest
Coulombs
Dammartin
Mauregard
St. Mard
Juilly
Barcy
Varreddes
Congis
Mary
Cocherel
Chambry
Penchard
Neufmoutiers
Villeroy
Charny
Changis
Ussy
ST DENIS
Meaux
La Ferté
Claye
Pantin
Villemareuil
Thorigny
Lagny
PARIS
Marne
Seine
Crécy
Aulnoye
Grand Morin
Coulommiers
Chailly
Tournan
Pézarches
Ormeaux
Rozoy
Vaudoy

Map No. 2

GENERAL MAP
FOR THE
MARNE CAMPAIGN 1914
1: 300000
Fère en Tardenois
Château-Thierry
Dormans
Epernay
Montmirail
Vertus
Fère Champenoise
Verlag von E. S. Mittler & Sohn, Berlin SW, Kochstr. 68 71.

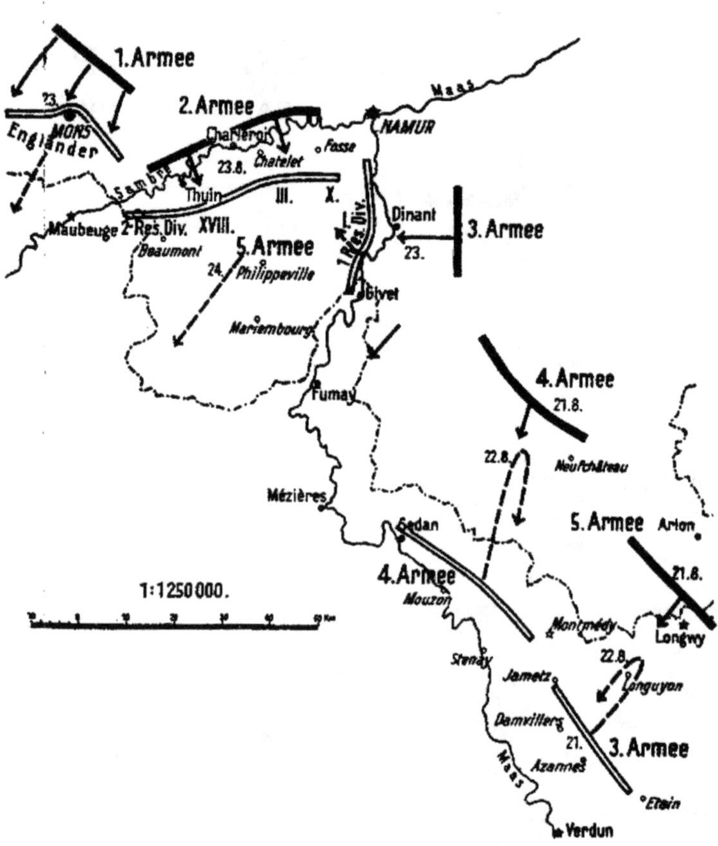

Sketch 1. Situation on August 22 and 23. Battle at Mons, Namur, Neufchateau and Longwy.

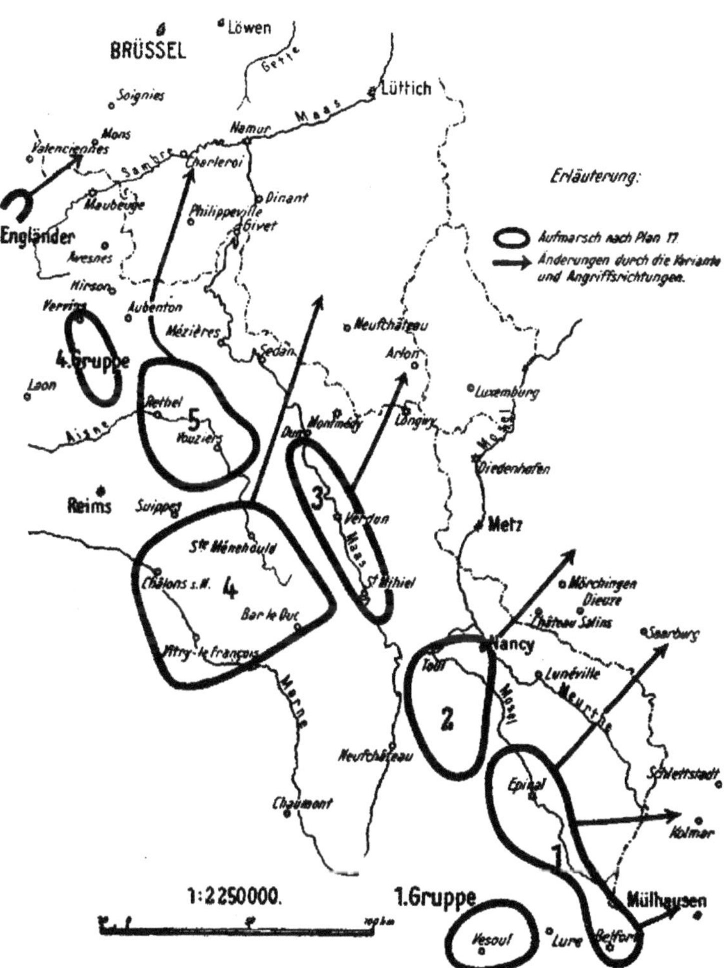

Sketch 2. The French concentration of 1914

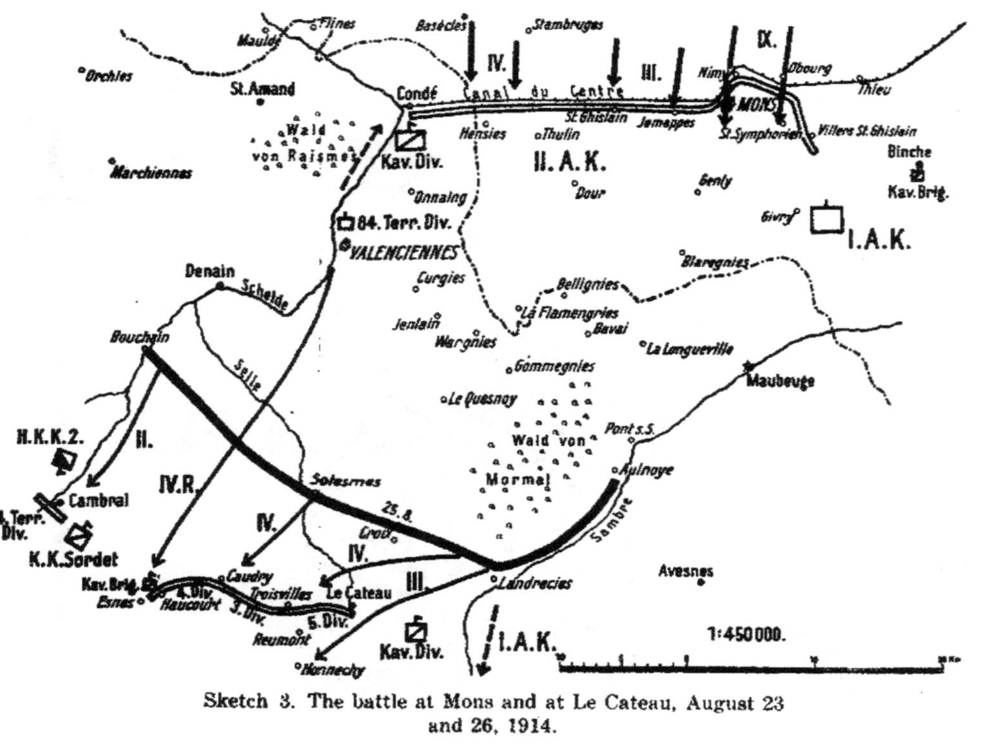

Sketch 3. The battle at Mons and at Le Cateau, August 23 and 26, 1914.

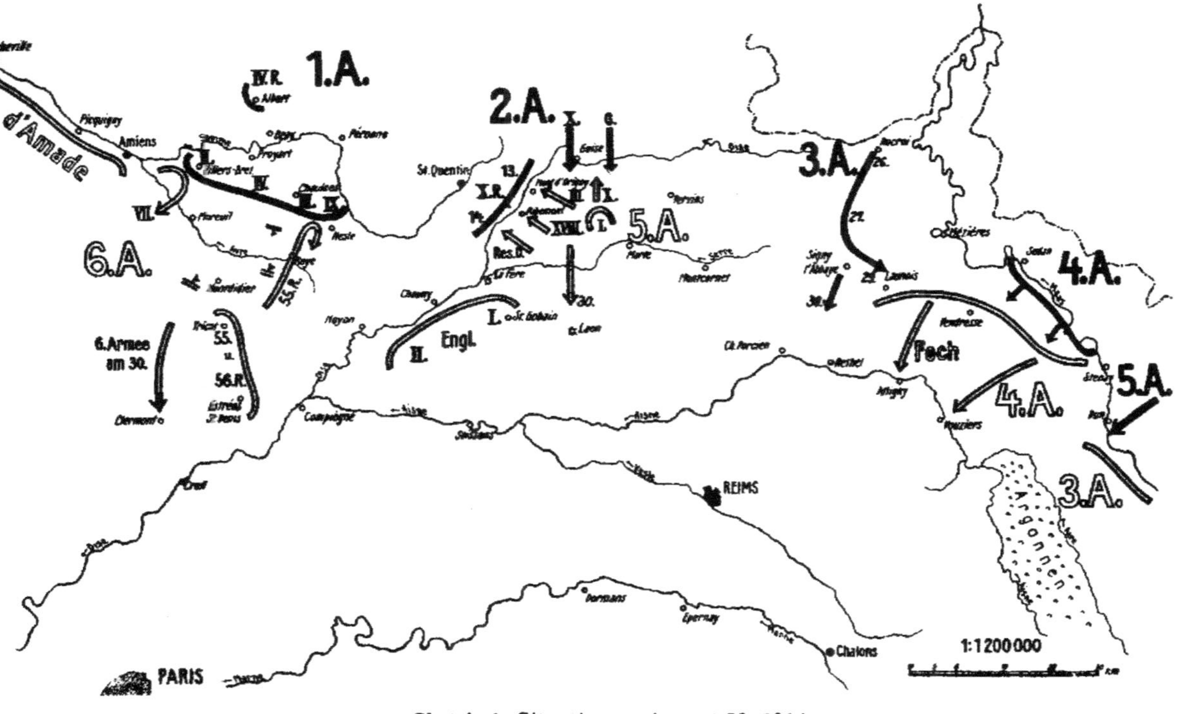

Sketch 4. Situation on August 29, 1914.

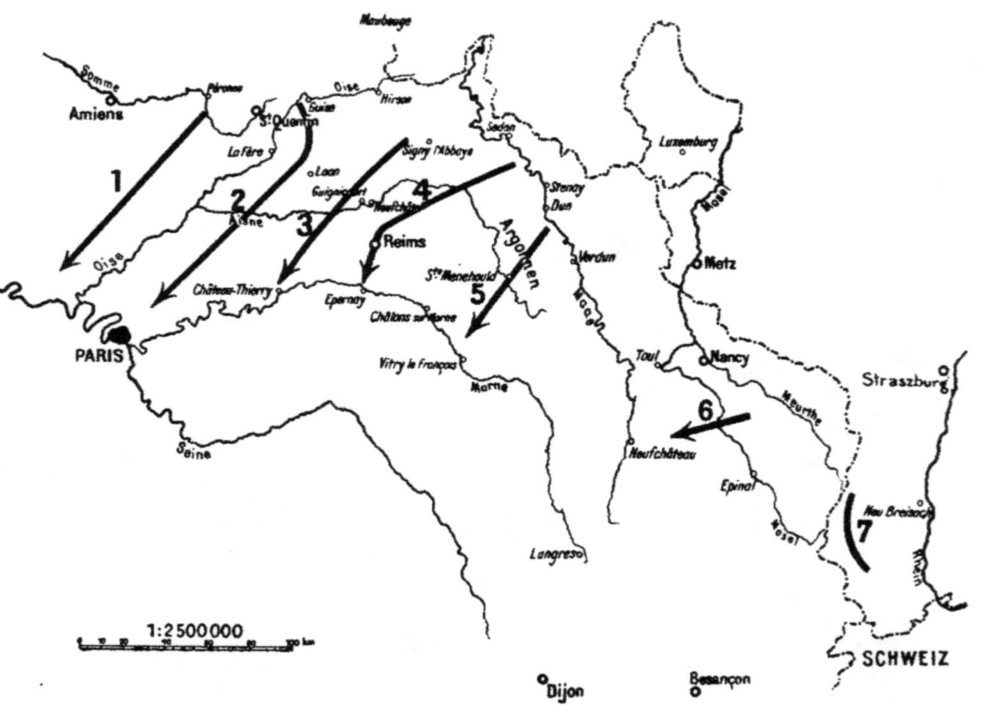

Sketch 5. GHQ Directive the morning of 27 August 1914

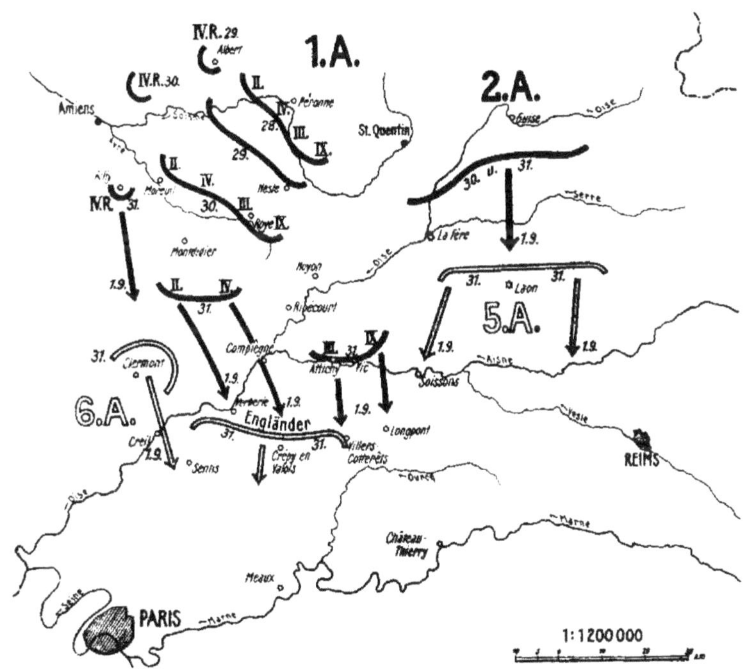

Sketch 6. Situation on 30 and 31 August, 1914.

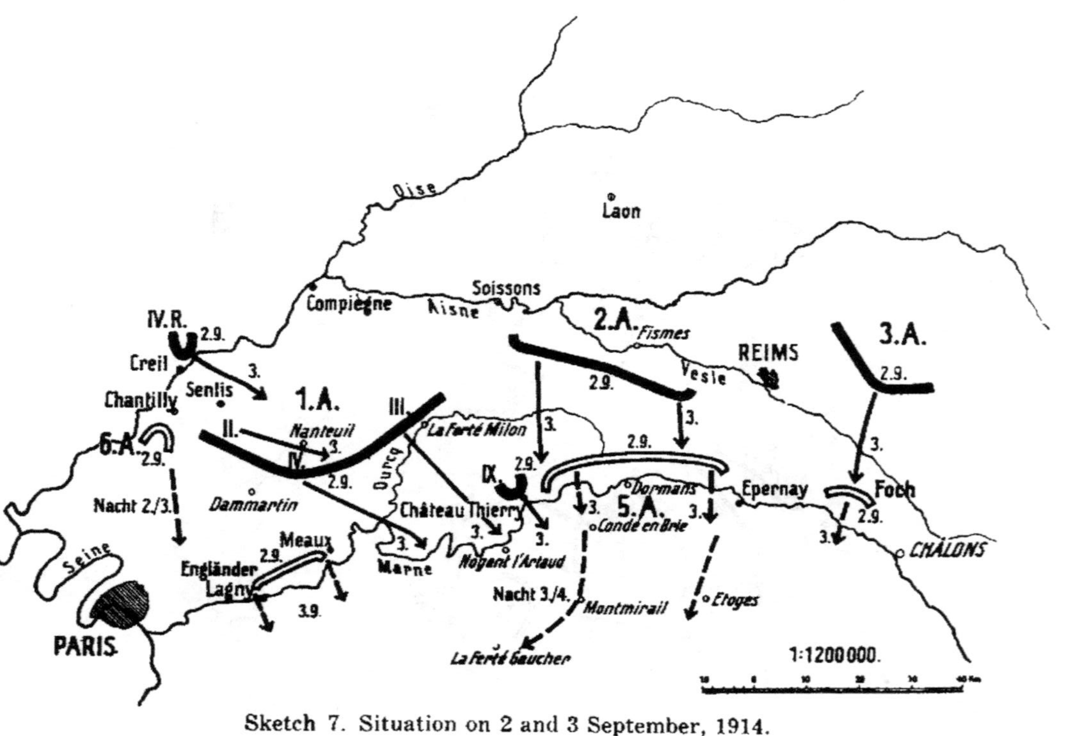

Sketch 7. Situation on 2 and 3 September, 1914.

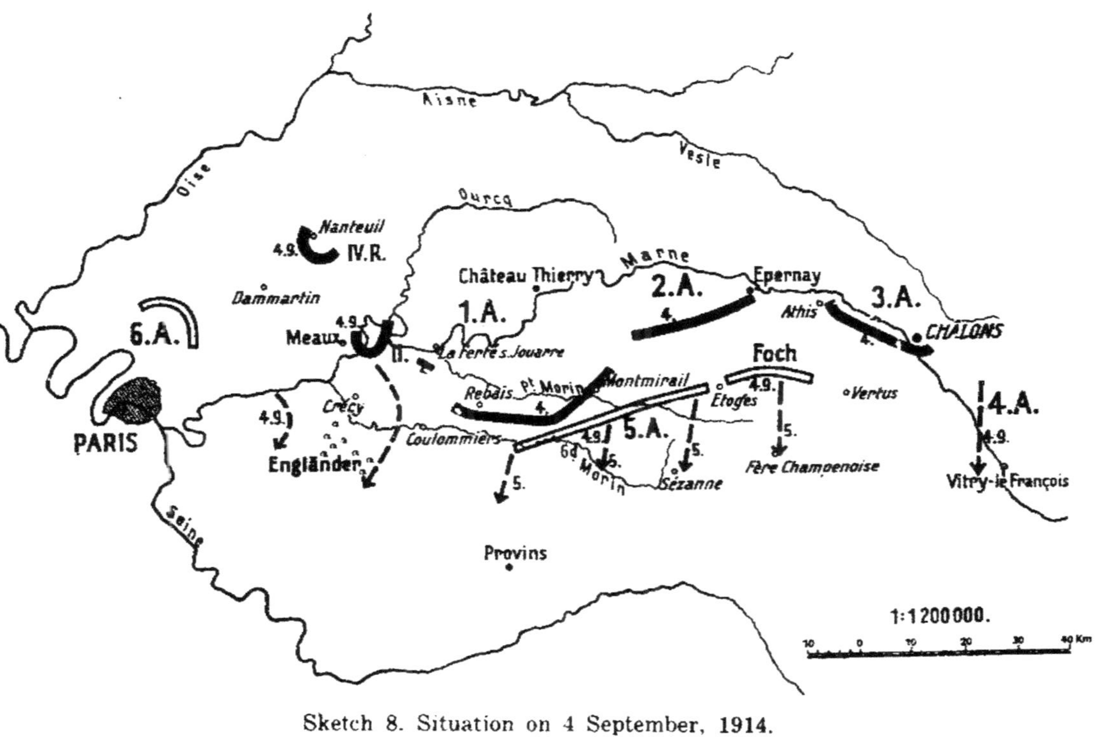

Sketch 8. Situation on 4 September, 1914.

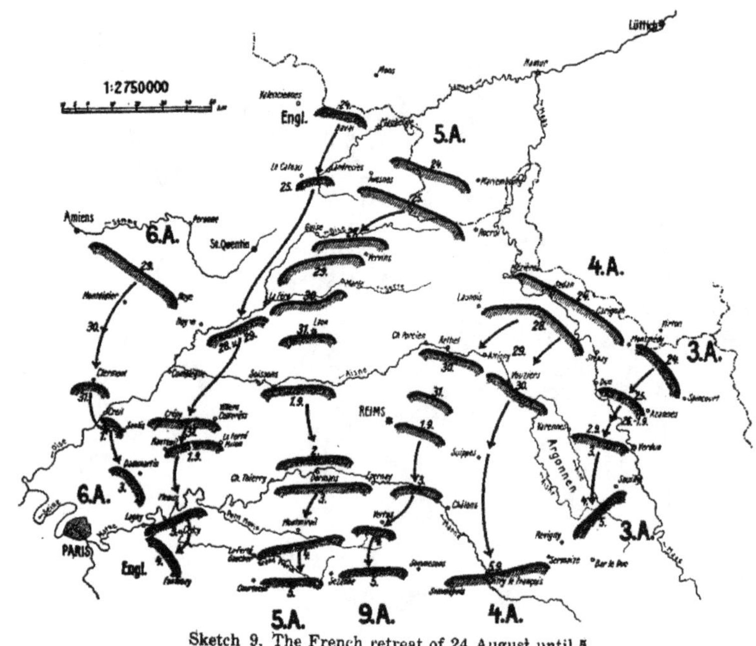

Sketch 9. The French retreat of 24 August until 5 September, 1914.

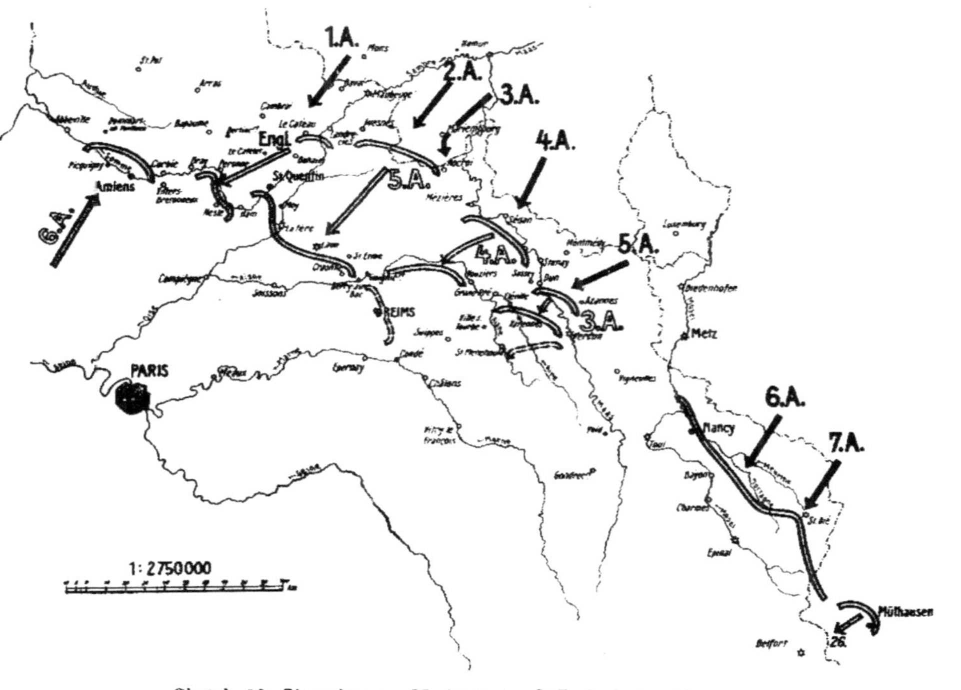

Sketch 10. Situation on 25 August. Joffre's instructions for that day.

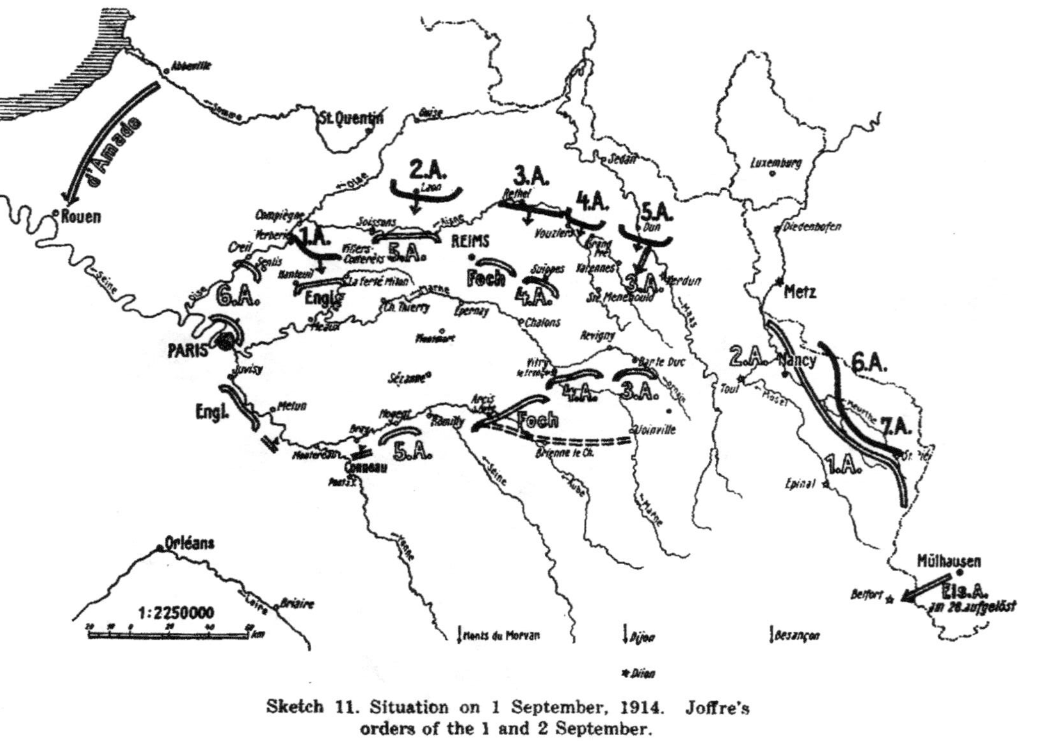

Sketch 11. Situation on 1 September, 1914. Joffre's orders of the 1 and 2 September.

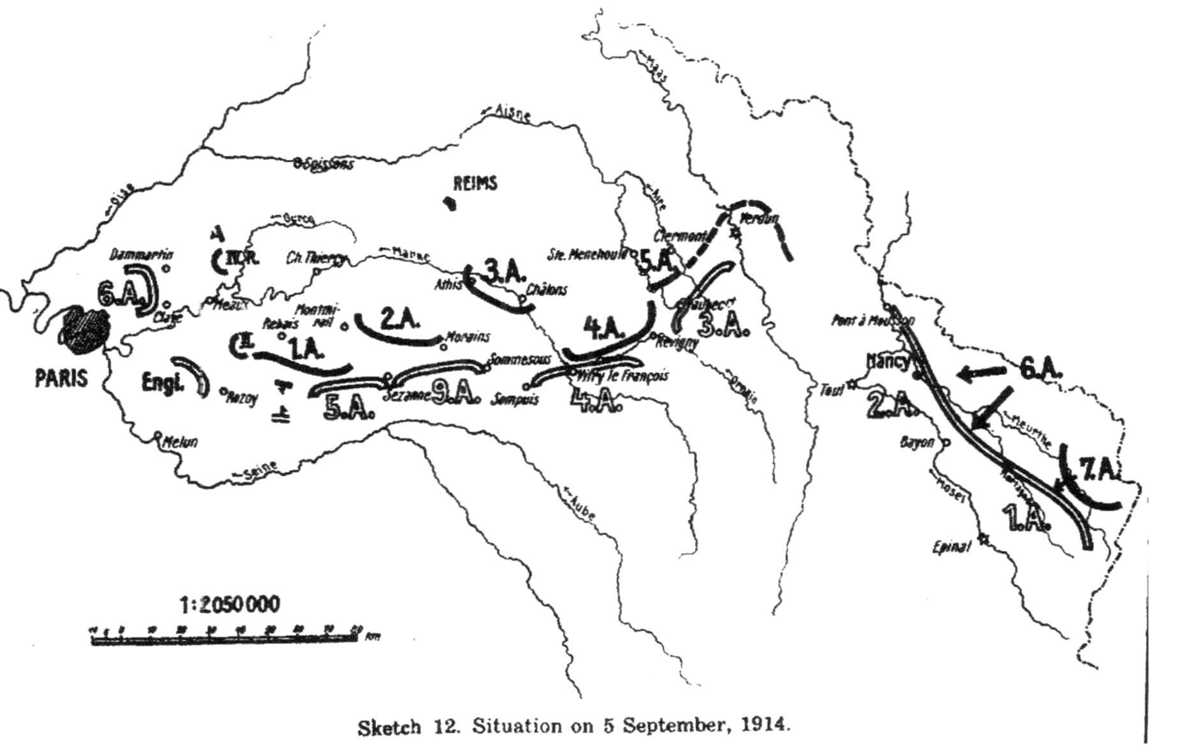

Sketch 12. Situation on 5 September, 1914.

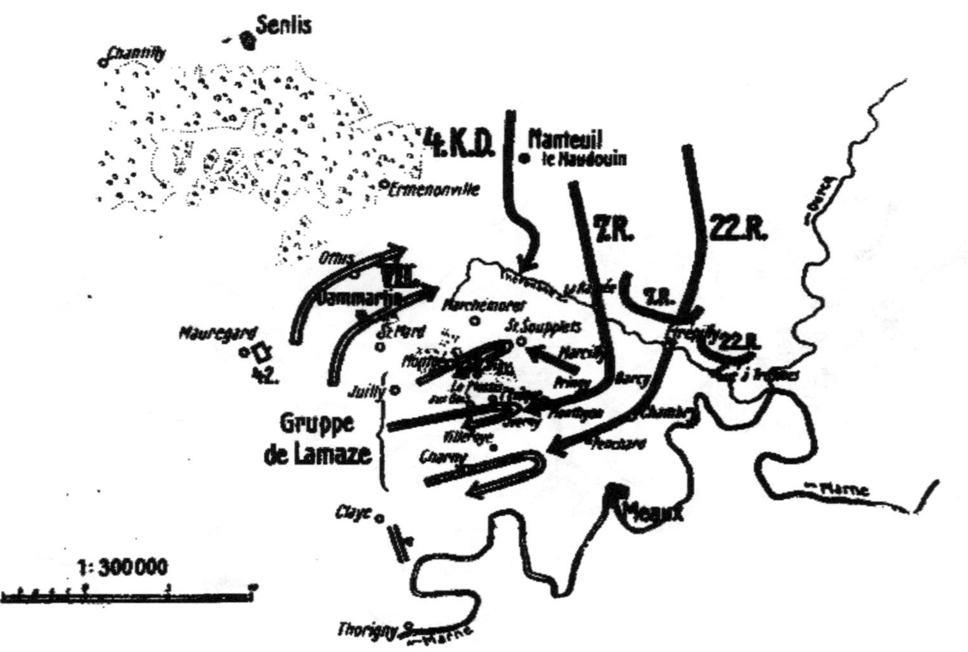

Sketch 13. The combat of the IV Reserve Corps on 5 September.

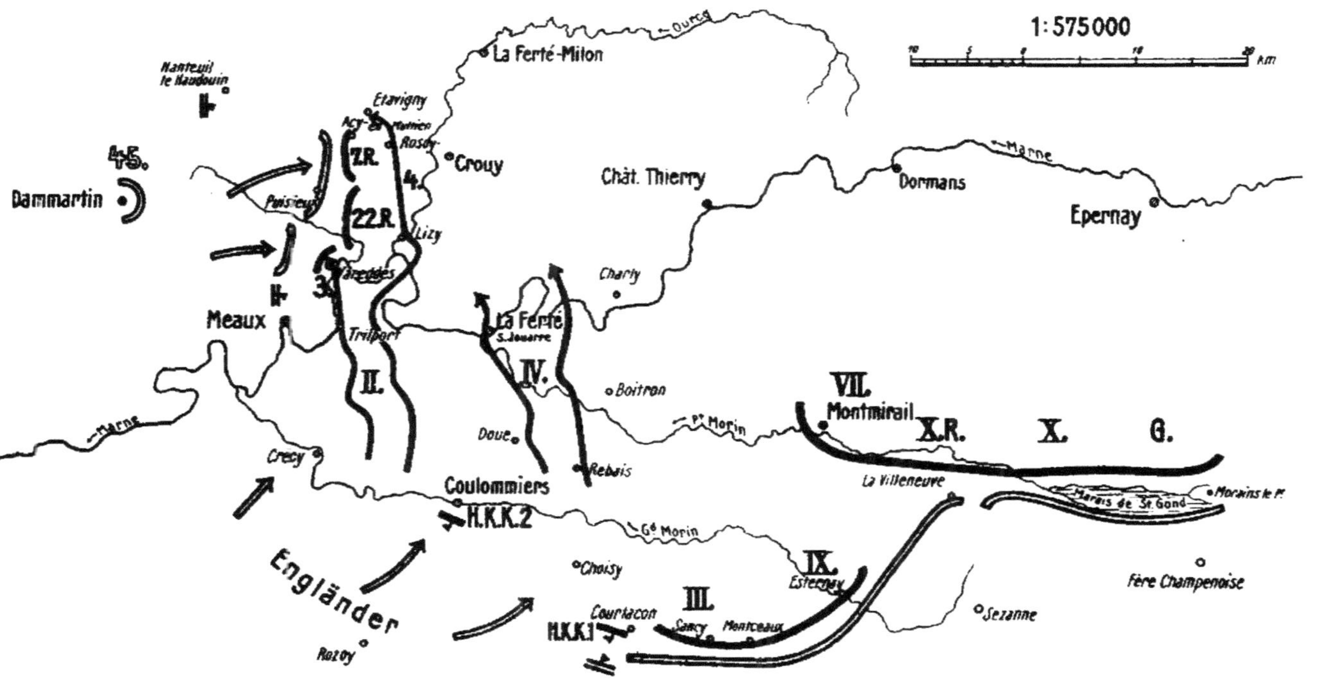

Sketch 14. Situation on 6 September, 1914.

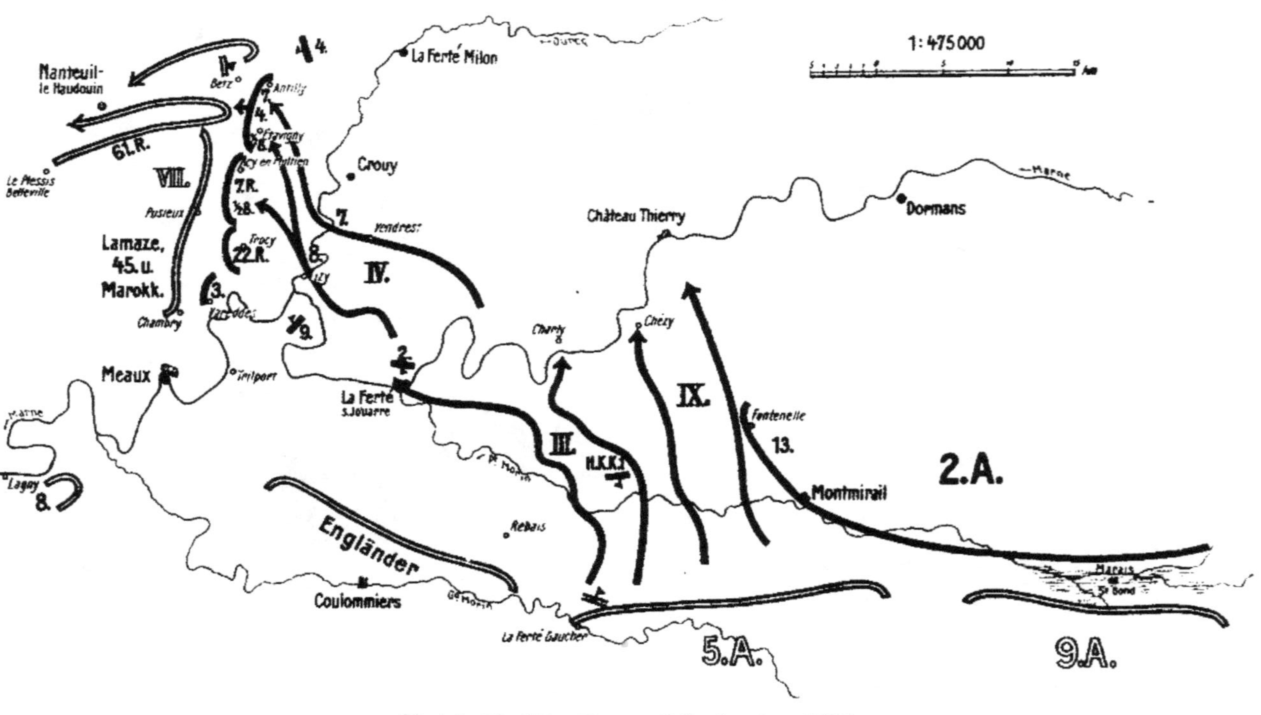

Sketch 15. Situation on 7 September, 1914.

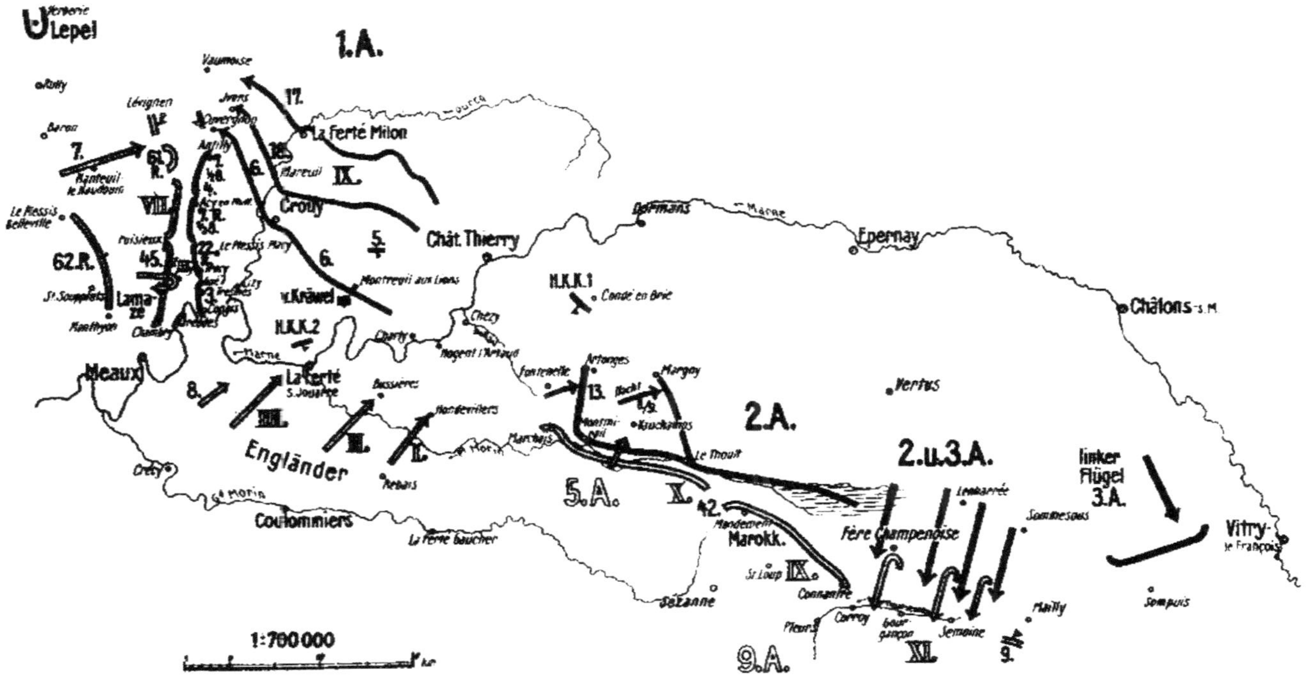

Sketch 16. Situation on 8 September, 1914.

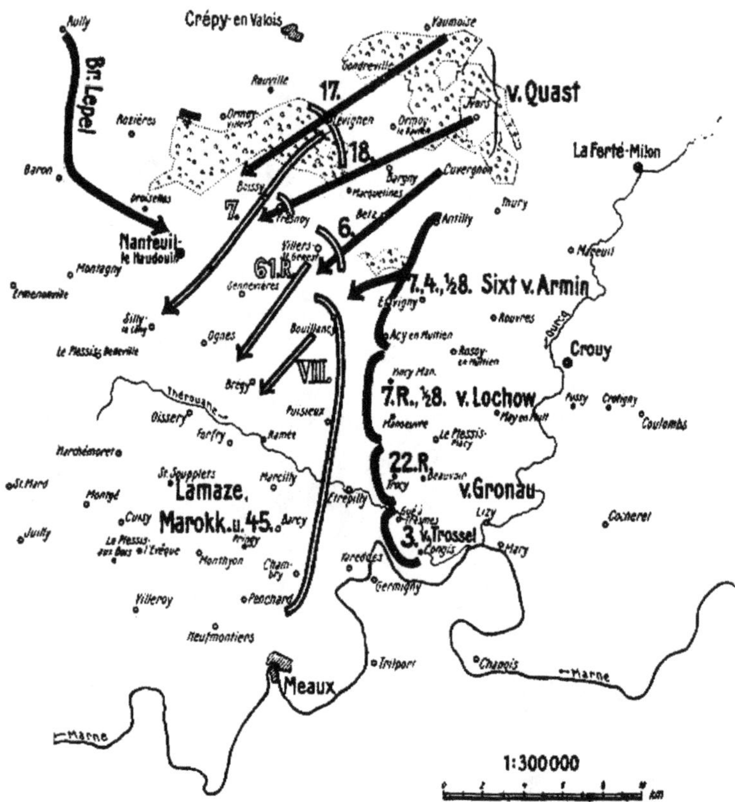

Sketch 17. The battle of the Ourcq, on 9 September, 1914.

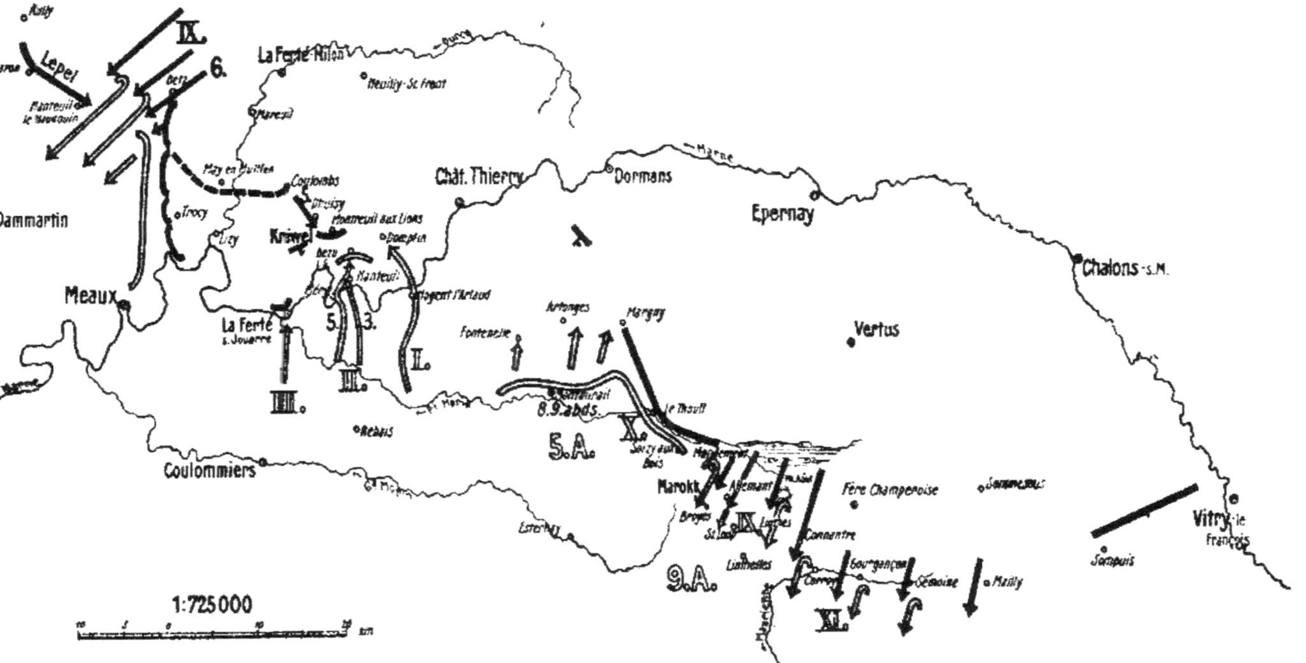

Sketch 18. Situation on 9 September, 1914.

About the Author

Hermann von Kuhl (1856-1958) was a scholar and staff officer. After receiving his Ph.D. from Tübingen in 1878, he joined the German army and spent time as a general staff officer under Count Alfred von Schlieffen. When the First World War broke out, he served as the Chief of Staff for the First Army under von Kluck, playing a key role in the Marne Campaign. After the war, von Kuhl became one of the foremost German historians of the Great War, publishing several books and serving on the Historical Commission of the Reich Archives.

CPSIA information can be obtained
at www.ICGtesting.com
Printed in the USA
BVHW052038261222
654951BV00015B/728